THE GREAT GLOBAL BUCKET LIST

ROBIN ESROCK

ONE -OF-A- KIND TRAVEL EXPERIENCES

Patrick Crean Editions

HarperCollins*PublishersLtd*

For Ana Carolina

Published by Patrick Crean Editions, an imprint of HarperCollins Publishers Ltd

First edition

HarperCollins books may be purchased for educational, business, or sales promotional use through our Special Markets Department.

HarperCollins Publishers Ltd
2 Bloor Street East, 20th Floor
Toronto, Ontario, Canada
M4W 1A8

www.harpercollins.ca

Library and Archives Canada Cataloguing in Publication information is available upon request.

ISBN 978-1-44344-236-7

Printed and bound in China
IMA 9 8 7 6 5 4 3 2 1

Contents

SOUTH AMERICA   1

NORTH AMERICA   63

ASIA   243

Introduction

Find the joy in your life.
—Morgan Freeman, in *The Bucket List*

We have always held an innate desire to accomplish certain goals before we die. It is a powerful drive that transcends culture, language, gender and age, and yet it was not until 2006 that a term appeared to perfectly capture this very idea. A silly term, almost nonsensical, that has nevertheless swept across the globe, so that most people are now familiar with a bucket list, even if they don't know exactly what it means. It's a riff, of course, on the more familiar idiom "to kick the bucket," which some historians believe dates back to the Middle Ages. Necks in a noose, condemned men were made to stand on buckets, the bucket then kicked out from under them. Although *bucket list* had been referenced in a few articles, it was the 2007 film of the same name that elevated the expression into the global lexicon. Morgan Freeman and Jack Nicholson portrayed two men of vastly different backgrounds who find themselves, terminally ill, in the same hospital ward. Nicholson discovers Freeman's bucket list, which includes general aspirations as opposed to particular experiences. Inspired, and with nothing to lose, they use Jack's extreme wealth to travel together for one last hurrah, ticking off one exotic adventure after another. Director Rob Reiner's sentimental film had influence beyond its modest box-office returns.

Every day, I receive a Google Alert of *bucket list* appearing in the news, from a US president's comments about visiting Stonehenge to pet owners indulging their dying pets to 101-year-old grannies skydiving on their birthdays. Thousands of people on seven continents have described their bucket lists to me, as if this universal term has always been with us, just waiting to sprout. With the increased sophistication of global tourism, affordable airfare and the interests of active boomers, millennials and all in between, the ripening power of the bucket list is no accident. *The Great Global Bucket List*, on the other hand, begins with one.

Approaching my 30th birthday, I looked back on a stuttering career in online development, media and the music business. Too often I would day-dream of the places I wasn't visiting, and the adventures I wasn't having. My job was stagnating, a long-term relationship had run its course and I truly had no idea where my life was heading. One morning, on my way to the office, a driver did not see a stop sign and drove her car through the intersection. Biking up the street, I slammed into the passenger door, did an impressive swan dive over my handlebars and cracked my kneecap. Just as starvation reminds one of the joys of food, a brush with death, however slight, makes one appreciate the fragility, and extraordinary opportunity, of life. Nine months later, I received a $20,000 insurance settlement. Not a million dollars, but just enough, if used sparingly, to book a solo one-year adventure around the world to finally chase those daydreams. I created a bucket list (though we didn't call it that yet) of ancient wonders, unusual cities, personal quests and bizarre activities, and set out to tick them off. To keep my friends and family updated, I produced a website to record as much as possible from the one wild year I hoped to live life at its fullest. Not only would I devote the year to adventure, I would commit to another passion I'd never seriously pursued—writing and photography. There was no serious intention to become a travel writer, but one newspaper bought a story, followed by others, and I suddenly found myself making a living of sorts, doing what I loved.

One of my favourite authors, Tom Robbins, writes: "In most of our lives, for better or for worse, there occurs a period of peak experience, a time when we are at our best, when we meet some challenge, endure some ordeal, receive some special recognition, have some sustained, heretofore unimag-inable fun, or just feel consistently happy and free."

That year was undoubtedly my peak experience, the guacamole to the taco chips of life. By the time it concluded, I had visited 24 countries and been published in newspapers on five continents. A year later, my Hail-Mary pitch for a TV show landed on the right desk at the right time, and seven months later, I found myself as a co-host, writer and producer for a 40-part adventure series filmed in 36 countries. Funded by television networks, I was tasked with seeking out experiences that conformed to my bucket list criteria:

- Is this destination or activity unique?
- Is it something I will never forget?
- Will it make a great story?
- Is it something everyone can actually do?

Tick off all those subjective items, and the journey began. Ukraine, Sri Lanka, Venezuela, Tunisia—I chased down bucket list experiences in the most unlikely of places. As a columnist for major newspapers and magazines, my pursuit of the Great Global Bucket List continued after the show wrapped. Ten years after my accident, my travels have now taken me to over 100 countries on all seven continents. *The Great Global Bucket List* draws together the best of these adventures, and I assure you, you've never read anything like it.

While you will certainly learn of new destinations and activities, you'll quickly realize that *this is not your traditional guidebook*. I'm fully aware that, in today's online world, you can find up-to-the-minute information on the Internet. Print cycles being what they are, no book can possibly compete with TripAdvisor, Google or travel blogs. Instead, I've focused on *inspiration*—the emotional draw of each experience—along with interesting history, trivia, context, humour and captivating real-life characters. One of those characters is me, an ordinary guy who never thought he'd run with bulls or sandboard off an active volcano. Someone, perhaps, just like you. I make no claims to be a gung-ho adrenalin junkie, a food and wine connoisseur or a learned historian. I am, however, blessed with an unusual amount of curiosity, a modest ability to capture experiences in words and images and, perhaps most pertinently, the immense good fortune to have specialized in a career chasing the extraordinary. Forgoing unrealistic hypotheticals, I present instead a road-tested and completely accessible bucket list, taking you to places you can *actually* go. Spending a night in a Maldivian ocean villa might cost a small fortune, but it's free to hike in Patagonia or run with bulls in Portugal, other than the costs of getting there.

If you think your job has challenges, try writing a hybrid guidebook that needs to remain relevant for years, even as the destinations it features shift like an Atacama desert dune. It's why I've done my best to stray clear of politics and current events, focusing on activities and destinations that are accessible regardless of which wingnut leader is in power. Granted, an earthquake might swallow the Taj Mahal, in which case it will still be of benefit to read about what it *used* to be like. Earthquakes, terrorism, killer viruses, political riots—read the news and you'd think it's a dangerous world out there. Tragedies do unfortunately occur, but worth mentioning is the fact that, throughout my journeys to every destination in this book (and many more besides), I have never been robbed, attacked or violently ill. Common sense, a respect for local customs and a smile typically see you through.

There is something here for everyone—for people of all ages and abilities, of all incomes and interests. Some of you might be inspired to tackle these adventures; others will be content to simply learn about them in your armchairs. But where is the Eiffel Tower? Where is the Statue of Liberty? These bucket list experiences steer clear of the obvious but include the must-haves. If we're going to visit the Great Wall of China (page 263), I'm going to show you where you can zipline off it. I'll be the first to admit there are woeful omissions, primarily because I am but one writer, with limited time, pages and financial resources. Also, bucket lists are a game of whack-a-mole. You tick one item off at the top, and three more pop up at the bottom. There are so many people to meet, so many miles to explore and so many adventures to jump into. Fortunately, you don't need a car accident to wake you to the possibilities that surround you (though it certainly helped in my case). *The Great Global Bucket List* is a compelling reminder that the world isn't going anywhere, but with each passing year, *we* most certainly are. Each chapter concludes with a "START HERE" URL. Perhaps more importantly, I'd suggest you START NOW.

How Many Countries Are There Today?

This book features 65 countries and regions. That is certainly not all of them, and nobody knows how many there actually are anyway. The United Nations currently has 193 members; the US State Department recognizes 195. FIFA has 208 members because it takes into account countries that are governed by other countries but can still kick a soccer ball. Most sources give the number at 196, adding Taiwan, still under dispute by you-know-who. Then you have dependent areas, disputed territories and celebrity egos that occupy enough media space to be considered nations unto themselves.

How to Use This Book

Practical information shifts with far more regularity than do print editions of a book. *The Great Global Bucket List* includes plenty of information but very little about prices, accommodation and restaurant options, nor about the best times to visit or official links. This is why I've created an extensive online companion to accompany the inspirational guide you hold in your hands. Visit **globalbucketlist.com** and you will find all the information you'll need to follow in my footsteps, along with bonus experiences, videos, photo galleries, reading guides, official links and the chance to weigh in through social media. In our digital era, I believe that inspiration belongs on a page and that information belongs online. Each chapter concludes with a direct link to the online companion, though you'll need to register first. It's free, quick and easy (and automatically enters you into bucket list prize draws). Just remember to add the book code GLOBALBUCK3TLI5T when you register to unlock all the experiences.

About the Icons

To help you find destinations that best suit your tastes, each entry is accompanied by icons that reflect the excursion's standout qualities. That is, some trips will appeal to nature lovers or history buffs; others will satisfy travellers with a passion for food or adventure. A complete list of icons is below:

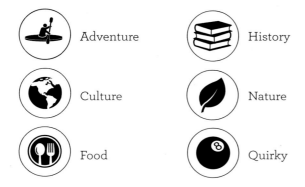

Adventure

History

Culture

Nature

Food

Quirky

Hike in Patagonia

ARGENTINA

As I hang by my fingertips on the edge of Cerro Lopez, too many thoughts preoccupy my mind. I am thinking that Patagonia, a fairy tale of deep-cut fjords, snow-capped mountains and gem-blue lakes, is so much more than a brand of outdoor clothing. I am thinking about last night's perfect steak, blackberry-red Malbec and Argentina's fantastic value for money. As my knuckle joints begin cramping, I have hot flashes of some of the gorgeous Argentine women I had met this week, followed by regret that I would likely never meet them again. Ah, the mysteries of nature, the joy of adventure! I think about anything to avoid dealing with the situation at hand, namely, that I am lost in the mountains and clinging for my life over an icy 40-metre crevice, with no ropes, safety guides or clue how to get out of this mess.

I had entered Argentina a few days prior, after a moustached border official typed *E-S-R-O-O-C-H* on my entry visa. I prayed the typo would not come back to haunt me, the way Maradona's hand haunts English soccer fans. The roller-coaster bust-boom-bust of Argentina's shaky economy makes the country a particularly delicious option for bucket listers. Here you can find a large, perfectly grilled filet mignon for less than the cost of a burger back home, and wolf it down with a low-priced bottle of high-value Malbec. While Bolivia is cheaper, it's what you can buy in Argentina that makes it the best deal in South America. Argentina clings to European tradition the way Americans cling to their Constitution. My first stop, San Martin de los Andes, could easily be mistaken for a ski village in the Alps, complete with gourmet chocolate stores, plump sausages and a large German population. Infused with renowned Argentine passion, Patagonia might be the bastard son of Marlene Dietrich and Che Guevara. *Viva la lederhosen!* Yet while Argentina's infrastructure is modern, its economy is often in shambles. Check out the bewildering black-market currency rates, and always remember, cash is king.

I arrive in Bariloche, a tourist town at the heart of Patagonia, and quickly get to work. That is, I spend a few days eating steaks the size of Mike Tyson's forearm. No small compliment: I believe that Argentine meat is the best in the world. *Parillas* (steakhouses) serve up a variety of medium-rare cuts. Do not dare tell a *parilla* master how to grill your steak, for you will insult his pride and honour. I don't know what he does but, somehow, the meat melts in your mouth like butter.

In winter, Bariloche becomes the Whistler of South America, with the nearby Cerro Catedral Ski Resort attracting people from all over the continent. I had arrived in autumn, but I still take a cable car up the slopes to see the mountain views. Joining me is a local named Alex, a climbing aficionado who conquered his first mountain in Patagonia over five decades ago. With the Tronador volcano looming in the distance, he tells me about his life during Argentina's turbulent history of civil wars, coups, dictatorships, economic collapse and revival. Of course, being Argentinean, he has to mention that the country has the world's most beautiful women. If I had a peso for every time a local tells me about the beauty of Argentinian women, I'd have a fortune—which I'd be sure to spend immediately, before the currency gets devalued.

In summer, visitors come to Patagonia to hike, horse ride, fish, climb and river raft. Which is how I meet a Danish traveller named Martin and an American climber named Des, who suggest we go on a day hike to check out the granite spires of Cerro Lopez. It starts innocently enough—a steep ascent up a switchback path, lunching at a mountain refuge with gobsmacking views. Forest foliage is in full bloom with all the bright colours of a Rastafarian Renoir. Despite the high sun, a crisp breeze blows in from Antarctica. In my daypack is a bottle of Malbec, reserved for the peak. Thirty minutes from the top, the trail signs disappear.

"I'm going this way," says Des, turning left with an air of authority. It makes perfect sense to follow the experienced climber, but I suggest to Martin we go right because it looks like an easier route, and because I'm an idiot, and idiots just *know* these things. At the time, I was oblivious to Cerro Lopez's reputation for claiming more lives of idiots than any other mountain in the region. In fact, a traveller had died on the very same trail just one week earlier.

Before long, rocks and ice are falling all around me. I have expertly climbed myself into an icy, dangerous corner. Martin has hung back with good sense, and Des is waving hello to me from a nearby summit. The only way to get out of the situation is to dig my fingertips into the adjacent ice wall and shuffle across the icy crevice to solid rock. One slip would see my promising discovery of Patagonia crash to an end. In retrospect, this singular moment was the most dangerous of all my travels. Bad things happen when we overestimate our abilities, make bad decisions and ignore the advice of people who know better. "Oh well," I psych myself up. "That wine isn't going to drink itself."

I lunge across the ice, stab my fingers into it, and pull a *Mission: Impossible* manoeuvre to repeat the process until I'm able to latch onto solid rock. Sliding down with the loose stones, I somehow catch Martin's walking stick. The look in his eyes tells me everything I need to know about the stupidity of what had just occurred. Fortunately, I still have the Malbec in my bag, and nothing

quells panic like half a bottle of good wine swallowed in one gulp.

I hope that, unlike myself, you don't risk your life exploring the wonders of Patagonia—or any item on the Great Global Bucket List. On the other hand, this is definitely one region you'll want to explore before you kick the mighty bucket, ideally with a belly full of steak, a bottle of red wine and a thirst for outdoor adventure.

START HERE:
globalbucketlist.com/patagonia

More Thrills, Less Risk

Here's what we like about mountain climbing: the epic views, the physical challenge, the pristine mountain wilderness. Here's what we don't like about mountain climbing: the danger of slipping, falling and being pulverized by the rocks below or, worse, having to use a pen knife to cut a trapped arm off. Fortunately, there's a place to climb in the middle. *Via ferratas* (Italian for "iron roads") are climbing routes where you can clip into secure wires and staples, and use a carabiner and harness to climb in places even traditional climbers can appreciate. Originally developed in the Alps to help soldiers scale over mountains, *via ferratas* have become increasingly popular in mountain regions. The longest

via ferrata in North America is CMH Summer Adventure's Mount Nimbus summit, accessible for guests via its helicopter fly-in from Bobby Burns Lodge. As you scale along a sheer rock face along the spine of the mountain, relax knowing that the 60-metre-long rope suspension bridge and all the iron rung ladders are designed to take 10 times the amount of weight you're putting on them. Relax knowing you're in the perfectly capable hands of expert guides and high-level gear. Relax knowing . . . oh, who are we kidding? Just because you're perfectly safe clinging to a rock face a kilometre above the ground doesn't mean you won't be quaking with fear.

Bike down the Death Road

The first time I mountain-biked down Bolivia's notorious Death Road, I almost soiled my shorts. The North Yungas Road, a 65-kilometre-long mountain pass connecting La Paz to Coroico, had the morbid distinction of being "the world's most dangerous road," causing an average of 150 deaths a year. Overcrowded buses and trucks tipped over the edge of the winding jungle road, plummeting 600 metres to the canyon floor below, with alarming frequency. Any number of factors could punch *my* ticket as I coasted through each blind corner of the narrow passes: an oncoming truck, an errant rock, a faulty brake, too much speed. Fortunately, I was in good hands. In 1998, a New Zealander founded Gravity Assisted Mountain Biking with the intention of safely guiding adventurous tourists down this beautiful, if deadly, pass.

Within a few years, biking down it had become one of the must-do activities on the Gringo Trail. The company has now guided over 50,000 cyclists, with zero fatalities. Competitors hoping to cash in on the tourist craze have not been so fortunate. Under their watch, more than a dozen tourists have been killed. When it comes to biking the world's most dangerous road, trained guides and quality bikes make a difference. This is not the road to cut corners on, for when it comes to Bolivian death roads, you get what you pay for. For a true one-of-a-kind bucket list experience, the going rate isn't much.

Tour shuttles depart daily from La Paz, driving high into the mountains to deposit riders at the top of the pass. The first 22 kilometres are an easy introduction, a rapid downhill thrill ride on smooth asphalt amid the spectacular snow-capped Andes. Four thousand metres above sea level, the air is crisp and sharp. All I have to do is hang on and slow down at corners, though the icy air freezes my hands despite my gloves, making braking unnervingly difficult. The group gathers itself every 10 to 20 minutes, receiving further instruction and advice about the forthcoming stretch. We cycle through a drug checkpoint (this part of Bolivia is a well-known smuggling route), then pedal up an exhausting, un-gravity-assisted hill and onto the more treacherous downhill muddy track. Now crosses, flowers and memorials line the road, marking where vehicles slipped off into the ravine. The demeanour of our guides becomes more serious. At each stop, they explain just what to expect ahead. There is incredibly little room for error when your tire is inches away from a cliff face. Quite frankly, I'm surprised more people *haven't* been killed. All it takes is a bump, a speed wobble, a bad, panicky decision. A woman in my group takes a tumble

over some loose stones. Shaken up, she retires to the support van behind us. Minor injuries are common enough, the severity dependent on how fast you choose to push it. We ride under waterfalls and over thick mud, surrounded by the forbidding jungle. Finally, the road levels out.

It's All Downhill from Here

Less hills, more thrills. Check out the following fun, beautiful and all-downhill rides.

Table Mountain Double Descent, South Africa: This is a two-and-a-half-hour ride, 90 per cent of which is downhill, on off-road trails and private roads down the front side of Cape Town's iconic mountain. Brake for stunning views of Table Bay, Robben Island, Lion's Head and the city itself.

Tasmania's Mount Wellington, Australia: This 21-kilometre ride starts with a 360-degree view of Hobart, the Southern Ocean and the surrounding area. Cruise down the paved, winding road through subalpine terrain and dense forest. Toast at the bottom with a pint from Cascade Brewing Barrel House.

Trail Ridge Road, Rocky Mountain National Park, USA: Kicking off at 3,650 metres high in alpine tundra, this 35-kilometre descent takes you down the east or west side of the ridge, eating up the highest continuous paved road in the United States. Chilly at the top, but magnificent views around every corner.

With more confidence, I increase my speed, my knees and elbows rattling as I stand on my pedals to avoid the saddle enema. Crossing two rivers, we arrive at a small village and to beer, congratulations and the customary T-shirt. My face is covered in mud freckles, my hands cramping from clutching the brakes so hard. Warm beer never tasted so good.

Hosting between 120 and 140 riders a day, Bolivia's Death Road has become an industry, bringing much-needed foreign dollars into the region. What's more, a relatively new paved highway to Coroico has significantly reduced the danger. Most trucks and buses use this faster, less-risky route, leaving the winding jungle road as an empty track ideal for bikers of all levels.

The only car I pass on my way down belongs to an American birdwatcher. "Watching all these bikers seems to be the most organized tourist activity I've seen in the whole country," he tells me. It's beyond him why anyone would want to bike a dangerous road in Bolivia. It's beyond me why anyone would want to drive it looking for birds.

In truth, the North Yungas is no longer the world's most dangerous road, and that suits us fine. Just because it is a worthy bucket list adventure doesn't mean we have to risk death ticking it off.

START HERE:
globalbucketlist.com/deathroad

Get Blessed on the Island of the Sun

BOLIVIA

Her name was Lola, she was a showgirl and she *never* visited Copacabana, located on the Bolivian shores of Lake Titicaca. This Copacabana is a small, dusty town with a distinctly bohemian-hippie traveller vibe and strong religious overtones. Argentinean hippies sell trinkets along the main boulevard; street vendors proffer traditional Bolivian ponchos, woollen hats and alpaca scarves; and cheap restaurants cater to a steady stream of travellers and pilgrims. Although most readers will associate Copacabana with Rio de Janeiro or Barry Manilow's hotel in Havana, this Bolivian town predates both of them and has long been a site of pilgrimage. Each weekend, you can watch Bolivians bless their cars, buses and equipment outside the white cathedral, typically by pouring wine and beer on the object, and lighting firecrackers. If it is blessings our bucket list desires, let's hop aboard a modern catamaran for an overnight cruise on Lake Titicaca, and gently make our way to the Island of the Sun.

For over 2,000 years, Andean cultures have revered the sun-bleached, almost Mediterranean-like Isla del Sol on Lake Titicaca. The Incan deity Viracocha is believed to have begun creation from Titicaca, while the first Incan couple, the Children of the Sun, are said to have founded the Incan Empire on this very island. The Island of the Sun—the "womb of the world"—has been connected to Atlantis, lost ancient civilizations and the source of all life on earth.

As the catamaran motors toward it, there's a conspicuous clarity in the early-morning light. Deep shades of Titicaca-blue reflect above. When Jacques Cousteau explored these waters—the highest navigable lake in the world—he discovered drowned ruins of ages past, and an unknown species of blind deep-water frog. Maybe the light was too pure for the poor frogs to handle.

I hop onto the pier and make my way up rocky stairs to a small spring, which, according to local legend, is the Fountain of Youth. Visitors typically help themselves to a swig, just in case the legend is true. Transturin, the company that operates the catamarans, has created its own museum complex on the island, where I learn about Incan mummification, agriculture, fertility idols and reed ship building. Did you know that in Incan and Mayan culture, it was believed that a long, elongated skull was classy? The aristocracy would strap boards to a baby's head to force the skull to lengthen into an oblong shape. When European explorers discovered such skulls, they thought they were of aliens.

I return to the catamaran for a welcome buffet, then sit back in a small wooden rowboat to visit another part on the island. An indigenous Aymara father and son row the boat together in silence, the rhythmic sound of wood in water (and a full belly) sending me into a blissful slumber. We're 4,200 metres above sea level, and perhaps the altitude is tiring me out too. At the wooden jetty, they awake me to explore the ruins and participate in a traditional ceremony. A robed priest with dark, leathered skin burns various objects over a fire. Muttering under his breath, he invokes the ancient gods with herbs, tobacco and pieces of cheap candy, then douses my head with water. Experiencing a solemn, spiritual tradition overlooking the mythical waters of Lake Titicaca? Blessed is our Great Global Bucket List, for taking us to unique historical places and skin-tingling sacred spaces.

10 Bucket List Sunsets

It's a tough hike up the steps of the Calvario, a steep hill that overlooks Copacabana and Lake Titicaca. Altitude sharpens the views of Titicaca's ultramarine waters but also makes for slow going up the hill. At the top, you'll find dozens of Christian and indigenous memorials, and scatterings of locals, travellers and vendors gathered for the day's majestic sunset. As the sun cracks the horizon, the clouds light up with shades of cherry nectarine. The moon's spot beam says hello. It's an epic sunset for the Great Global Bucket List. Here you'll find others:

- Africa House Hotel, Stone Town, Zanzibar
- Anjuna, Goa, India
- Atacama Desert, Chile
- Le Morne Brabant, Mauritius
- Mount Nemrut, Turkey
- Petra, Jordan
- Santorini, Greece
- Sihanoukville, Cambodia
- Sunset dune, Jericoacoara Beach, Brazil
- Taj Mahal, India

START HERE:
globalbucketlist.com/titicaca

Cross the World's Largest Salt Desert

Call it Planet Salt, thanks to flat plains of sodium chloride stretching as far as you can see. Or perhaps Planet Mineral, in honour of the bright green and blue lakes, surrounded by pyramid volcanoes. Some might prefer Planet Thermal, because of the boiling rocks, steaming mud and hot-peach skies. Bolivia's Salar de Uyuni looks remarkably like an alien planet, but rest assured, you're still on planet Earth.

Crossing the world's largest salt desert is a well-marked signpost on the Gringo Trail. Travellers typically use it to journey from Bolivia into the Chilean Atacama or vice versa. There's certainly a lot of transport involved. First a four-hour bus ride from the capital La Paz to Oruro, followed by a seven-hour train to Uyuni, an outpost town from which tours depart. As it nears the town, the train is elevated above unnerving flatness. Submerged in shallow water, a big desert reflects a big sky, creating one vast mirror, which is why scientists use the Salar to calibrate satellites. With water on either side of the tracks, the train feels more like a boat. On the horizon, lightning crackles between violet shades of sunset.

Water dries up around Uyuni, the launch pad for exploring 10-billion tons of bright, white salt, up to 16 kilometres deep. Tour operators offer one- to three-day excursions crossing the desert, gathering parties of six into well-corroded Land Rovers. Sleeping bags, food and gear are loaded onto the roof. A strong sun reflects off the salt, some 3,656 metres above sea level, turning the sky a rich shade of blue. Our first stop is a train cemetery, where rusty steam engines lay abandoned from failed mining projects in the 1940s. In this distinctly post-apocalyptic setting, I explore old, decrepit engines, half expecting to bump into Mad Max polishing his sawed-off shotgun.

There are no roads in the Salar. Our driver just points the car in one

Picture This

Few places in the world offer the incredible photo ops of the Salar de Uyuni. Play around with perspectives and mirror-perfect reflections in the water. You'll definitely want to pack extra batteries for your camera, though. There is extremely limited access to electricity in the surrounding villages, and few, if any, places to charge your gear.

direction, until eventually we reach something interesting to look at. We hop out at a salt mine, where indigenous Aymara men gather and process salt. It's physical work, and given the heat, I gather that each worker is worth more than his weight in salt. The car continues into the desolate nothingness, which might resemble ice if it weren't so hot outside. A hill floats like a mirage in the distance, an island refuge in this endless sea of salt. It's called the Isla del Pescado, translated as "Fish Island." Giant cacti spike into the sky, some of them hundreds of years old. Climbing up

smoothly eroded rocks, I stare out over this alien landscape. Several historical wars have been fought over the procurement of salt. Those armies would have lost their minds in the Salar de Uyuni.

Once we leave the island, there's nothing whatsoever to bump into. One could fall asleep at the wheel for hours, and apparently some drivers do. Eventually, our wheels enter deep puddles of brine, evidence of the November-to-April wet season. Soon enough, the saltwater is up to the passenger doors. How these vehicles survive such conditions I don't know, and frankly, I am too afraid to ask.

SOUTH AMERICA

Gratefully reaching the skirts of the desert, we drive into a dusty Aymara village called Bella Vista, where we will spend the night in a simple dormitory, on cots with creaking bedsprings. The temperature plummets at nightfall. I have to stop chasing woolly llamas around the quiet village dirt roads and return to the dorm to play Uno by candlelight.

The Land Rover continues south, passing small villages and a military post. Thanks to various minerals, the white salt turns into a silt of many hues. Red, blue and green mineral lakes appear, the colours vivid, as if angels have been tie-dying T-shirts in rock pools. The blue-green algae and brine shrimp are perfect fodder for flamingos, which gather by the tens of thousands. Perfect conical volcanoes let off steam in the distance.

We pass further signs of life, like wild vicuña, llama-like creatures prized for their soft fur. There's a pee- and photo-break next to unusual rock formations caused by volcanic activity, including an aptly named Rock Tree. When the salt makes way for red sand, I feel like I'm in the cockpit of the Mars rover. The second night's rustic accommodation is in a desert reserve with old dorms. Altitude and lack of light deliver intense stargazing—for as long as I can stand the icy wind. An early morning on the final day gets us to Sol de Mañana for sunrise. I strip down in the pre-dawn freeze to watch the sun rise from the warmth of a shallow thermal spring. Bubbling geysers and boiling mud are scattered about, so we're advised to walk around carefully, and dip only into those springs the guides know are safe for bathing. It's still several hours to the Chilean border. We pass more volcanoes, lakes and desert formations, including a section appropriately called the Salvador Dali Desert. Rocks appear as bent and twisted as his imagination.

At the border, an exchange takes place. Bolivian companies cannot cross, so travellers from Chile hop into our Land Rover, and we jump onto their bus. Dirt tracks turn into tar roads, prices triple and I continue onward to the Chilean town of San Pedro de Atacama. I'd spent three days in the world's largest salt flat, off the grid, on another planet. A bucket list adventure to be sure, but we all have to come down to earth sometime.

START HERE:
globalbucketlist.com/salar

16

Dance inside the Sambadrome

In the world of spectacles, it doesn't get any bigger, brighter and hotter than Rio de Janeiro's annual Carnaval. Every year, nearly 1 million tourists invade the city, crowding the beaches, dancing in the streets. Hundreds of *blocos*—street parties—sprout up all over the city, open to all. Drums clang in the neighbourhoods of Copacabana and Ipanema. Summer energy crackles in the sweat-soaked, frenetic city, and beating at the heart is the legendary Sambadrome. Up to 90,000 people will cram into the cement stands and private booths of this 700-metre-long stadium, to watch thousands more parade with lavish costumes and jaw-dropping floats. Some will come for the show, others for the party, but as the fireworks continue to explode close to sunrise, nobody goes home disappointed.

My wife, Ana, is telling me to get some rest. Tonight, Carnaval kicks off in the Sambadrome, and we won't get home until at least 7 a.m. Having grown up in Copacabana, Ana is all too familiar with this annual madness. By most accounts, the festival has its roots in a pagan celebration, which was co-opted by the Catholic Church and is held just before Lent. The word *carnaval* literally means "a farewell to meat"— and it's the last chance to revel before a 40-day period of introspection and abstinence of worldly pleasures. For the religious, Carnaval represents a massive bender before things get solemn. For everyone else, no excuses are necessary. The heat, crowds and noise may be exhausting, but this is the highlight of Brazil's social calendar.

As I prepare for the evening ahead, spending as little time on my feet as possible, Ana explains the mechanics. Each samba organization, known as a school, represents a local community; they range across the social and economic spectrum. Up to 4,000 members perform for the school, which chooses an overall theme. Each member pays a costume fee, with choice positions priced accordingly.

It might cost US$50 to walk on the floor, or thousands for a marquee spot atop a float. Some of these positions are also made available for connected tourists. Incredibly, the average school spends around US$3.5 million each year on its parade. Carnaval is, therefore, a self-sustaining industry, employing thousands of people to make it all possible. With 12 samba schools parading over two nights, I am eager to experience what US$42 million can buy.

We are invited to a *camarote*, one of the private booths that overlook the parade street. The spectrum of Rio's socio-economic life is reflected in the event's ticket prices. The low-income sections, open to people from the *favelas*, are reserved for just US$5 a seat. In the stands, where most tourists will end up, the average ticket price is about US$60, though that goes up to US$150 depending on your view of the action. Six-seat open booths cost around US$2,500 per night, while *camarotes* (think corporate boxes at a sports event) reach up to US$40,000 per night. Security is tight. Each *camarote* hands out special designed shirts that must be worn at all times, along with

ID cards. As is the custom, we use scissors to redesign our shirts into something more fashionable, which in Brazil translates as "show more skin." Contrary to worldwide popular belief, stemming perhaps from the sight of all the hair-thin bikinis, nudity is publicly condemned in Brazil. Women sunbathing topless on the beach can be fined or arrested. But for these two special nights in the Sambadrome, all bets (and plenty of bras) are off.

We successfully navigate multiple levels of security. The atmosphere is one of a frenzied major sporting event: crowds, vendors, plastic cups, booming announcements on loudspeakers. Judging booths line the parade street, the judges awarding points for themes, costumes, floats, music and performances. The winning school achieves national acclaim, along with high-paying sponsors and illustrious new members. The awards are televised live across the country, amid a passionate debate over who deserves to enter the pantheon of Carnaval greats.

A massive round of fireworks signals that the first school is entering the street. It has just 82 minutes to get to the end of the stadium, crossing the iconic arches of the Sambadrome, or it will face stiff point penalties. Having been to Mardi Gras in New Orleans, I thought I knew what to expect. Oh no, this is something else entirely.

It is pure scale. Floats up to 10 storeys high, with dancers shaking their booty on the top—no ropes or safety nets. Shiny sequins and fake feathers by the millions. Platoons of drummers marching in perfect unison. Animatronics competing with anything you'll find at Disneyland, accompanied by giant effigies depicting legends of Brazilian sports and literature. A huge glowing robot shakes its head as a half-naked Amazonian bombshell dances the samba above its head. There is so much stimulation, your mind just gives up, to let your body involuntarily join the rhythm.

Each float seems to outdo the others, and they keep coming, up to a dozen per school. Interspersed are hundreds of revellers in themed costume, singing and shouting and noticeably laughing, having the time of their lives. Providing the rhythm is the *bateria*, the drum corps, pounding the signature samba beat with a chorus singing over top. The school's song is repeated until the very end of its parade, by which time everyone knows the lyrics and the crowds have joined in. The entire event is broadcast on television around the country. Tomorrow, half the country will be singing the most popular songs. The Queen of the

Bateria are gorgeous Brazilian goddesses, flashing their muscular thighs, vibrating on their stilettos, blowing kisses and smiles as the crowds cheer in adoration. I am covered in sweat from dancing, exhausted from the spectacle and amazed there are still *five* more schools to come—and this is only the first night. Coming up are the

Meanwhile, outside Rio

Each spring, Carnaval sweeps across South America, and you don't have to be in Rio to experience it. In northern Brazil, the city of Salvador hosts a wild street carnival on three parade circuits. Colombia's Barranquilla hosts the second-biggest carnival on the continent, a riot of dancing and colour. Bolivia's Oruro claims to have held a carnival for over 2,000 years, soaking the Christian and Andean traditions together (water fights are everywhere). Over in the Caribbean, Trinidad holds one of the world's biggest carnivals, vibrating with calypso. The Bahamas funks up Boxing Day and New Year's Eve with its annual Junkanoo parade in Nassau. Aruba exorcises evil spirits on its own Fat Tuesday, while French-speaking islands like Guadeloupe, St. Barthelemy and Martinique hold boisterous parades and parties leading up to Ash Wednesday.

neighbourhoods of Beija-Flor, Portela, Salgueiro, Vila Isabel, Imperatriz and—Ana's favourite—Mangueira. "They don't have the most money," she explains, "just the most heart."

Madonna is in attendance this year, as is actor Gerard Butler. Earlier that week we had bumped into French actor Vincent Cassel at the prestigious Magic Ball at Copacabana Palace Hotel, along with several Brazilian A-listers indulging in an *Eyes Wide Shut*–like orgy of hedonism. Several balls take place throughout the city, and it's worth getting into one if you can hustle up a ticket. Scrawled in my notebook from that evening: *Half-naked women on stilts, famous artist in drag on roller skates, overflowing champagne, lizard people*. I meet a fading French beauty queen dripping in jewellery, her lipstick blood-red. "All the money in Europe is so old, but look, *chéri*—in Brazil, the money is young!" Old European

money is here with fangs out, ready to suck the rich blood of South America. My literary hero, Dr. Gonzo, would have loved the place.

Back in the Sambadrome, dozens of Brazilian media celebrities are parading on floats. I look over to see Paris Hilton taking photos from the next *camarote* over, and for once she's not the centre of attention. Some of the schools are circuses, with trapeze acts and stunts. Some use floats and costumes to recount great moments in Brazilian history.

Forty-eight hours later, my tingling nerve sockets are blown. There are black rings around my eyes where the fuse ignited. Too much stimulation, too much samba, too little sleep. I could now judge the performance of the dancers and debate the merits of the themes. Later that week, I will sit with my in-laws, riveted to the TV as results are announced. Only in Rio could parading become a sport. No wonder the city got to host the FIFA World Cup finals and Summer Olympic Games just two years apart. When it comes to hosting parties, Rio de Janeiro is the Carnaval Queen.

START HERE:
globalbucketlist.com/carnaval

Get Wet in the World's Largest Wetlands

BRAZIL

There shouldn't be any problems rappelling 30 storeys into a cavernous abyss, watching a faint glimmer of light reflecting off a crystal-clear pool at the bottom. By now I've rappelled on several continents, and just the day before, I had lowered myself 90 metres alongside a spectacular waterfall known as the Mouth of the Puma. But the Abismo Anhumas, sheltering a subterranean aquatic wonderland, comes with a neat little twist. If I hope to see the glorious sun again, I'll have to climb *back up* the very rope I rappelled down. Hand over hand, inch by inch, breath by breath.

Caves are plentiful here in Brazil's Pantanal, the world's largest wetland. A huge compression in the earth's crust has created a 150,000-square-kilometre freshwater flood plain, stretching into Bolivia and Paraguay. With so much water, the Pantanal is one of the most biologically diverse regions on the planet, a birders' and wildlife paradise. It has also been under threat, since over 95 per cent of the land is privately owned and rich waters make the wetland fertile for crops and cattle—and, of course, mosquitoes. On the other side of the mountains that frame the wetland, a small town named Bonito has reinvented itself to become one of the most popular ecotourism destinations in South America. Besides being the starting point for trips into the Pantanal—where tourists can enjoy night safaris, river cruises, hikes and horse rides in protected areas—Bonito is also a launch pad for visiting caves and waterfalls, and for several tasty adventures. The latter includes dining on unusual dishes, like grilled caiman and piranha stew, in local restaurants.

After years of destruction of the Amazon, Brazil is making an effort to protect the Pantanal's fragile environment. New laws have been passed and tourism standards created, and farm owners have increasingly begun to see the value of ecotourism over traditional cattle breeding. Take Rio da Prata, where 80 per cent of the farm's revenue comes from its extraordinary attraction.

The riverbed filters a clear-as-glass freshwater tributary, making it clean enough to drink from. Donning wetsuits and snorkelling gear, you hop into the river and flow gently with the current amid thousands of incredible freshwater fish. Some of them, like the golden dorado, are as big as sharks. Others are just large and curious. Amazing underwater flora adds to the ambiance as you float down the river like a pixel in an underwater screensaver. Some of the low underwater rocks are sharp and could snare you, and the current can drag you at quite a pace, but this all adds to the fun. Kicking is not allowed (and unnecessary), guides are friendly and well trained, and groups are limited in size so that traffic remains at a minimum. After three hours, you join up with the main river,

where visibility deteriorates considerably, and a truck is waiting to return you back to base and an excellent buffet.

Floating among giant river fish is one for the bucket list, but so is exploring the Anhumas Abyss. There are daily tours from Bonito; guides test their clients the day before to see if they can hack the return ascent. Anyone can be lowered down, but climbing up a 72-metre-long rope through a narrow rock shaft requires an adventurous kind of stamina. Don't worry; if you can scale up

the 7-metre-high in-store platform, you're set. Discovered in 1984 and opened to the public in 1999, the Abismo Anhumas has an unparalleled draw. Inside the cave is an 8-metre-deep pool, lifeless save for tiny fish but home to massive underwater cave structures that can be explored by scuba diving or snorkelling. While normal-size stalactites form above, some of the conical underwater stalagmites grow an incredible 20 metres tall.

The descent is easy enough, in a terrifying "I'm only alive because of a wet rope" kind of a way. Once

I arrive on the bottom, I put on a wetsuit, and with flashlight in hand, float weightlessly above an alien underwater world. It feels like a scene from a fantasy movie, a waking dream. Unless you're into hardcore underwater cave spelunking (and arguably have a death wish), you won't have seen anything like it. Unfortunately, now you'll have to strap into a belay device to begin the long climb back up. The modified harness cuts into my water-softened flesh as I heave with my legs and steady with my arms. After 10 minutes, muscles are burning, but if I need incentive, all I need to do is look down. The darkness below looks like a watery grave. Connected as a backup to another tourist up ahead, the rope shakes as he quakes with fear. But each thrust brings more light, until finally, after squeezing through an unassuming crack in the rock, I reach the top. Having spent the day drifting down a tributary and floating in the calm water of an abyss, I find the heat and humidity of the Pantanal coming on thick. I'm still sweating bullets that evening on a drive to spot capybaras and caimans.

Underwater or not, bucket list adventures await your arrival in the world's largest wetland.

START HERE:
globalbucketlist.com/pantanal

Man-Made Underwater Marvels

British sculptor Jason deCaires Taylor took his art below sea level to create the world's first underwater gallery in the warm Caribbean waters off Granada. The Molinere Underwater Sculpture Park, opened in 2006, is accessible by snorkelling, diving or glass-bottom boat. The cement sculptures, mostly of people, cover an 800-square-metre area and have been an environmental boon, relieving pressure on surrounding reefs. Taylor followed this success with his Cancun Underwater Museum, or MUSA, using pH-neutral concrete to create over 500 life-size human statues in the shallow waters of Cancun's National Marine Park.

Climb an Angry Volcano

It is a sunny yet ominous day in the Chilean lakeside resort town of Pucón. At the tour-booking offices, TV crews are looking for sound bites from gringo travellers booking their one-day hike up Villarrica, a nearby active volcano that has decided this week to grumble. All I can say in Spanish is *bueno,* which somehow makes it onto the nightly national news. I have no idea what the reporter is asking, but it must be along the lines of "Don't you think you're being a little stupid to climb an erupting volcano?" To which my answer translated roughly as "Cool!"

Visiting Villarrica has been a popular activity for over three decades, when William Hatcher started offering guided tours up the volcano's steep, snowy slopes. Today there are more than a dozen operators in Pucón, some of dubious quality when it comes to equipment or safety, not that headwear means much against a waterfall of lava. Pucón is cabin country, located in the Lake District popular with Chileans for fishing, rafting and geothermal hot springs. Villarrica itself tends to attract mostly international bucket listers, drawn like moths to a lava lamp.

"The Chileans come for the lake, the gringos for the volcano, and neither seems to want the other," explains Willie in an indistinguishable accent.

Like me, travellers I meet have arrived for the volcano, discovering Pucón's other attractions almost by accident. Subsequently, a weekend outing turns into a week filled with river rafting, tree canopying, horse riding and lazing about in beautiful and highly social thermal springs. At 2,860 metres high, Villarrica looms in the distance like Mount Doom, glowing pink in the afternoon sun. It resembles an upside-down ice cream cone, vanillary snow leaking out the top. Nobody appears too concerned with today's front page of the local newspaper. A blurry photo shows people running from the rim as lava erupts from the crater. Willie thinks the authorities are being ridiculous.

"Every time it grumbles, they go crazy," he says reassuringly.

At the time of my visit, Villarrica had seriously grumbled only three times in the last 50 years, and not to a level that has ever seriously threatened the town of Pucón. With this in mind, I see no reason not to sign up, headlines and TV crews be damned. We are told that government authorities are restricting hikers from reaching the crater, but like the weather, we'll have to see on the day itself.

That night, I sleep restlessly, dreaming of a premature exit at the hands of an angry mountain. Backfiring trucks on the main road outside my hotel window do not help the cause.

We leave shortly after sunrise, supplied with waterproof shells, razor-sharp crampons, backpacks, ice picks and a protective helmet, since hair doesn't react well to chunks of exploding lava. Our senior guide, Oscar, has been hiking Villarrica for 10 years and is a member of the Chilean National Rescue Team. Times like this, you count on more experienced adventurers to know better; although, let's face it, that didn't work out too well for the Franklin Expedition. The bus drops us off at the bottom of the cone, where we hitch a ride on an old ski lift, taking a well-appreciated hour off the ascent.

It is a two-hour uphill slog over ash and granite before we reach the snow line. Rewarding us is a magnificent view—snow-capped mountains, shimmering lakes and, in the distance, another volcano. As the mid-morning sun burns away the clouds, I strap on my crampons to start the physically exhausting ascent on snow. It's single file and slow going, and I have new-found respect for anyone brave enough to do this at altitude, in the Himalayas, for example, where the air is as thin as eggshell. Finally we pause, just 300 metres from the crater, the limit set that day by the authorities for approaching hikers. Although I see wisps of smoke emerge from the crater above, it seems calm enough. Oscar seems on the fence. Having come so far, my group, consisting of

More Volcano Vacations

Bucket listers in search of hot spots will get a seismic kick out of these destinations:

Arenal, Costa Rica: Arenal is one of Central America's most accessible volcanoes, shadowing the Costa Rican town of La Fortuna. Hot springs, ziplining and river rafting have made the town an ecotourist hot spot. Until recently, you could drive to various viewpoints around the town at night to watch lava rolling down the sides of the cone. Unfortunately, rainforest weather often masks the volcano in a thick cloud and the volcano is now resting in a quiet phase.

Eyjafjallajökull, Iceland: This is the geological boil that shut down air traffic over Europe in 2010. Hovering over the tongue-buster Eyjafjallajökull crater makes for a jaw-dropping helicopter ride. The scarred, blackened remains contrast with the lush, green surrounding farmland, which benefited from the fertile volcanic ash. Nearby are two other active volcanoes, Hekla and Katla, which promise to cause even more havoc.

Kilauea, USA: Big Island's Kilauea, located in Hawai'i Volcanoes National Park, is one of the world's most active volcanoes. Easily accessible and therefore popular with tourists, the park lets visitors drive up to several calderas, explore a 500-year-old lava cave and hike 240 kilometres of trails.

Mount Etna, Italy: Europe's most active volcano is one of Sicily's most popular attractions. Visitors start from the 1,800-metre base and then hike, cable car or 4x4 bus up another kilometre for guided walks on the volcanic ash. Etna has four summit craters, sulphuric steam rising from vents. Hike the barren landscape in summer, or ski down the slopes in winter.

Mount Mayon, Philippines: This Mount Doom–looking cone is the country's most active volcano, with an aesthetically pleasing, pack-a-day smoking cone. Being a volcano, it's also killed thousands of people over the years, with many more evacuated when the lava starts to flow. ATV operators from the nearest city of Legazpi take you right up to the solidified lava, which vanquished surrounding palm plantations.

not to think about these things when hiking on active volcanoes.

Pacaya, Guatemala: Pacaya is a popular tourist volcano, even if it occasionally erupts, causing havoc. Three thousand people were evacuated in March 2014 when it blew its lid. Volcano junkies can go on day hikes from nearby Antigua or Guatemala City, and walk close enough to the lava to poke a flaming stick in it. In 2010, seven people were killed during an eruption, including a CNN reporter. You try

Sakurajima, Japan: Ash explodes every day on Sakurajima, located close to the city of Kagoshima, in southern Japan. Authorities prohibit anyone from climbing the volcano, and for the sake of the city's 600,000 inhabitants, seismic activity is closely monitored. Most volcano tourists head to Yunohira Observation Point for the view, followed by a traditional *onsen* for a peaceful soak.

English accountants and Australian teachers, decides we know better than an experienced mountaineer.

"Let's make a dash to the crater!"

Oscar, perhaps seeing his tips melt away with the snow, agrees on the condition that we drop our packs first and spend no more than a few minutes at the crater. A news helicopter is circling overhead, and I imagine the coverage, a nation

glued to its TV sets, eagerly hoping the crater blasts these gringos all the way to Peru.

Exhausted from the climb, I find that merely putting one foot in front of another at this point requires supreme effort. But I'm channelling Frodo. We are not tourists. We are warriors armed with ice picks crossing the Misty Mountains, pursuing orcs at our heels! That is, until I reach the top and suddenly have to concentrate really hard on not wetting my waterproofs. The sound of a volcano on the verge of eruption rattles your spleen. It is a hungry lion roaring in your face, the sonic boom of a jet fighter in the pit of your stomach. It is loud, deep and primal, and if I listen very carefully, I can just make out the words: *Get off the volcano, you moron!*

Contrary to my expectations, there is no river of red-cherry lava in the crater, but rather, a chocolate rocky filling letting off steam like a geyser. The crater blows a little steam, followed by a loud explosion that spews drops of lava and ash 50 metres in the air. After a few seconds it cools off, perhaps deciding whether now is the perfect time to kill everybody or maybe just grumble some more. We hastily collect our gear, our guides discussing the descent among themselves until the ground shakes and we are all reminded that we are on top of a volcano in the midst of a seismic orgasm. Fortunately, getting down the volcano is the most fun you can have on two cheeks. Narrow channels have been carved out for our butts to bobsleigh, reaching impressive speed as we fly down the banks using our ice picks as brakes. It takes just 20 minutes for this frozen waterslide to deliver us safely to the bottom. I arrived at the snow line covered in ice and grateful for not having impaled myself with my ice pick.

For all their fear mongering, the newspapers were right to call Villarrica a disaster waiting to happen. In March 2015, the volcano erupted in spectacular fashion, spewing lava 1,000 metres in the air, resulting in the panicky evacuation of Pucón. Damage was minimal and things settled down shortly afterward. Villarrica is once again open for bucket list business.

START HERE:
globalbucketlist.com/villarrica

Ask Questions on Easter Island

Easter Island is a riddle wrapped in a mystery inside an enigma surrounded by 50 metric tons of solid rock. Maybe. The island is steeped in the unknown, the only certain fact being that nobody is quite sure of anything. Polynesians colonized Easter Island a thousand years before a Dutch explorer named it on the date of its European discovery. They called this tiny, triangle-shaped Pacific island Rapa Nui (Big Island) or Te Pito o Te Henua (the Naval of the World) and how they ended up here in the first place is one of many mysteries. We're talking about a sliver of land in the Pacific Ocean, 24 kilometres long by 12 kilometres wide, located more than 3,500 kilometres off the coast of Chile and 2,000 kilometres from its nearest neighbour—the just-as-batshitcrazy-remote island of Pitcairn. Finding this island by canoe, as the Polynesians would have done, would be like throwing a dart behind your back, blindfolded, off a 50-storey building in Hong Kong and having it hit the eyeball of a dingo in Brisbane, Australia.

There are various competing theories as to how ancient Polynesians got here, but it's a distinct certainty that they did, because they left behind 887 giant statues, called *moai*, of people, deities or aliens—depending on your source of reference. If you're a fan of Erich von Daniken's (comprehensively debunked) book *Chariots of the Gods*, then it's little green men all the way. Several modern archaeologists believe the *moai* were more likely created in homage to paramount chiefs. Regardless, the lush tropical island that once boasted 16 million trees now has none—the slash-and-burn agriculture and feverish demand of the islanders to build and raise these mammoth tributes/works of art/

religious symbols/alien spaceship marshals saw to that.

Carved in a local quarry, these heavy *moai* statues were somehow transported to ceremonial platforms (called *ahu*) around the island. Captain Cook believed islanders, also called Rapa Nui, used stones and scaffolding. Local legend has it that the *moai* walked to their resting places with the help of a supernatural priest. Some 288 made it; the rest were abandoned in transit or back at the quarry. Many were destroyed. Barely surviving to present times are the Rapa Nui themselves. Some theories hold that their environmental destruction ultimately led to the collapse of their civilization, resulting in famine and civil war.

An estimated population of

20,000 was reduced to just 5,000, and further annihilated when Europeans brought the gifts of slaving, smallpox and rats. Less than a century after their meeting with the rest of humanity, the Rapa Nui had been reduced to an estimated 100 indigenous survivors. The mopey eyes of the *moai*, long stripped of their white coral or obsidian, watched on in stony silence.

Easter Island's remoteness makes it neither particularly accessible nor affordable. Serviced by LAN Airlines, you'll have to endure a long-haul flight from Chile or Tahiti before settling into your accommodation in the island's one village, Hanga Roa. A permanent population of just over 5,000 (about half of them of Polynesian descent) is primarily focused on tourism. Despite calls for independence, the entire island remains a national park of Chile. So little is known about its past, or how to decipher ancient Rapa Nui writing, that some archaeologists regard the traditional dress and dances you'll encounter as more of a reinvention—an interpretation of what might have been.

On the other hand, Tapati, an annual festival that takes place during the first two weeks of February, feels wonderfully authentic, largely because it is organized by and for the locals. Men covered in traditional body paint don boards for races down a large, grassy hill and into the surf. Without trees, the island's plains appear not unlike a picturesque sheep farm. Not surprising, since the Chilean government leased Easter Island to a Scottish firm, to use as a sheep farm—right up until the 1950s. On each corner of the triangular island hangs an extinct volcano. Hiking Rano Kua delivers views and history, for this is where the ruling elite behind the *moai* statues was replaced by the cult of Birdman in the 17th century. Or maybe they coexisted—nobody knows for sure.

Despite cultural events, and epic surfing, hiking, biking and horseback riding, it is the *moai* that deservedly steal the spotlight. At Ahu Tongariki, 15 sentinels face the island, as if protecting the land from the power of the Pacific wind. The *moai* at Ahu Nau Nau have intricate carvings on their backs and each is topped with a red headdress made of a different stone. The how's and why's of this are unknown, of course, but the buzz from sipping chardonnay on the grassy mounds of Anakena Beach as sunset explodes behind the statues needs no further explanation. Spend some time exploring Rano Raraku, the quarry where *moai* were constructed, and you'll instantly see the scale of the enterprise. Nearly half of the island's *moai* are found here, some finished, some abandoned long before completion. One statue, nicknamed El Gigante, is 21 metres high, weighing between 160 and 180 metric tons. Such is its size that it is unlikely it would ever have been raised. That so many *moai* were toppled over here and around the island suggests a rejection of all they might have represented, though it is possible we may not ever know the reason for sure.

Easter Island is often used as an example of what can happen through humanity's reckless regard for its environment. By demolishing their trees, the Rapa Nui decreased their chances to thrive under the fierce Pacific sun. The island may also serve as an example of what happens when the masses realize an entire belief system is built on myth as a means of control and distraction, for the benefit of the elite. Who wouldn't riot when discovering the truth about false idols? Juicy stuff, and much to ponder as you chew on hot-stone-cooked ahi tuna and sweet potatoes that were baked in an earth oven. Why were the *moai* built and later abandoned? What did they represent? How did the first settlers find this island? When did they build the statues? Who built them? Where did they learn such craftsmanship? So many damn questions, but at least one courts no controversy. Does Easter Island belong on the Great Global Bucket List? Absolutely.

START HERE:
globalbucketlist.com/easter

More Ancient Mysteries for the Bucket List

Did a technically advanced ancient civilization exist before the last ice age, giving rise to the legends of Atlantis, and even Noah's Ark? Did aliens mark a desert in Peru and the English countryside with a celestial landing strip? Come up with your own theories at these sites:

Göbekli Tepe, Turkey: Six thousand years *before* the construction of Stonehenge, before humanity had discovered pottery, agriculture or the wheel, Stone Age primitives built a sophisticated temple complex with 20 *T*-shaped limestone towers, elaborately decorated with carvings of animals. It is the oldest surviving temple (or monument) in existence, and its origins and purpose remain a mystery.

Stonehenge, England: Sometime between 2000 BC and 3000 BC, somebody decided to build a massive megalithic structure using stones weighing around 25 metric tons each, some of which were transported from a quarry 240 kilometres away. We don't exactly know when they did it, we don't know who did it and we don't know why they did it. To protect the structure from Griswolds (see *National Lampoon's European Vacation*), you'll have to ponder this mystery from the surrounding walkway.

The Nazca Lines, Nazca Desert, Peru: Landing strips for spaceships? Tributes to the gods? Markers for primitive astronomy? An irrigation scheme? Nobody knows the origins of these grand and elaborate ancient geoglyphs. Take a scenic flight to spot enormous animals, plants and geometric designs, the longest of which stretches almost 15 kilometres across the plains.

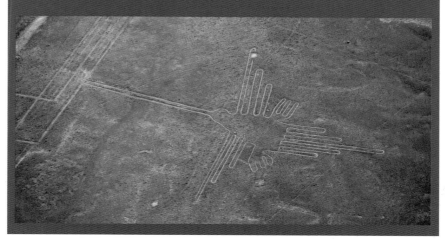

Submerge in the Mud Volcano of Youth

This one is straight out of Willy Wonka's sweet imagination. About an hour's drive outside Cartagena lies a natural phenomenon known as Volcán de Lodo El Totumo, a volcano with thick, mineral-rich, chocolate-textured mud bubbling in its crater. Formed by various geological forces, mud volcanoes, free of hot lava but saturated with sedimentary sludge, are found around the world. Several volcanoes are featured in this book, and bucket listers should take great care not to fall into their craters. This particular volcano, on the other hand, wants us to jump right in.

Locals have long enjoyed the therapeutic benefits of dipping into El Totumo's mud. Lately, the pool-size crater has been seeing a lot more foreign bodies, which make the journey from the cruise port of Cartagena. First, dispel the image of Mount Doom. This is no lava-crackling cone towering in the distance, shooting gases and molten rock into the sky. In fact, when you first encounter Volcán de Lodo El Totumo, it looks like an overgrown termite hill, or a 15-metre-high pile of elephant dung. More than one bucket lister will shake his or her head disappointed, wondering if this is just another tourist scam, a two-bit natural wax museum. Well, don't judge a book by its cover, a volcano by its lava or a Colombian taxi driver by his choice of car (trust me on that last one).

I climb a slippery path to the top, holding on to rickety wooden beams, quickly ascending high enough to gaze across lush tropical vegetation and a tranquil lagoon below. Several thatch huts at the base offer blessed shade from a scorching equatorial sun. Volcán de Lodo is operated by an association from a nearby village, the villagers rotating duties of collecting entrance fees, selling bottled water and offering massages (for tips) or lagoon rinses (for more tips). The crater itself is the size of a small pool, if you can imagine a small pool full of dark, creamy mousse.

I arrive early, before the crowds, and a single villager beckons me in. The sun is already beating down hard, so I hang my shirt on the wood and eagerly immerse myself in the cool, thick slop. I loved *Charlie and the Chocolate Factory*

(the original, not the remake), and I've always fantasized about swimming in a pool of milk chocolate. Not anymore. This mud is so thick it suspends my body as hair gel would, comfortably invading my pores with natural mineral goodness. The mud is solid enough to support my head when I lie back; the crater, deep enough for me to stretch out in every direction and relax every muscle in my body. Within seconds I feel like vanilla soft-serve dipped into melted chocolate, with goggles of bare skin around my eyes. The mousse masseuse effortlessly spins me over and roughly exfoliates my back by rubbing his hands up and down. Like most Colombians I have met, he is only too eager to share his culture's genuine hospitality.

Refreshingly cool in the mid-morning sun, the mud envelops my body as if it were liquid black latex. Buses of tourists arrive and the small crater quickly fills up, a bowl of black-bean soup with floating white potatoes. A splash of mud gets in my eye, but fortunately another villager is on hand to wipe it away with tissue paper. Tugging on our arms and legs, the masseuse parks us around the crater, making sure everyone gets a spot. After 30 minutes, the mud has sucked up whatever toxins it could find, and I begin to feel light-headed. Emerging from the silt porridge, I make my way down to the adjacent lagoon, where village women await with tin bowls for the messy cleanup. My rinse-lady is fearless. She dunks me into the warm lagoon, scrubbing me with her hands. Before I know it, she's ripped off my shorts too. Female tourists yelp as they cling to their bikinis for dear life. Within seconds, I'm mud-free and, after awkwardly replacing my shorts beneath the water, emerge from the lagoon with rejuvenated skin glistening in the sunshine.

Local legend calls it the "Volcano of Youth," where a 50-year-old might enter the crater and leave 20 years younger. Whatever the medical or mythical benefits of this volcano may be, it's most certainly one for the Great Global Bucket List.

START HERE:
globalbucketlist.com/
mudvolcano

More Fountains of Youth

The legend of 16th-century Spanish explorer Juan Ponce de León's quest for a magical spring has long captured popular imagination. Drink or bathe in these waters and, voilà, your youth is restored! Unfortunately, de León's search may be as mythical as the fountain itself, since there's no actual evidence he ever went on one. Still, several springs are claimed, despite all scientific evidence, to be the real deal, including:

Coamo, Puerto Rico: These mineral-rich hot springs have long been thought to be the *original* Fountain of Youth, thanks to indigenous legends.

Isla del Sol, Bolivia: After climbing 206 steps to the village of Yumani, fill your water bottle from the sacred springs believed by some to grant everlasting youth. Note: I've done it twice over the years, but the grey hairs are still sprouting.

Punta Gorda, Florida, USA: Feel the glow of youth from these artesian waters in Charlotte Harbor. The fountain pays tribute to Juan Ponce de León and also warns drinkers that

the waters exceed the maximum contaminant level for radioactivity.

Sanliurfa, Turkey: The father of monotheistic religions, Abraham is said to have lived to age 175. Might it have something to do with these sacred springs that quenched his youth? Visitors to the Cave of the Patriarchs (a.k.a. the Sanctuary of Abraham) can take a swig from a handy water pipe.

Evolve in the Galapagos

ECUADOR

Some movies are critic-proof. Big-name director, huge stars, compelling subject matter, perhaps a superhero or two—film critics can only stand back and let the box-office dollars flow. Likewise, there's no debate about the Galapagos. It's a renowned no-brainer for the bucket list. As for me, the mythical and remote archipelago has been the burning flame to my moth's imagination for over a decade. Now, having finally found myself booked on a week-long island cruise, I'm battling the Demon of Expectations. I'm not wild about birds. I've seen plenty of volcanoes and sea lions and sea turtles. Will the Galapagos Islands live up to my heady expectations?

Groups of birdwatchers are twitching with excitement waiting for the delayed flight from Ecuador's Guayaquil to Baltra Island. The Galapagos comprises one of the world's largest marine reserves, recognized by UNESCO and protected across various categories, but the archipelago is not quite as remote as one might think. Although the islands are located 1,600 kilometres off the coast of Ecuador, over 25,000 people call them home. After a six-hour delay, the plane finally touches down to the grateful applause of tourists from around the world. We will all pay a hefty park fee, then scatter to awaiting ships and ferries. Mine is Haugan Cruises' *Ocean Spray*, the best small boat I could find, a 34-metre luxury catamaran with huge staterooms, walk-in showers, private decks and fantastic staff. Joining me are 16 bucket listers from England, the United States, Austria and Australia. Everyone is glowing with the aura that surrounds those who finally, at long last, realize a dream. We introduce ourselves over the first of many superb meals and then head to the upper deck to starbathe beneath the glittering Milky Way. A warm, humid breeze hugs us like a comforter. Eventually, exhausted after my 28-hour transit, I retire to my stateroom and dream of Darwin.

Twenty-six-year-old Charles Darwin landed in the Galapagos Islands in 1835. He was the

naturalist aboard HMS *Beagle*, part of a British expedition on a voyage of discovery around the world. Darwin spent just five weeks of his five-year journey aboard the *Beagle* in the Galapagos, but these five weeks inspired the theories of natural selection and evolution that revolutionized our understanding of the world. Darwin correctly ascertained that each of the 13 species of finches found on the islands had a common ancestor and had adapted over time to their individual environments. Likewise, black marine iguanas had evolved from land iguanas to survive on the harsh rocky coastline. And as with these creatures, so for

the rest of us. There is no shortage of books explaining the history, details and significance of Darwin's work. Instead, let me focus on what it's like to see marine iguanas with Galapagos penguins and giant sea turtles and sea lions and flightless cormorants and blue-footed boobies and bright orange Sally Lightfoot crabs in the same viewfinder—that is, in the *same* frame. All there, together, everywhere you look.

We had sailed from Baltra to the northern tip of Isabela Island, crossing the equator early in the morning to anchor at Punta Vincente Roca.

There, we hopped aboard a motorized dinghy (called a *panga*) for our first excursion, which skirted a steep volcanic cliff, where dark cracks in the rocks turned out to be bathing black marine iguanas. The fauna of the Galapagos is famously unperturbed by human presence. Over the next week, I have to watch myself not to trip over the fierce-looking iguana dragons—or lazing sea lions and skittish lava lizards. Our group is still buzzing from our first wildlife encounter when Morris, our onboard naturalist, spots a massive manta ray breaching the surface. Its fin is 5 metres across. As we head toward a nearby sea cave, there's so much wildlife, I don't know where to look first. Underwater, as it turns out, for the first of several incredible snorkels.

I swim alongside an iguana, watch an underwater cormorant mating ritual and almost bump into a huge green sea turtle, while a squadron of penguins gracefully scream past. Moments later, a curious sea lion circles around me, maintaining puppy-dog eye contact. No other wildlife encounter has come close to this, and we're just getting started.

Our first shore landing is at Punta Espinoza, on the youngest island in the chain, Fernandina. Now we're stepping over hundreds of marine iguanas (described by Darwin as "Imps of Darkness") snorting white streams of salt from their specialized salt-excreting glands. We do a short walk on a designated route, sticking to the

trail to minimize our impact on the environment. Under a tree, a baby sea lion barks for its mother, endemic mockingbirds sing overhead. Morris leads us over the jagged lava flow to his favourite spot, where four sea turtles bathe in the sunset and a silhouetted lava huron plucks fish out of the water.

"Thank you, Morris. This has been one of the finest days of my life," says Brian, a retired Anglican priest from London, England, in a voice that sounds uncannily like that of David Attenborough. We all nod our heads in agreement.

We awake each morning to soft music on the intercom, and Morris's briefing of the day ahead. "Bring sun protection and water, and wear comfortable walking shoes or sandals," he says in a soothing *sotto voce*. We

Survival of the Fittest

Flightless cormorants, swimming iguanas, tropical penguins, a rat-eating centipede—the Galapagos' isolation allowed creatures to evolve with unique traits—traits you won't find anywhere else. Birders will encounter the world's entire population of waved albatrosses gathered April to December on Española Island. Look out for the colourful painted locusts, keeping their buggy eyes out for endemic lava lizards and the Galapagos hawk. Other creatures that have evolved on the islands include the Galapagos mockingbird, sea lion, giant frigate and more than 50 species of fish. Diving, most famously with schools of large but harmless hammerheads, is primarily focused around Wolfe and Darwin Islands, in the north.

have arrived at Tagus Cove for a hike up to Darwin Lake, and onward to a sweeping viewpoint of the surrounding volcanoes. Finches flutter about. The birdwatchers among us are enthralled by the avian action that accompanies every step. Still, a century of graffiti on the harbour rocks jars with the isolation of the island. Morris explains that protecting the Galapagos is no short order. Invasive species of pigs, goats, insects and rats, along with fungus and human development, have wreaked havoc across the islands. Illegal shark finning and fishing in the reserve is a real issue, and public officials have passed increasingly lax laws (large-scale resort development has recently been approved).

The human population is growing, placing further pressure on the environment with the ongoing threat of more invasive species. Some argue that an increasing number of tourists will ultimately destroy the paradise, whereas others (myself included) believe responsible tourism can salvage the future. Each visitor will have his or her own thoughts on the matter, thoughts that will likely subside when snorkelling with spotted eagle rays, and green sea turtles, and hieroglyphic hawkfish, and blue chin parrotfish, and rainbow wrasses and dozens of other tropical fish. Every snorkel gets better than the last.

We land on the black sands of Urvina Bay for our first encounter

with yellow land iguanas, larger and more territorial than their marine cousins. More birds, more sea lions, more dancing hermit crabs and bright orange-yellow Sally Lightfoot crabs, which one could watch for hours. Giant frigates glide like pterodactyls in the slipstream above our sun chairs as the *Ocean Spray* continues onward. As for the sunsets, if only one could bottle them in this part of the world. Along with the stars.

Having explored the sharp lava field before dinner (walking on tendon-like *pahoehoe* and glass-sharp *ah-ah* lava), we receive our evening briefing and the news that tonight's sailing to the main island of Santa Cruz will be a little rough. Up on the deck, the boat pitching and rolling, I gather with my new friends as nausea blows a cold wind down my neck. Fortunately, it's a thick barf bag away from the

Drake Passage that laid me low in Antarctica.

I awake after a bouncy night to find the *Ocean Spray* anchored in the calm, blue-green waters of Academy Bay, gazing upon a strip of civilization. Puerto Ayora is bustling with tourists, dive shops, restaurants, boutiques, souvenir stores and hotels. It's not what you think of when you hear the word *Galapagos*, but the local population is as much a part of the islands as the wildlife. A sea lion sits at the feet of the ladies chatting on their cell phones at the fish market, while baby iguanas bask in the sun on the sidewalk.

We visit the Charles Darwin Research Station, where various species of giant tortoises are bred before being released onto their respective endemic islands. Having sustained centuries of hungry sailors, four tortoise species are

now extinct. Where once there were millions of tortoise, now there are an estimated 20,000. With the passing of the legendary Lonesome George in 2012, the current hero is Super Diego, a male who arrived from a San Diego zoo and has since sired some 1,500 offspring. At over 100 years old, he looks positively prehistoric. The walk through town back to the boat reminds me what

I'll be missing: unreal scuba diving with schools of hammerhead sharks in the north, the unique landscapes of islands further east. My six-day itinerary has been nothing short of magical, but in the Galapagos, magic is in no short supply.

START HERE:
globalbucketlist.com/galapagos

Visit the Equator

Ecuador is named after the equator on which it sits, an imaginary line equidistant from the North and South Poles, dividing the globe into its northern and southern hemispheres. La Mitad del Mundo is a tourist attraction outside Quito with a big yellow line painted on the pavement to represent the equator, a gift shop, a 30-metre-tall monument and some fun experiments to play with. The actual equator is 200 metres away, a screw-up discovered only with the invention of the Global Positioning System, and long after the monument was built. Close enough. Fill a basin with water and watch as it swirls down the drain clockwise when positioned on one side of the line, and in the reverse direction—counter-clockwise—when positioned on the other side of the line (thanks to the Coriolis effect)—but with no swirl at all when right on the line itself. On the equator, you can also, apparently, easily balance an egg on the head of a nail. Although, having never attempted to balance an egg on a nail anywhere at all, I suspect they might be making that last one up.

Explore the Amazon in Style

PERU

I n this book are adventures by foot, bus, bike, ship, helicopter, plane, ferry, camel, submarine, horse and train. Occasionally, we have travelled on faith, desire, fear and curiosity too. Now that it's time to delve deep into the ultimate jungle, our bucket list calls for travelling on a vessel as distinct as the world's richest biome—something luxurious to contrast the hostility and heat of the sweltering jungle juju. Which brings us to Aqua Expedition's floating penthouse, the *Aria Amazon*.

Most Amazon adventures traditionally kick off in Brazil's Manaus, but whereas Brazil contains 60 per cent of the 5.5-million-square-kilometre rainforest, 60 per cent of Peru—an area larger than Spain—is pure Amazon jungle. Serviced by flights and ferries, remote Iquitos is therefore our Peruvian port of call. As our LAN Airlines flight from Lima approaches this city of half a million inhabitants, I see a jade carpet of dense, impenetrable foliage stretched to the horizon. A meandering muddy river coils through an endless sea of trees. Leave the sanctuary of the waterway and the jungle will swallow you. In the airport arrival hall are four *Aria* nature guides we will get to

know well over the next four days. They are local guys, raised in tiny communities along the river's edge, enthusiastic to share their knowledge of the jungle's flora and fauna. Joining me are 24 passengers from the United States, United Kingdom, Australia, Japan and Austria. Humidity clings to our necks like melted toffee between the teeth.

We tour the city, stretching our legs in the main square as the setting equatorial sun casts a pink glow on the old tiles that decorate the former mansions of rubber barons. On our way to the port, we navigate a busy street market with vendors selling piranhas and manioc root and all manner of tropical fruits I can neither name nor

describe. Three-wheeled bike taxis are honking; families of four straddle the backs of scooters. Crowded knick-knack stores paddywhack into each other. Peruvian cities are a riot of colour. Wait until you get to the jungle.

As a skiff scoots us over to the awaiting *Aria*, warm air dances between my fingertips, moist from the spray of the mighty Amazon River, which flows an amazing 6,400 kilometres. The Amazon has a resumé that qualifies this region for any Great Global Bucket List. Unfolding across nine nations, it is the world's largest rainforest, home to over 2,000 species of birds and mammals, 950,000 identified species of insects and 3,000 types of fish. During the wet season, it can stretch over 190 kilometres in width. Despite the ongoing concerns of deforestation, the Amazon basin still generates 20 per cent of the world's oxygen. The Amazon has many plants, animals *and* people unknown to modern civilization, and more than a few creatures that can kick your bucket—anaconda, jaguar, piranha, poison frogs, malarial mosquitoes, electric eels and the odd rabid vampire bat. Don't let comparing that with the monsters you'll find in any urban sprawl scare you. Especially given that your floating hotel has air conditioning, hot showers, flush toilets, king-size beds and gourmet chefs preparing local delights. It's not cheap, mind

you, but the vision and execution of the *Aria* is quite extraordinary. The resident bartender, Robinson, greets us with a cocktail made of freshly squeezed camu-camu, a cherry-like Amazonian fruit that contains 60 times more vitamin C than an orange. Smiling cabin stewards show us to our rooms on the 45-metre-long vessel. I told my wife we'd be comfortable, but her eyes still pop out of her head. With just 16 suites, she didn't expect a jungle riverboat to have cabins with floor-to-ceiling windows, cabins as large and well-appointed as rooms in a luxury hotel. There's also a gym, Jacuzzi, bar, sun deck and 24 crew members to cater to our every whim.

We gather in the low-lit panoramic lounge on the top deck for a briefing, followed by the first of the trip's extraordinary Amazonian fine-dining menus. Armoured catfish broth with tapioca and wild cilantro. Fresh corn cake with freshwater shrimp salsa and crème fraiche. Rib-eye steak with peanut sauce and jungle greens. Grilled Amazon ceviche. Granitas of passion fruit and caju and lemongrass and new fruits with wondrous tastes. Ingredients you won't find back at home, prepared by award-winning local chefs into dishes you'll hope to have the good fortune to taste again.

"We hope you enjoyed seeing just a little of Iquitos—no mosquitoes!—and we promise you that you're not gonna *like* this trip, you're gonna *love* it!" says George, an easygoing guide with jokes and quips timed to perfection.

Each day will have two or three excursions, with guests split among four comfortable motorboats. On the skiffs, we see a world as exotic as it is abundant. Parrots, vultures, hawks, flycatchers, woodpeckers, birds with multicoloured feathers flocking together. Pairs of blue and yellow macaws glide in the expansive sky. We exit the muddy, milk-chocolate waters of the main river and explore blackwater tributaries, darkened by organic debris. Beneath us, in this part of the river, swim nearly 700 species of fish, including giant catfish and feared piranha. A three-toed sloth dances ever so slowly to a soundtrack of unrelenting birdsong. Beneath the sloth are flowers and trees and other plants exploding a wild cacophony of biodiversity, as one would expect given the 40,000 plant species found in the Amazon.

Just beyond the protected borders of the 20,000-square-kilometre Pacaya-Samiria National Reserve are many villages too, built on stilts and flooded during the wetter months. It rains 250 days a year in this part of the world, but the rivers recede enough from May to September for thousands of villagers to migrate forth from terra

firma (ground that doesn't flood) in order to plant crops like yucca and banana. Some villages have a dozen families, others over 500 people. They wave from their wooden dugout canoes—same world, different planets. Ironically, for all the wasteful slashing and burning of the jungle, high heat and rainfall make Amazonian soil ill-suited for agriculture.

We choose a spot for piranha fishing, catching a few guppy-size fish with our wooden sticks. My wife bravely brushes a large spider off my back. In the jungle, as in life, you kind of just have to go with it. Our guide, Ricardo, gives us cool towels to wipe off with, and colder beer to refresh with. A memorable buffet lunch on the *Aria* (Dorado catfish brochettes, braised goat in corn beer), a siesta, and then we head out again on the skiffs in the late afternoon. Squirrel monkeys do the jungle boogie-woogie, an otter comes up to the boat for a belly scratch. Evening brings out the bugs, and the nocturnal animals that feed on them. We watch the sunset from the middle of the river, toasting with mimosas and snacking on jungle nuts. Pricks of starlight illuminate the heavens, while a bright

blood moon rises through the trees. Now we use a spotlight in search of reflecting eyes. Ricardo plucks a baby caiman from the swampy edge, not far from a larger mother deeper in the bushes. We're on the lookout for anacondas and jaguars, but in an area so vast, seeing these creatures is unlikely. A shooting star sizzles above our heads as we return to the welcoming, cool and bug-free *Aria*. The crew call it "the mothership." She embraces us in her protective bosom.

We awake to a half-dozen pink dolphins splashing about outside our window. Some of the group had gone off on an excursion in search of these mythical river mammals, but it turned out the dolphins had come fishing around the boat instead. Not a bad morning view. The afternoon's excursion is on terra firma, where a local villager plucks out a poison dart frog, a too-large-for-comfort boa constrictor and a palm-size hairy tarantula. Nice jungle, wouldn't want to live in it . . . though many indigenous people and *mestizos* do, including an estimated 50 tribes that have never had any contact with the outside world. My wife chats in Spanish with Manual, a local villager, as we paddle up the river in his dugout canoe. He tells her about his three wives and three children, and his faith in the river. "The more money, the more problems," he says. I'm sure many of the wealthy guests on board the *Aria* would agree. We swim in the refreshingly cool and perfectly safe blackwater tributary before returning to the *Aria* to float between the convergence of three mighty rivers and the headwaters of the Amazon itself.

Ranging from 22 to 80 years old, our eclectic, friendly group of bucket listers dance to the tunes of the makeshift house band on our final night, relishing the good company and better fortune. However one chooses to explore the Amazon— king-size bed or hammock, luxury riverboat or local jungle ferry—it's

Amazon: Not Just an Online Retailer

Cashew, macaw, cayenne, cougar, jaguar, tapioca and *piranha* are just some of the words we use today courtesy of the Tupi-Guarani languages spoken in the Amazon rainforest. Ironically, the word *Amazon* is not one of them. When Spanish explorer Francisco de Orellana encountered the vast river system, he battled tribes of both male and female warriors. Inspired by the fierce female Amazonian warriors of Greek mythology, he named the region Amazonas.

sure to be a highlight on the Great Global Bucket List.

START HERE:
globalbucketlist.com/amazon

Hike the Inca Trail

PERU

The streets of Cuzco, the historic and tourist capital of Peru, are paved with tour operators, hostels, restaurants and the subtle fragrance of fresh urine. Here you will find international tourists in droves, shuffling along to the soundtrack of panpipes, gearing up for the 45-kilometre bucket list hike known as the Inca Trail.

Booking well in advance, one is advised to arrive in Cuzco a few days early to acclimatize to the altitude. Having grown up in Johannesburg, some 2,000 metres above sea level, I am hoping my body remembers life at altitude, muscle memory on a molecular level. After three days (and one crazy night in a wild club called Mama Africa), I'm still chasing breath, my hands lightly trembling. The air is as thin as the hair on Patrick Stewart's head. Each breath robs me of oxygen I have long taken for granted. The good news is that tomorrow I depart on the four-day hike, which climbs *another* 1,000 metres up the Andes. Truthfully, it's not all bad, this altitude business, not unlike being constantly excited. After a few days, your body learns to breathe air with limited oxygen, relieved to escape the smog-churning taxis that clatter the streets of Cuzco.

Joining me are nine trekkers, two guides and 13 porters. Government regulations require you trek with reputable guides. Cuzco is thus lined with companies offering one-, two- and four-day trips to the mysterious ancient wonder of Machu

Picchu. I recommend Peru Treks & Adventure, an outfit known for treating and paying their porters well. Collected on a crisp, early morning, our group meets for the first time. We will come to know one another well in the next week, breaking bread, hiking hard and chewing the coca leaf.

Once registered with authorities, we gradually and easily ascend through a valley, already apprehensive about day two, notoriously known as The Challenge. Six hours of hiking up uneven rocky steps at 4,200-metre elevation is not everybody's hot chocolate, especially those of us who consider walking a shopping mall a day hike. I packed as light as I could, but it doesn't take long for my daypack to weigh heavy on my shoulders, as if the shoelaces holding my sleeping bag and mattress together were guilty of a crime. As for our porters, they have feet of cement and lungs of steel. Unlike porters in Nepal, who are not regulated and can carry as much as 50 kilograms each, Inca Trail porters have a union and strict guidelines. They carry our tents, food, gas, equipment and water, and are responsible for our three meals a day. This allows us to stumble

exhausted into camp with our tents set up and tea ready to be served. God bless them. Especially Apu, our chef, who manages to cook delicious meals, Lord knows how, well into the trek—without refrigeration, and with only a tent for a kitchen. Good food always translates into good morale, and spirits are appropriately high for the altitude.

The pace is leisurely but steady, with one guide at the front, another at the back. There is always time to catch our breaths, to be inspired by the porters who leave later and arrive earlier, passing on the right with unnerving pace and rock-hard calves. Day two is every bit as challenging as we expected. The rock path ascends to the highest point, Dead Woman's Pass, by which stage each step requires intense motivation and energy. A Himalayan veteran in our group explains the importance of walking slow and steady, the tortoise versus the hare. Eventually, we summit with burning muscles, our backs dripping with sweat but cooling fast in the exposed mountain winds. Our rush of accomplishment is rousing but, because of the icy gust, understandably brief. Replenishing with chocolate, we descend on an uneven

rocky path, seemingly designed by the Inca to tear knee ligaments to shreds. Although, considering the trail is part of a 400-year-old, 32,000-kilometre road system that once connected the Incan Empire, it has held up remarkably well. We slug into camp elated that the worst is behind us, though with plenty more hiking to come.

On every trek, you reach a point of Zen, a moment when everything comes together. Now that your body is over the shock of what you're doing to it physically, you begin to appreciate where you are, what you are doing, and why the sacrifice has been worth it.

The trail levels out on the third day, cutting through the dense jungle that spreads to the Upper Amazon. Hummingbirds zip overhead, hikers are smiling. Different seasons have different pros and cons for trekkers, and since I'm here in April, one of the very definite cons is the prospect of rain. Drops the size of manhole covers turn the rocky path, already worn from centuries of use, into a slippery mountain slide. As the clouds open, we snap on our waterproof ponchos and quicken the pace downhill to the campsite. Before long, I find myself running, a silly way to travel given the conditions, but an exhilarating way too. Life is all about moments. This is the moment where I'm running down an ancient Incan rock path in an Andes downpour.

Camping facilities on the final night offer hot showers, cold beer and a healthy dose of extra-strength ibuprofen. Our porters join us for a multicultural party, each member of the trekking group regaling us with a song of his or her culture. Refreshed after its late-afternoon shower, the jungle awakens with the songs of birds and insects, planets dancing above the heads of stargazing parrots. For the first time on this trek, I sleep soundly, if not for long. We are awoken at 4 a.m. to pack up one last time for the two-hour walk to Machu Picchu.

Arriving at Sun Gate just after sunrise, we finally glimpse the fabled lost city in the distance. Machu Picchu was discovered by American

5 More Hikes on the Great Global Bucket List

Annapurna Circuit, Nepal: Although trekking to Everest Base Camp hogs the glory, this multi-week circuit is regarded as the classic Nepal hike, offering an incredible variety of landscapes, rich cultural encounters and mountains tall enough to tickle the tummies of angels.

Mount Kilimanjaro, Tanzania: At 5,995 metres high, the "Roof of Africa" is also the world's highest "walkable" mountain, so while you may not need ropes to summit Uhuru Peak, you'll definitely need more air in your lungs.

Torres del Paine Circuit, Chile: Eighty-two kilometres, 10 days, and more eye candy than your retinas can handle, this trek circles the famous granite monolith spires of Chilean Patagonia, leading you to glaciers, lakes, forests and rock chasms.

Tour du Mont Blanc, France/Italy/Switzerland: A 160-kilometre loop around the highest mountain in Europe delivers the best views of the Alps, with the bonus of staying in comfortable mountain huts, feasting on fondues and fine wine.

West Coast Trail, Canada: This infamous 75-kilometre trail on the wild west coast of Vancouver Island immerses you in rugged wilderness, a physical challenge rewarded with waterfalls, tidal pools, beaches and old-growth forest.

explorer Hiram Bingham III in 1911, and nobody is quite sure who lived here, why they lived here or why they disappeared without telling anybody. Theories abound: it was home to high priests and witches; it was home to royals who abandoned it in the hope of returning to it after the Spanish invasion. It was not until Bingham hacked his way through the jungle that the city was discovered, to be later faithfully restored and now one of the world's most beautiful and mysterious ancient settlements. Tourists can catch buses and trains from Cuzco and make it a day trip, but as the destination after three hard days trekking, Machu Picchu delivers its famous spectacle. You truly feel you have arrived someplace extraordinary.

An advantage of hiking in is the few hours you have to yourself before tour buses arrive. We admire the Temple of the Sun without the distraction of crowds—its amazing craftsmanship, terraces and surroundings. We are fully exhausted and sweat-stained, somewhat resentful when the clean, camera-happy tourists arrive en masse.

Tired, wrecked and stretched, I amble through the ruins, play with roaming alpacas and eat a horrifically overpriced sandwich from the onsite restaurant. I try to climb Huayna Picchu, the mountain that overlooks Machu Picchu and is seen in all the postcards, but my swelling kneecap, formerly broken, has other ideas. I pop another ibuprofen and take a pass. Finally, our group catches a bus down the snake-coiling road to the town of Aguas Calientes, where we enjoy a final meal before a four-hour train ride back to Cuzco. After four days in the mountains, the dusty city feels like a metropolis of civilization. It is hard to believe that I watched the sunrise over Machu Picchu that very morning. Sinking into a soft hotel bed, I don't get up for 14 hours. A physical challenge rewarded with beauty, friendship and a mysterious wonder of the ancient world, the Inca Trail is a bucket list adventure that lives up to the hike.

START HERE:
globalbucketlist.com/incatrail

ARCTIC OCEAN

NORTH

Baffin Bay

AMERICA

Juneau

Inside Passage

Canadian Rockies

Hudson Bay

CANADA

Churchill

Haida Gwaii

Jasper

Banff

Great Lakes

Bay of Fundy

PACIFIC OCEAN

ATLANTIC OCEAN

Black Rock City

Yellowstone National Park

Niagara Falls

UNITED STATES

Coyote Buttes ■ ■ Monument Valley

Grand Canyon

New Orleans

Gulf of Mexico

Havana

MEXICO

CUBA

Santiago de Tequila

Mérida ■ ■ Chichén Itzá

Caribbean Sea

Mexico City

San Cristóbal de las Casas

BELIZE

■ Caves Branch

Pacaya ■

GUATEMALA

León

NICARAGUA

Arenal

COSTA RICA

N
W   E
S

| 0 | 500 | 1,000 Miles |
| 0 | 500 | 1,000 Kilometres |

Swim beneath an Underground Waterfall

For hundreds of thousands of years, fire-blackened caves provided shelter for our ancestors. Perhaps that's why we're still drawn to caves, though most tourist caverns feature coloured spotlights, crowds, damp wooden boardwalks and limestone formations with cringe-inducing nicknames. Mickey's Hump? Snoopy's Doghouse? Jabba the Hutt?

On the other end of the dark tunnel are spelunkers, those adventurers who use specialized ropes and harnesses to seek out cave systems that run for dozens of miles. Caving requires contortionist techniques, rock-climbing skill, the instincts of a navigator and arguably the motivation of a lunatic. In central Belize, I discovered it's possible to hoist yourself somewhere in the middle— an authentic cave adventure for us leisure tourists.

Canadian Ian Anderson opened his Caves Branch Jungle Lodge as an alternative to the sanitized resorts on Belize's Caribbean coast. Sitting on 23,500 hectares of property, it's a tropical jungle paradise for birdwatchers, nature lovers and anyone who prefers a subterranean flavour to their adventures. Caves Branch rests on a foundation of soft limestone, which, together with regular tropical rainfall, creates perfect conditions for the formation of hundreds of miles of caves and underground river systems.

Beyond its luxurious suites and modern treehouse accommodation, Caves Branch offers multiple caving excursions, tailored to different levels of fitness, physical skill and confidence. Guests can choose the cave-tubing option: sitting in the middle of doughnut-shaped rubber tubes to float down an underground river. Or there's the Black Hole option: a 60-metre abseil deep into a sinkhole, where you can camp overnight, not far from the bones of Mayan sacrifices. The resort's activity list is a menu of thrills, and my eyes are hungry. I settle for the Waterfall Cave Expedition, a dark and wet combo to contrast the bright jungle heat.

Torrential rain has swelled the river that runs alongside the lodge,

so a heavy-duty farm tractor is needed to transport us to the mouth of the cave. All Caves Branch guides are members of the Belize Association for Search and Rescue, and thanks to their combined decade-plus experience in the caves below, I'm in safe hands. Two guides accompany every group, and we're each provided with a waterproof headlamp, hard hat and life jacket. Standing in the trailer, we rumble alongside a tranquil orange grove, buttressing the jungle and limestone ridge. Vultures fly above in the citrus-tanged sky, their shadows sweeping the ground in circles. Twenty minutes later, we dismount

Don't Forget the Hot Sauce

There's little that's bland about Belize, and I'm not just talking about the coral reefs or Mayan ruins. Marie Sharp started out in her kitchen with a recipe for homemade hot sauce, and today her company manufactures some of the finest sauces, jams and jellies a chili head can find. I brought 14 bottles home with me, and went through every one of them. Combining local grapefruit or orange pulp with habanero peppers has created a terrifically tangy condimental masterpiece.

and head along a thin path that quickly disappears into the dense jungle. My guide, Pablo, points out a large camouflaged peanut bug and some aggressive fire ants. Bugs, snakes, spiders—no wonder people took refuge in caves.

Trappers and hunters discovered this particular cave in the 1950s. Further exploration in the 1970s revealed that the Maya had used the system centuries before, with ancient artifacts and even human remains found deep inside the system. Although Caves Branch owns the land above and outside, the government owns all subterranean rights in the country. Still, you won't find any tour buses pulling up here.

We gear up and descend into darkness. Immediately, I am acquainted with some of the extraordinary creatures that inhabit this world of darkness. Harmless fruit bats dash above my head, using sonar to avoid, at the last possible moment, collisions with rock and human. Pablo picks up a giant scorpion spider, possibly the most frightening insect I've ever encountered. Although harmless, it is 20 centimetres long, with two sharp pinchers, resembling a scorpion

with long, hairy legs. He puts it in the palms of my hands. Best I turn off my headlamp and not see these things.

It is a one-hour hike to reach the waterfalls. As we pass narrow, slippery channels, we're careful to avoid touching or breaking any of the thousands of stalactites dripping from the ceiling, formed at the glacial pace of just 1 millimetre every year. Often we must crawl on our hands and knees, hard hats scraping the low, muddy ceiling. Layered white limestone rock forms stunning natural formations, with water flowing from layer to layer like champagne over a glass pyramid. There are no cute names for these landmarks, no red lights painting a cavern as the "Devil's Kitchen." We are deep inside the earth, our headlamps providing the only comfort from the void.

A series of six waterfalls signals our arrival. I put down my bag, don a life jacket and dive headfirst into the cold pool below. Water gushes hard from the schism above, and it takes some effort to heave myself up, using holds in the rock to conquer this first challenge. The second will not be so easy. Pablo climbs up ahead to secure the rope.

In the confined space of a cave, the noise of the first, 6-metre waterfall is deafening. It soaks up my strength just swimming against the current, water crashing alongside me as I harness my carabiner to the rope as a precaution and begin to struggle and slip to find grips, my feet clumsily seeking out footholds as the gush of water pounds my thigh. I finally hoist myself to the top, where I scream in triumph, drenched and utterly elated. Scaling the waterfalls that follow is less physically demanding, as they are smaller and less intimidating. At the final pool, it is time to turn around. While this spectacular cave system does have another mouth, the waterfall path is a dead end. What goes up must come down, and what goes in must come out.

An hour later, I emerge from the silent cave into the dark jungle. It takes a few seconds to realize that night has fallen, and that a dense thicket has replaced limestone rock. The sounds of the jungle tickle my ears awake. As the tractor returns us to the lodge, I gaze up at a clear night sky, pinpricks of brilliant stars brushed together in that wild stroke called the Milky Way. Warm air tastes sweet; firebugs dance between the plump oranges. You don't have to be brave, crazy or fit to experience the true pleasure of a caving adventure. Providing, of course, there's light at the end of the tunnel.

START HERE:
globalbucketlist.com/belize

Bucket List Natural Landmarks

One could spend lifetimes chasing the world's most iconic natural landmarks. Unlike man-made landmarks, these natural wonders will likely be here long after our human experiment is over. Those not listed below are discussed elsewhere in this book. Grab a pencil and start ticking:

☑ Bay of Fundy, Canada

☐ Giant's Causeway, Northern Ireland

☑ Grand Canyon, USA

☑ Halong Bay, Vietnam

☐ Mount Everest, Nepal/Tibet

☐ Mount Kilimanjaro, Tanzania

☐ Niagara Falls, Canada/USA

☐ Old Faithful, Yellowstone National Park, USA

☑ Uluru (Ayers Rock), Australia

☐ Yellow Mountains, China

Feel the Hot Breath of a Polar Bear

It is a peculiar dichotomy: the largest carnivore on earth—a ruthless predator that can sprint, swim, climb and shred our bones with razor-sharp claws—and the cute, cuddly, perfect ambassador for soda-pop commercials. The last thing you'd ever want to encounter is a hungry 500-kilogram polar bear in the wild, unless you happen to be on a customized Tundra Buggy above 1.6-metre-high tires inside a protected viewing platform. Which is exactly where I found myself, wiping condensation off my camera lens, the droplets formed by the hot breath of a large polar bear.

Many a Canadian has told me that at the top of their bucket list is a visit to Churchill, Manitoba. It's a northern outpost town that sits on the edge of Hudson Bay, wholly unremarkable save for the wildlife that visits its shores. In the summer, up to 3,000 beluga whales gather in this part of the bay, a whale-watching gold mine where one can hop off the boat and snorkel with the white ghosts of the Arctic. For six weeks in the fall, Churchill lies directly in the migratory path of the world's most southerly population of polar bears. Nearly 1,000 bears awaken from their summer slumber and hang about, waiting for the bay to freeze. Once it does, they begin their long journey north on the ice in search of food. The result is a bonanza for polar bear scientists, conservationists, photographers and bucket listers who want a face-to-face encounter with this magnificent, beautiful and somewhat terrifying creature. Terrifying that it can look so damn cute yet be so damn deadly.

Frontiers North Adventures' charter plane touches down in Churchill, where the large group of international travellers who were aboard are met by a weathered school bus.

Above the driver's seat is a shotgun, and we are immediately reminded that it is polar bear season. This means sticking to lit roads in town, adhering to polar bear warning signs and not stepping foot off the Tundra Buggy Lodge, our home for the days ahead. Within a few minutes, we spot our first bear, ambling over some rocks. It stands up on its hind legs like a meerkat, prompting about 8 billion photos from our group. We are an experienced group—many of us have been to the Masai Mara, Antarctica and Galapagos—and yet this first encounter is viscerally emotional. One woman breaks down in tears.

"Oh, don't worry, you're going to see a lot of polar bears, and a lot closer than that," says our driver, Neil, who has seen this all before.

We spend one night in town, learning how Churchill keeps its population safe with cameras, bear traps and a special bear jail for repeat offenders. Kevin Burke, who has been driving buggies for three decades, explains: "The bears follow their noses, [smell being] their keenest sense. Their curiosity gets them in trouble. We're not a food source, but we are easy pickings, especially if they're starving. We live on their turf, so we can't be blasé about it. I've trained my wife to use a firearm. I've got two young kids. You have to be bear aware." There have been remarkably few bear attacks in Churchill, and the town has become a model of how humans and wildlife can share the same habitat. Walking to the hotel from the restaurant on a dark, freezing night, I still have to steel up to face the bears in my mind, waiting to pounce from behind every parked car.

Tundra Buggies take visitors on day trips into the bears' domain, or you can spend several nights in the 100-metre-long buggy lodge. Secure atop its high wheels, we will sleep, eat and lounge on several connected train-like carriages, serviced by a small crew whose feet won't touch ground for the duration of the eight-week season. Smaller buggies, heated by propane fireplaces and with anti-fog windows, dock on each end like spaceships, allowing us to explore different parts of the bay.

We don't have to look far to find bears. Twenty metres from the heated dining room, two adolescent males are sparring on their hind legs, practising for the difficult months ahead. Largely solitary creatures, they are learning the behaviour they will need to survive on the ice. Another bear, a large scar across his nose, casually walks up to the buggy and pops up to look

inside the windows. He is not threatening or aggressive, but having not eaten in months, Harry Potter (as Neil calls him) would have no problem finding the meat beneath our Canada Goose parkas. We see Arctic fox, hare and ptarmigans, all residing in the shadows of the bears. Neil was right—there are a lot of them, and we see them often. One crosses an ice lake, backlit by the sun. Another is playing with a cub, a photographer's dream. They appear innocuous, which is perhaps one of the reasons we're so attracted to polar bears but fear grizzlies. Climate change is bringing both species closer together. With warming temperatures, the ice on Hudson Bay is freezing later, but nobody informed the biological clocks of the local bears. This may be the most accessible population of wild polar bears, but it is also the most threatened. There have been reports of polar-grizzly hybrids (nicknamed "grolar bears") as grizzlies head north in search of food and polar bears have no ice on which to hunt. Our onboard interpreters and bear experts explain all this, along with bear behaviour and why conservationists do not intervene, even if the bears are starving. Feeding

The Best Animal Encounters in Canada

Bison: Stampede your way to Alberta's Elk Island National Park.

Caribou: Track herds in Yukon's Ivvavik National Park or northern Labrador.

Elk and Bighorned Sheep: Gaze over the Albertan Rockies.

Grizzlies: Sniff out BC's Great Bear Lodge.

Moose: Paddle your way into Ontario's Algonquin Provincial Park.

Salmon: Witness the world's largest sockeye migration up BC's Adams River.

Whales: Explore the Bay of Fundy, Gwaii Haanas National Park Reserve or Cape Breton. For belugas, head to Churchill in summer or Nunavut's Arctic Watch Wilderness Lodge.

Wolves: Howl at the moon inside Saskatchewan's Prince Albert National Park.

bears can make them dependent on humans and lead to aggression and, ultimately, an inability to survive in the wild. Even on the tundra, a fed bear is a dead bear.

Once viewed as a nuisance for local industry, polar bears have become vital to Churchill's economy. The eight-week season is short, and the town's hotels and two buggy lodges book up fast, despite the steep prices. Temperatures at this time of year can drop to -40°C. Thanks to our fascination with

polar bears, and bucket lists, we pay no heed. A ride on a Tundra Buggy during the annual polar bear migration is without doubt something to do before you die. With melting sea ice and rising sea levels—increasing threats to the polar bears' natural habitat—you might want to act before the polar bears of Churchill sadly die first.

START HERE:
globalbucketlist.com/polarbear

Experience the Rockies

I'm not one to ignore accolades for the Alps, Andes and Himalayas, but in the Mountain Olympics of my heart, nothing beats the Rockies. In particular the Canadian Rockies, which boast gold medals in several categories. First of all, you can't legally ski within any other UNESCO World Heritage Site, nor could you find one with the jaw-dropping views of Banff National Park. Lake Louise, Sunshine Village and Banff Norquay are not the largest nor the best ski resorts in Canada, they just happen to be the most magnificent.

Next on the podium is surely the world's most stunning drive. Highway 93, also known as the Icefields Parkway, connects Banff and Jasper National Parks, and essentially consists of one postcard stapled to another. It will take you only five hours to drive it, but you'll most likely stop to ogle at the turquoise lakes, stroll on the Columbia Icefield Glacier or wobble on the glass horseshoe-shaped viewing platform of the Glacier Skywalk. If it's a summer day, you're obligated to swim in at least one glacial lake, just because everyone needs an ice-cold slap in the soul. Banff and Lake Louise are lovely little towns, blessed with two of the world's iconic mountain hotels—Fairmont's Banff Springs and Chateau Lake Louise. Moraine Lake Lodge, Fairmont Jasper Park Lodge, the Post Hotel and Emerald Lake Lodge are pretty exceptional too. If you'd like to cross-country ski back in time, book a night at Skoki Lodge, the oldest backcountry lodge in western Canada, which lacks bathrooms and electricity but does have the glorious veneer of how things used to be (and a fantastic chef).

There are better places in the world to hike, play golf or canoe. You can go flightseeing through the mountains in New Zealand, Alaska or Iceland, though I doubt you'll find the quality of heli-yoga offered by Rockies Heli Canada. Point is, you can find snow-capped mountains and jewelled lakes in other places, but you won't find them as accessible, well serviced and glorious as in the Rockies of western Canada.

START HERE:
globalbucketlist.com/rockies

Stand beneath the Totem Poles in Haida Gwaii

I spent several years travelling across Canada—coast to coast to coast—and many bucket list moments are discussed in my other books. Horseback riding among the bison in the prairies, kayaking alongside icebergs, jetboating the world's highest tides, snorkelling with migrating salmon—Canada is bursting with unique experiences. Yet when friends ask me about personal Canadian favourites, a whimsical glaze comes to my eyes as I think about an alluring Pacific archipelago in northern British Columbia. It is called Haida Gwaii, and there's nowhere else on earth quite like it.

The Haida were once a feared seafaring nation, compared in their prowess and aggressiveness to the Vikings. Their two clans, the Eagle and the Raven, were governed by traditions that balanced power in trade and civil life. They still speak a language you'll find nowhere else on the planet, and their bold, distinct art is world-renowned. With the arrival of European settlers, the Haida nation was all but exterminated through a combination of disease and cultural annihilation. Of a pre-contact population of 10,000, by the early 1900s, just 350 Haida remained. Their hallowed habitat became known as the Queen Charlotte Islands, their seas plundered for whales and sea otters. The archipelago's remoteness offered some measure of protection, and today, the Haida are staging a dramatic comeback. In 2010, the islands were officially named Haida Gwaii ("Islands of the Haida people"). An impressive $26-million Haida Heritage Centre now greets visitors in the main hub of Sandspit. The Gwaii Haanas National Park Reserve uniquely protects 138 islands, from the ocean floor to the mountaintop, creating an environment of such pristine wilderness it has been called the Galapagos of the North.

Visitor numbers are limited, and the only way to explore Gwaii Haanas, and visit the UNESCO World Heritage Site of Anthony Island, is on the water. After Parks Canada's mandatory orientation, I board Bluewater Adventures' 21-metre-long *Island Roamer* for a week sailing the islands. We'll visit towering old-growth forest, drift alongside pods of transient orcas and other whales, and meet the Watchmen, Haida men and women who volunteer on a half-dozen islands to guide visitors into the absorbing world of Haida culture.

S'Gang Gwaay, once a thriving Haida village on Anthony Island, is represented today by the remains of cedar longhouses and cracked century-old totem poles facing the wind. James Williams, who has volunteered as the island's Watchman for over a decade, explains how the Haida attribute supernatural qualities to the creatures of the islands—the ravens, eagles, bears and whales—and to the trees themselves. Totem poles from Haida Gwaii sit in museums in Victoria and Ottawa, but these last remaining mortuary poles carry a lot of weight in their splinters. UNESCO recognized the village's historical significance in 1981; indeed, there's an intangible quality to the place. It might not be as old as other ancient wonders discussed in this book, but the same energy permeates the air: this is all that remains of a time that will never be the same again.

Sailing these remote islands in the simple comfort of a yacht is a world-class eco-adventure, one that is steeped in a sincere appreciation of the environment. When we discover washed-up ocean garbage on Kunghit Island, the passengers are mobilized to gather it all up and return it to the boat for later disposal. A black bear feasts on salmon swimming upriver, unperturbed by our cameras capturing the moment. Famously unpredictable weather cooperates during the week, the protected waters calm for our Zodiac expeditions. Our chef somehow whips up incredible dishes from the confines of her tiny galley, including fresh halibut gifted by one of the Watchmen. On board, I share a tiny bunkroom in the bow of the ship with a retired gentleman in his 70s, the epitome of the bucket lister. It doesn't matter that we share a small room on a small boat with 20 other passengers. What matters is the true one-of-a-kind experience.

The year 2013 saw the raising of the first new totem pole on Haida Gwaii in over a century. It stands three storeys high and weighs 3,000 kilograms. Master carvers spent a year delicately adding symbols to it, depicting the unique custodial relationship of the Haida people to their land. The totem was raised to celebrate the 20th anniversary of the agreement that allows the Haida and Canadian government to jointly administer and protect the island. Symbolically, the totem represents the promise of a nation's re-emergence of the glory of its past. Tears swelled up in the eyes of the hundreds of locals who attended the raising.

This infusion of culture, history and nature stuck with me during my visit, and sticks with me still, an intangible quality I wish I could share with everyone I know. Including Haida Gwaii in a book about the world's very best experiences will have to do.

START HERE:
globalbucketlist.com/haida

Tour Havana in a Classic Convertible

As the modern world reaches Cuba, many things will change. Exploring Havana from the backseat of a classic American convertible will hopefully not be one of them. There are some 60,000 vintage American cars in the country, driven not as collectors' playthings but as a necessary form of transport. Due to the trade embargo, these prize vehicles have been elbow-greased with non-original parts and converted to diesel to save money. Dozens of freshly painted Fords, Chevrolets, Plymouths, Oldsmobiles, Buicks, Mercuries and Cadillacs line up at Havana's Parque Central to offer tourists rides around the city. Basking in sunshine, you'll see sights like the impressive Capitolio, the Plaza de la Revolucíon, the Necrópolis Cristóbal Colón and Chinatown. Feel the sea breeze ruffle your hair as you rumble down the Malecón, Havana's famed esplanade. Should you feel the need to light up a fine Cuban cigar, you can be assured of its quality. Some things never change.

START HERE: globalbucketlist.com/cuba

Swim in a Cenote

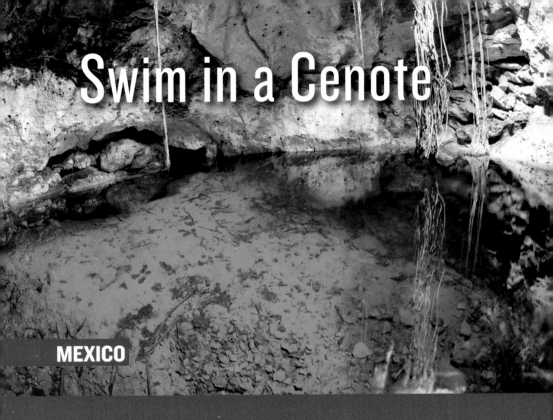

MEXICO

Posh resorts will tell you that *Cancun* means "end of the rainbow." In Mayan, *Cancun* means "snake pit," a more accurate description of the massive resorts that coil around the coastline, constricting sun-starved tourists and squeezing out hard-earned dollars. I ask the hotel shuttle driver if he knows the weather forecast. Since I don't speak Spanish, this involves me making sounds of splashing and blowing wind, and pretending to sunbathe, all badly.

"Señor," says José (for that is the name on his badge), "it will rain for 11 days."

"Good thing I'm leaving in the morning, then," I say proudly, irritating fellow passengers. Nothing wrong with an all-inclusive resort vacation, but I'm here to explore the Yucatan Peninsula, which means getting the jalapeño out of Cancun.

For authenticity's sake, I forgo the comfortable tourist shuttle for a local long-distance bus, on which I am entertained by poorly dubbed American action movies blaring at high volume. First stop is a treat of the ancient world, Chichén Itzá, not to be confused with chicken pizza, which happens to be delicious. A giant Mayan pyramid sits in a jungle clearing, each stone perfectly positioned to create an incredibly accurate cosmic calendar. This is Mayan country. The Maya still constitute the largest indigenous group in Mexico yet it is a mere shadow of the mighty empire that ruled before the Spanish invasion in the 16th century. Along with their advances in astronomy, sophisticated city states and impressive stone temples, the Maya invented a precursor to soccer, basketball and tennis called *pok-a-tok,* in which two teams battle to get a rubber ball through an elevated stone circle without using their hands. Competing on a walled court—Chichén Itzá's is the size of a football field— the captain of the winning team would be sacrificed, which is a rather strange incentive to be the team's leader. Imagine ripping out Sidney Crosby's heart as reward for winning Olympic hockey gold. Yes,

humanity has come a long way.

Human sacrifice was viewed by the Maya as an honour, even for the elite. Still, historians describe a huge, lowly population working for a wealthy class of priests who forbade them to look at the stars, or even use the wheel. Sacrifices—the heads of the lucky "chosen" rolling down the pyramid steps—kept the masses in place. As for why the Maya suddenly disappeared in the area, evidence suggests that bodies were dumped into nearby water sinkholes, or cenotes, which poisoned the drinking supply. People were getting sick and dying, so to appease the gods, there were more sacrifices, and soon enough everyone was either dying or being sacrificed, a vicious circle that ultimately left Chichén Itzá in ruins.

Any visit to the region has to include the other cenotes, found outside the lovely colonial city of Mérida. The water in these cave pools is sparklingly clean and terrific fun to swim in. To find them, I take a one-hour bus ride, passing small Mayan villages where heat bakes the earth and toothy kids play traditional games in the streets. My transit, arranged through a local tour operator, continues by horse cart, pulled along a narrow gauge rail to the first sinkhole. Catfish are swimming in the warm, clear water. A wooden platform lets me dive into the blue, as deep and bright as if someone had stirred in colour therapy bath salts. I visit three different cenotes, scaling the walls of each cave as stalactites slowly drip their way from the ceiling. Giant roots from trees above descend through the limestone. One cave has a small opening for a 12-metre jump into the dark waters below. You can easily forgo the launch platforms for the wooden staircases descending gently into the pools. If you do decide to jump, mind your *cojones*.

Another loud bus ride drops me off in San Cristóbal de las Casas, once a volatile stronghold of the revolutionary Zapatista Army of National Liberation, now the image of a leafy Spanish colonial postcard. I visit the Mayan villages of Chamula and Zinacantan, which provide a fascinating intercultural encounter. Where else will you see live chickens sacrificed in a church, or Coca-Cola worshipped along with the saints? The bizarre integration of Christianity into Mayan paganism has created a spectacle, to be witnessed respectfully (or else shamans will confiscate your camera).

Late-night salsa dancing at local bars, gorging in cheap taco joints—oh yes, it's a joy to drown in swamps of Yucatan guacamole and flash floods of lime-soaked beer. After I visit the ruins of Palenque, one final adventure finds me speeding up the Rio Grande on a boat beneath the kilometre-high cliffs of the Sumidero Canyon. The Maya once jumped off the edges to avoid being captured as slaves for the Spanish. I see a large crocodile swimming just 50 metres from children playing in the river. The *cocodrilo* is clearly not into Mexican food the way I am. The guide on the boat is machine-gunning facts in Spanish, so I sit back and just appreciate that I'm outside the hotel bubble, exposed to a culture unique to the world and surrounded by a beauty authentically, and distinctly, Mexican. I expect some readers will prefer the all-inclusive option in Cancun rather than the Yucatan adventures I had, and there's nothing wrong with that. Travel, like a bucket list, is a personal decision. One person's end of the rainbow is another's snake pit.

START HERE:
globalbucketlist.com/cenote

Cheer for a Luchador

Metalium has tied me into a human pretzel. He's pinned one arm behind my neck and looped my leg behind my back, resulting in a lock designed to separate one's shoulder from one's body. In an unfortunate case of my intended meaning being lost in translation, the boisterous wrestling student mistook "Skinny travel writer wants to learn wrestling moves" for "Gringo warrior wants to fight." The moment I enter the practice ring, I am thrown against the hard ropes, picked up, slammed down, flung about, T-boned, elbowed, body kicked and kneecapped. I'm slapping the floor with my one free palm, the frantic wave of submission, writhing in equal parts pain and shock. Serves me right for trying to get under the mask of a luchador.

Lucha libre refers to the high-flying world of Mexican professional wrestling. Much like its WWE counterpart in North America, it involves colourful characters (the luchadores), theatrical violence, multi-team tournaments and rabid fans of all ages. Yet lucha libre (literally "free wrestling") is also known for its acrobatics, as well as its associated tradition of masks and heroes.

It's Friday night, and Mexico City is throbbing. Often overlooked by tourists because of its intimidating size, this is a city with deep pockets of culture and art, sport and music—all connected by choking lines of traffic. Outside Arena Mexico, the sidewalks are choked too as vendors sell masks, toys, T-shirts, food and all manner of wrestling paraphernalia. It takes me a few moments to relax around grown men wearing the masks of their favourite luchador—they look like flamboyant bank robbers. The kids are out in force too, for despite the physical violence, wrestling has always been good fun for the whole family.

Lucha libre was born in Mexico in the 1930s, but it wasn't until the 1950s that it took off, with the

advent of television. The rules are simple: opponents lose if they are pinned to the mat for 3 seconds, removed from the ring after 20 or disqualified for illegal holds, groin strikes or the removal of a luchador's mask. It is the mask that gives each wrestler his character, personality and mythical allure. The public has adored these masked men ever since El Santo, the most famous luchador of all time, stepped into the ring with a silver mask. It does more than just conceal the identity of the wrestler (who will never be named or make a public appearance without it). It represents their honour, to be protected at all cost. Battles take place between arch-rivals for the right to remove the mask. There is always a good (*técnicos*) hero and a bad (*rudos*) villain, though role switches are not uncommon.

I had yet to pick good or evil when I stepped into the training ring wearing a customized luchador mask, the word *ESROCK* in red sequins glued across the top. It's a gag for my TV show, but Metalium isn't laughing. Under the eyes of his watchful trainer, he is hungry to show off his skills, and La Cobra de Lentejuelas a.k.a. The Sequinned Cobra a.k.a. Robin Esrock proves easy fodder. According to his trainer, Metalium will soon be ready to enter the main ring, but it will still be some time before he earns the right to wear his own mask. Choosing the right mask to resonate with the buying public can make or break his career.

I ask Metalium just how fake are the fights. He explains that moves, holds and blocks are taught so opponents know how to absorb the blows, land safely and avoid getting hurt. What moves the two luchadores decide to use can be rehearsed or improvised. Since he initially believed I was a wrestler myself (some luchadores are from the United States, Canada, even Japan), he assumed I would know how to block his high-flying kick to my chest. I assumed my ribs were only bruised, not broken.

That evening, the announcer hypes up the packed crowd with a deep voice, while beautiful girls in bikinis line up behind the ring. We are not so much ready to rumble as we are to marvel at the acrobatics. The hard ropes of the ring are designed to provide extra spring for the luchadores, who are regarded as the most agile and versatile of all wrestlers. Their somersaults and leaps add all the excitement of a Cirque du Soleil performance.

Teams are battling each other

in the 16,000-seat stadium, and it's pretty easy to determine the crowd favourites. The *técnicos* play by the rules, receive their acclaim with honour and always seem to come back after receiving a horrific beating at the hands of the *rudos*. A midget luchador in a white mask seems destined for punishment, until he pulls off an incredible manoeuvre, spinning with his legs around the necks of his opponents and then throwing them out of the ring altogether. Kids are screaming

their approval, the atmosphere is electric and, while the contest seems to have shifted from camp to the bizarre, the evening's entertainment value is top-notch. The best of three rounds always goes to the wire, the bad guys always threatening to remove the mask of the good guys, and in one case they actually do. It appears to be a wardrobe malfunction. The unmasked luchador clutches his face wildly and is led from the ring before his true identity is revealed to the masses. For unlawful unmasking, the villain is disqualified; justice is served.

Lucha libre is a form of physical theatre designed to steam up our emotions, wow our senses and provide dazzling entertainment. With its freewheeling high-flying kicks and refreshing lack of pretension, weekly tournaments in Mexico City are guaranteed to thrill any bucket lister. Just don't step into the ring before you've earned your mask.

START HERE:
globalbucketlist.com/luchalibre

The Legend of El Santo

They don't get any bigger than Santo, Mexico's most beloved luchador. Santo's silver mask concealed his true identity for more than 40 years, much like a real-life superhero battling countless (fictional) villains. Rodolfo Guzmán Huerta wasn't pretending to be Clark Kent pretending to be Superman. He truly was El Santo (The Saint), a powerful hero who battled corruption and lawlessness of villains inside the ring, in movie theatres and in the pages of comic books. Such actions held immense appeal for the masses of Mexico. A star of over 50 films, Huerta went to great lengths to protect his identity at all times—including eating and flying with it. He unmasked himself shortly before his death in 1984, a date that continues to be celebrated by Mexicans around the country.

Barber an Agave Plant in Tequila

MEXICO

Rows of blue agave cover Jalisco's highlands, their sharp, waist-high spikes piercing the sky like mohawks at a punk-rock show. As his grandfather and father did before him, Izmael Gama uses a machete to hack away the leaves of this hardy plant, leaves so sharp they were once used as weapons. Gama is a third-generation *jimador*, an agave harvester who works the plantations for Jose Cuervo, the world's largest tequila manufacturer. Operating the oldest distillery in the western hemisphere, the company has over 50 million plants in the region. The process of turning hostile agave into the world-renowned party-starter is not an easy one. Izmael hands me his machete and gives me instructions on how to barber the agave to its valuable pine, which will be collected and processed at the nearby factory. He worries I might accidentally hack my fingers or toes off, or impale myself on an agave spear. No lime or salt necessary.

Beneath a punishing sun, *jima-dors* barber up to 400 plants a day, or lightly trim thousands of others. Their name has its root in the Spanish word for "moaners," and I can see why. I am pierced by needle-like edges and sprayed with the plant's poisonous sap. Once the spikes are removed, Izmael picks up a steel *coa*, a heavy tool shaped like a pizza-oven spatula, with edges sharp enough to split a skull. He jams the edge into a pine, breaks its roots free and effortlessly topples it onto its side. Pines take 8 to 12 years to mature, at which time they have an average weight of 40 to 60 kilograms. This one, freshly cut, is sticky with resin, and I can barely

pick it up. My friends in college always told me I had a problem holding my liquor.

Most tequila is produced in this region of Jalisco, in and around the town of Tequila itself. Mexico's national drink has its roots with the Aztecs, who produced a fermented potion called *pulque* from agave. When Spanish conquistadors ran dry of their imported liquor, they adapted this drink to produce mescal, the name still given to a variety of liquor produced from agave. Tequila is therefore a type of mescal produced only in this particular region, refined and perfected—much like cognac, as opposed to just any brandy. Jose Cuervo began production clandestinely in 1758, officially in 1795. The company's La Rojeña distillery is the oldest distillery in Latin America. The town of Tequila, located about 60 kilometres from Guadalajara, is surrounded by fields of blue agave and lined with shacks selling hundreds of brands of tequila produced in the region. Bottles are packaged in anything from award-winning original art to 5-litre plastic containers, the latter perhaps best left to the brave or already blind.

A UNESCO World Heritage Site that is protected and promoted by the Mexican government, Tequila offers an impressive 18th-century stone church, as well as Mexico's National Museum of Tequila. Other towns in the region, including Arenal and Teuchitlán, are included in a "Tequila Route" that allows bucket listers to explore agave fields, processing facilities and tasting rooms. Among these is La Rojeña, where Jose Cuervo offers a daily factory tour.

Jose Cuervo translates as "Joe Crow," which explains why a huge sculpture of a black crow greets visitors at the plant. The tangy, pungent smell of tequila permeates the air. I am warned that, in some parts of the distillery, the air is so thick with alcohol that flash photography could ignite a fire and is therefore prohibited. In just 24 hours, La Rojeña produces over 65,000 litres of tequila, churning

through 350 metric tons of agave. Men in overalls heave and hook the heavy pines into stone ovens, where they are steamed for 24 to 36 hours, depending on the type of tequila being produced. This process transforms the pale yellowish agave heart into a rich brown fibre, dripping a sweet, candy-like juice ready to be extracted. A washing and crushing process presses out the juice into a liquid called *aguamiel* (honey water), to be distilled and aged in wood barrels. I taste samples of tequila at different stages of fermentation, learning how sugar is added for some products and how time in the ovens differentiates others. Cuervo Gold is a *mixto*, with 51 per cent of the alcohol coming from agave, the rest from other sugars. This product is supposed to be used exclusively for mixed drinks like margaritas, whereas 100 per cent agave tequila should

always be sipped and enjoyed slowly, like a brandy.

Rows of French-oak barrels, stacked 10 high, contribute the key ingredient that mellows the taste over time, fusing aromas and softening the palate. For the oldest family-run business in all the Americas, time is something Jose Cuervo does well. The tour descends into a dark cellar (or *cava*) where visitors can sample the Familia de la Reserva— the finest tequila they have. The Reserva is blended using the finest three-year-old tequilas, made from only the best agave, and extra time is allocated for the distilling process. Illustrious visitors have signed some of the barrels. I see the signatures of Bill Clinton and Paris Hilton, perfectly demonstrating tequila's wide appeal.

Dipping directly into the wood barrel, I ladle the rich, full-bodied elixir into a cognac glass, swirling it to release its complex fragrance. My humble experiences with Mexico's national drink relate primarily to late nights in cheap bars and deep regret the morning after. Here in the private cellar of tequila's most famous family, I realize just how far up the ladder one can climb in the appreciation of the finer things in

What's Up with the Worm?

Much like learning that Coca-Cola invented our modern version of Santa Claus, you'll find the story behind finding a worm in a bottle of tequila disappointing. It started as a marketing gimmick in the 1950s and factors in mescal only, not tequila. If butterfly larva has bored into the pine, the pine is considered unfit for harvest. If you do find a worm in your bottle of tequila, you might want to ask for a replacement.

life. Instead of barbed hooks down my throat, I lubricate my taste buds with a tang of sour and sweet, the base tones of the tequila I know, but with an intricate smoothness I didn't know existed. Soon enough, my head is spinning, possibly because I'm literally inhaling alcohol.

A nasty rash appears on my arm the next morning, accompanying a nastier but well-earned hangover courtesy of the bars of Guadalajara. Raw agave has properties not unlike poison ivy, which gringo tourist *jimadors* might want to keep in mind before picking up a cone. Barbering was fun, but bucket listers will enjoy the final product more. Like most things in life, tequila tastes a lot better once you see how much work, science and history goes into its making.

START HERE:
globalbucketlist.com/tequila

Sandboard down an Active Volcano

NICARAGUA

Luminous orange overalls flap in the strong wind, an egg-yolk sun cracks against the horizon. It's been a physically tough hike, stumbling over loose rocks, my face caked in black volcanic dust. Atop the cone of Cerro Negro, one of the youngest active volcanoes in Central America, the countdown has begun. All that's left to do is sit down on my wooden board, lean back, grit my teeth and hurl down the cone, zero to 40 km/hr in eight wild seconds.

You can tell the "next big travel thing" by watching the trends of budget travellers. They're heading in droves to Nicaragua. The beaches, colonial towns and accommodating locals and prices, along with bucket list activities like volcano boarding, are a backpacker's dream. From the roof of León's cathedral, the largest cathedral in Central America, you can see 11 of the 13 volcanoes surrounding the city. They sit like a chain of pearls on a necklace, and when they erupt, as Cerro Negro did as recently as 1999, they might cover León in a layer of fine ash. Not that it bothers the backpackers at Bigfoot Hostel. When I inquire about the

conspicuous absence of waivers for volcano boarding, the hostel's affable owner explains some of the legal differences between Nicaragua and the United States. If tourists want to pay 20 bucks for the opportunity to throw themselves off an active volcano, that's their problem! Even though the volcano is at the tail end of its regular eruption cycle and could explode any day, Bigfoot is doing a roaring trade with about a dozen clients of all ages heading out daily, wooden sleigh in hand, anticipating a bucket list ride of a lifetime.

It took the staff at Bigfoot some time to figure out the right apparatus to accomplish such a feat, with everything from fridge doors to second-hand mattresses tested to find the right balance of speed and relative safety. One thing is certain: although from afar Cerro Negro appears to have soft, sandy steep sides, the granite dust is as sharp as broken glass. Wearing protective overalls and eye goggles, and remaining seated (as opposed to standing upright, as in traditional sandboarding), is essential. Wiping out would mean being torn to shreds.

It's a 40-minute drive to Cerro Negro National Park, and it's no accident that sandboarding trips

take place during late afternoon. November through June, night after night, the sunsets in this part of the world are atomic. Our group pays a small fee to enter the park, grabs some boards and starts the climb up the rear of the ominous-looking black pyramid. As we begin our steep ascent, the wind picks up considerably. Blackened lava from the last eruption sits like thick oil spilled over the countryside. At the back of my mind, I'm well aware that nobody can sandboard fast enough to beat an erupting volcano.

The loose rocks are sharp, but we scramble over them, shifting the awkward weight of our boards from arm to arm. Half an hour later, we arrive at the outer edge of the crater to find steaming-hot sulphuric ash. You can burn your hand on the ground here, so we keep walking around the lip, saying a silent prayer that the monster below us remains asleep. With the sun perfectly poised near the horizon, our guide, Gemma, explains how to use our feet to break and steer.

"Keep the mouth shut unless you want to chew rocks for dinner. Back straight, lean back and smile for the radar gun at the bottom!"

A thin metal sheet has been affixed to the bottom of the wood, along with a piece of plastic that increases speed. As I begin the

500-metre slide, the grate of granite against metal sounds like an engine revving fast. Rocks and sand attack my goggles, stab my lips, siege my shoes. I'd scream but it's wiser to keep lips pursed and board straight (cone-burn awaits those who flip).

Active volcanoes have intrigued many a bucket lister, but only in Nicaragua will you find one so creatively accessible. Safely back at the bottom, the group cracks open celebratory cold beers and compares experiences. "Now that's something to do before you die!" says one back-packer. I certainly agree.

START HERE:
globalbucketlist.com/leon

The Bait-and-Switch Wonder of Central America

How did the region's most magnificent cathedral find its way to northwest Nicaragua? Covering a full city block, León Cathedral is the largest in Central America and blessed with an elaborate neoclassical facade. Construction commenced in 1747, but no one is quite sure why. One theory is that the Spanish, en route to Lima, mixed up plans for cathedrals, consequently rewarding León with a cathedral beyond the city's stature. Another is that local clergy deliberately misled the Spanish with alternative plans for a more modest structure and, once those plans were approved, switched the designs. Inside you'll find masterpieces of colonial art, a black Jesus and stairs leading up to the domed ceiling. Stand beneath the statues holding up the arches and large bell facing the square below. It's one of my favourite spots on the continent.

Catch Beads at Mardi Gras

Snakes in the bayou do the cha-cha when Mardi Gras comes to town. New Orleans, the Big Easy, transforms from a steaming powder keg into a steaming powder keg with a lit fuse. I am en route to the mansion of none other than a Louisiana Supreme Court judge during that special time of year when the city lets itself go, like an intoxicated Grim Reaper doing handstands on the crest of a neon rainbow.

Through a friend, I'd found accommodation in the mansion, just a block from St. Charles Avenue and bead-hurling distance from the Fat Tuesday processions. With a clown suit in my luggage, I arrive to fanfare at the Louis Armstrong New Orleans International Airport. Actually, the fanfare is for D-actor Luke Perry, who happens to be on my flight and is scheduled—along with Britney Spears, Harry Connick Jr. and Whoopi Goldberg—to crown the parades that year. Although it's still springtime, Louisiana's heat encloses me like thermal underwear in a sauna. As ever, a helpful cabbie is on hand to furnish me with useful socioeconomic background.

Sixty per cent of the population of New Orleans is African-American, and 90 per cent of the city's wealth belongs to 10 per cent of its population (90 per cent of whom are white). Some folks had great-great-grandparents who owned slaves; many more had great-grandparents who *were* slaves. As I watch weathered projects transform into tree-lined suburbs with art deco mansions, the divisions become clear. The judge, a renowned social activist,

lives in a three-storey house just two blocks from the projects. This cocktail of racial and economic tension, fuelled by alcohol, religious celebrations and costumed ribaldry, gives Mardi Gras an undeniable edge. There's tension, but Mardi Gras is the painkiller—an event that will continue come hell or high water. The year after Hurricane Katrina, routes were limited and some parades were smaller, but Mardi Gras was as festive as ever.

I am greeted with famous Southern hospitality, then given a key to the house and a drawling debriefing as to how Mardi Gras works. Essentially, there are huge organizations representing different political, social and economic communities. They spend from US$25,000 to US$750,000 each year on decorative floats; the event itself generates over a billion dollars for the city. Throughout the week, parades follow a route through the city, ending at the edge of the French Quarter, where everyone toasts the mayor. On top of each float, inebriated donors throw Chinese-manufactured beads and cheap carnival toys into the mob that lines the streets. Donors have paid handsomely for this privilege, so forget

about jumping aboard. Each float reflects a different theme or story, but most people on the streets are too busy yelling for beads to know what they are. It all leads to Fat Tuesday, the horn-blowing climax of Mardi Gras. Moving between floats are local groups, school and army bands, cheerleaders and dance troupes. You haven't seen sweat until you see an overdressed, overweight kid with a tuba walking 15 miles across town in the oppressive Louisiana heat.

New Orleans is among the few places in the United States where you can drink open containers of alcohol in the streets. Glass bottles are, however, a no-no, because they make a terrible mess every time they break, which happens about every 10 seconds during Mardi Gras. Float participants throw large plastic cups into the crowd, which revellers promptly fill with liquor. Everyone is looking for a place to pee, which is impossible to find. All shapes, colours and sizes of beads line the necks of revellers. Beads have both social and aesthetic value. At first you'll want to collect them all, but it doesn't take long for Mardi Gras virgins to learn that some beads are not worth the effort. One day in and most trees and power lines along the procession route are littered with plastic rejects, sparkling in the sun.

Long known as the haunting grounds of vampires, drunks and men in tight dresses, the French Quarter is the tourist mecca of New Orleans. Parades do not actually enter the Quarter until the last day of Mardi Gras, but it is packed with overexcited lunatics, and those are just the celebrities. Decatur and Royal Streets fret buzz nightly with infectious jazz. The Quarter is guaranteed to smell funky—a stew of rotting vegetables, urine and decomposing seafood. Speaking of which, the judge is ploughing me with gumbo, jambalaya (this week's leftovers mixed with last week's leftovers), turtle soup, alligator, oysters, beignets and that lovable mudbug of the Mississippi, the crawfish. Turtle tastes like chicken, but then again, doesn't everything?

I make my way slowly through the crowds to Jackson Square, where riverboats on the Mississippi are blowing their horns and the sun beats down its rays. New Orleans: where even the weather has rhythm. I encounter locals who are lovable but occasionally scary, like someone else's pet Rottweiler. During a short break from the festivities, I take a

Drinking in the Streets

If you enjoy drinking Hurricanes on a crowded street, head to the few other US destinations that allow open containers of alcohol in public:

Beale Street, Memphis, Tennessee: Specially exempted from the statewide ban.

Butte, Montana: Heck, there are no open-container laws in the entire state.

Fredericksburg, Texas: In case things get too spirited, only beer and wine are permitted.

Las Vegas, Nevada (pictured below): There are no limits downtown on Fremont Street, though the strip does sometimes require only plastic containers.

Power and Light District, Kansas City, Missouri: Plastic containers only in this eight-block loop.

Savannah, Georgia: One open container with no more than 16 ounces, ma'am.

boat trip to the bayou, where the words *deliverance* and *banjo* swill in my head. Someone asks the captain if it's true that locals eat beavers. "Them beavers, I don't stop eating till them eyes cave in," he replies seriously. Then he points out an alligator, and shocked German tourists start smiling again.

I hear the loud drumbeats of Fat Tuesday while lying in bed, nursing a vicious Hurricane hangover. Made with rum, gin, vodka and the sweet burning lava of hell, the Hurricane's a drink that perfectly complements its origins. You won't know how much trouble you're in until it's too late. It's still early in the morning, but the streets are already jammed with locals with tents, air mattresses and portapotties on the back of pickup

trucks. Zulu and Rex floats conclude the parades, funded by the cream of the city's bourgeois crop. Everyone has a blast, although after one full week of this, there's a distinct sense of exhaustion. The city's police stand back during Mardi Gras until exactly midnight on Fat Tuesday, when they move in with riot gear to begin an intense 48-hour cleanup. By Friday, the only evidence of the week's excess are a few beads glittering atop the tallest trees. The edgy history of the South makes Mardi Gras more than just a carnival. Anywhere else in America they would call it a riot; here, it's just one heck of a party.

START HERE:

globalbucketlist.com/mardigras

Witness the Temple Burn at Burning Man

Burning Man is famously impossible to describe, so I'm not even going to try. I won't talk about flying from Vancouver to Vegas to rent an RV for the 10-hour drive to Black Rock City. I definitely won't get into my passing a massive US military installation in Hawthorne, Nevada, since, along with nearby Area 51, it has severe access restrictions. I can, however, tell you how, upon arriving at this sprawling cultural festival, we virgins are made to roll around in the white-flour dust of the playa, embracing the dirt we'd mentally prepared ourselves to combat. It takes mere seconds for the dust to cling to our clothes, skin and psyche. I've spent years waiting to get to this legendary festival, and I am as nervous and apprehensive as anyone. Nothing to buy? No taps, showers or garbage bins? Fifty-thousand-plus people in a hostile environment, and somehow this is meant to be fun? All these adventures over the years, and just when I think I've seen it all, along comes Burning Man to clobber my mind with an existential baseball bat.

It is many things to many people: an art festival showcasing thousands of sculptures, modified cars and creative installations; a music festival with hundreds of professional and makeshift venues for DJs and musicians; a giant costume party, everyone wearing something extraordinary, if they choose to wear something at all; a conference for the mind, offering lectures and educational seminars from thinkers across the creative arts and social science spectrum; a religious festival, steering clear of organized dogma and veering into the outer realms of spiritual expression, open worship of the universe and a deep reverence for the beauty of diversity; a love festival, where nudity is accepted, sex is acceptable; a community of like-minded individuals gathering in a remote place to avoid the confused, ignorant reaction of those who simply don't get it and probably never will; a backlash against corporate America, with no brand advertisements, promotion or even commerce allowed. It's the wildest, most hedonistic party you've ever seen. And most of all, Burning Man is none of these things at all.

It started in 1986 with a small group of artists in a hostile desert, challenging their creative limits and engaging in a form of self-reliance and personal responsibility—this in a nation drunk on liability. There are countless ways to get yourself

killed at Burning Man, from exposure to extreme weather to getting toasted by a rogue art piece. It's your responsibility to stay alive, even though just about everyone you meet will gladly help you out (including volunteer rangers and medical staff). Community membership is viewed as a privilege. If you don't get it, please don't come. You'll hate every second of it.

For all my travels, I just didn't expect the scale of the event to be so huge, the creative energy so vast. Black Rock City emerges overnight as the second-largest city in Nevada. It is shaped like a clock, organized by the hands of the hour and 12 long, circular promenades. With the city stretching more than 8 kilometres across, bikes are essential if you want to see all that's on offer. Hundreds of camps and villages are set up along the grid, tribes ranging from a few members to several hundred. Each camp offers something of value to the casual passerby: free cocktails, hot tamales, engaging conversation. Free massages, games of tennis, bowling, a mechanical bull ride. Free rides, free bad advice, free hugs, free kisses, free help. Free beds, free art, free costumes, free decorations for your bike. Everyone seems to bring more than they need and need less than they want. It's a free-for-all, and it takes a while to recalibrate my capitalistic conditioning so that

I stop asking, "What's the catch?" There isn't one. "Where am I?" It doesn't matter. "Who are you?" A Burner just like you. "Where are we going?" I don't know, but there's no rush, so let's take it slow.

I see things that shock, surprise, dazzle and delight. Moments of beauty, moments of overstimulation, moments of bewilderment. Every time I stop to ask "How on earth did they get that giant [fill in the blank] here?" I am reminded to stop questioning and start accepting. My guides are friends old and new, veteran Burners and virgins like myself. As much as this is a community event, every single Burner develops a unique personal response to the environment. Some thrive in the heavy dust storms that blind and sting. Others, including hundreds of families with young kids, thrive in the theme camps and villages. Some prefer the scorching hot day, others the cool, LED-lit night. Drawing it all in together is the Man himself, erected on a wooden platform at 12 o'clock, gazing out

over the playa. His design changes annually; this year the Man stands 30 metres tall, regally awaiting the Friday-night climax of the week-long event—his destined combustion. Any second now he's going to erupt into a giant fireball. Sometimes the Man burns fast, sometimes he burns slow. A huge dust storm sweeps in, blowing fiery ash into the crowd. This is not cause for concern. The crowd is well prepared with the right gear and attitude. Only at Burning Man do harsh elements become cause for celebration.

There's a monkey chant at Center Camp, hypnotically blending voices to become a cacophony of sound. Hippies and corporate sharks, artists and number crunchers, Silicon Valley millionaires and homeless wanderers. Is the guy playing the flaming tuba really one of the producers of *The Simpsons*? Are those bikes among the thousands donated by the founders of Google? Was that Bono who just walked past me? Is that Mark Zuckerberg's theme camp? What does it matter? I spend a half-hour looking for a friend at Center Camp, then realize that even if I walk right past her, I probably won't recognize her

and she won't recognize me. I am wearing red underwear with eyes printed on it, blue wings made out of recycled water bottles, a bright shock of green wig, ski goggles and a dust mask. Costumes allow anybody to become anyone or anything, and they do. Superheroes or furry animals, desert squid or neon robots. Women can be naked or topless without fear of harassment, as Burners won't stand for young, drunken frat boys. The community is a self-regulating system, an entropic organism that shakes out the dust and arises.

"Is this the real world, or is the real world out there?"

My friend, Burner veteran and filmmaker Ian MacKenzie, is never shy to initiate a philosophical debate.

"Perhaps the real world should be more like Burning Man," I ponder.

"Look, it's all well and good until the food and water runs out, and then it will quickly turn into *Lord of the Flies*," says Vancouver-based sculptor Bruce Voyce, never shy to speak up.

Applying the lessons of Burning Man is a common theme at many workshops. Taking away the sense

of community—of environmental responsibility, of respect for those around you—has led to dozens of regional "Burns" and "Decompressions" around the world.

The Temple is the spiritual soul of Burning Man. Anyone who visits it will instantly recognize why there's so much more to this festival than flame-breathing dragon cars, stilt bars and half-naked discos. The Temple is a sacred act of wood, a solemn place to say goodbye to loved ones lost, dreams abandoned or anything that needs to be released. People write on its walls, in the cracks, on the wooden platforms. It soaks with energy so intense you can feel it throbbing. I gaze at life-size photos of Burners lost before their time. Tears drip off the face of people in private confessions, sad waters hitting the dust like syrup leaking from a maple tree. I can only stand and watch, aware and grateful

that this week marked a personal beginning and not an end. It is here, in a camp dome surrounded by my tribe, that I ask my girlfriend to marry me, and it is here that our lives moved to the next step. Mourning at the Temple can wait as long as I can help it. On the final night, with thousands already returned to the real world, the Temple is set aflame, a raging inferno of emotional relief. We can feel the heat from far away, its unmistakable energy rushing through us, ash soaring into the starlit sky. It is beautiful, it is sad, it is magic.

Like other items on the bucket list, this one is not for everyone. It requires a significant mental shift, but one I believe people of all ages, incomes and interests can make. In recent years, Burning Man's influence has hit a tipping point, and this little-known gathering is now featured across major media outlets, in sitcoms, as a punchline in

late-night TV monologues. Tickets sell out in hours, and there is deep concern within the community that it has got too big, is at risk of losing its spirit, being shut down by the authorities. Time will tell. As for my own efforts, my description of Burning Man barely wipes the surface dust. If anything you've read so far intrigues you, do some reading, visit a couple of websites and, as they say on the playa, welcome home.

START HERE:
globalbucketlist.com/
burningman

The 10 Principles of Burning Man

Written by founder Larry Harvey as guidelines for regional events, Burners debate and interpret these 10 principles as if they're the Talmud:

- **Radical inclusion:** Anyone may participate; all strangers are welcome.
- **Gifting:** Unconditional gift giving, without the expectation of an exchange for something of equal value.
- **Decommodification:** No commercial sponsorships, transactions or advertising.

- **Radical self-reliance:** The individual is encouraged to discover, exercise and rely on his or her inner resources.
- **Radical self-expression:** Deep respect for the individual, while respecting the rights and liberties of all.
- **Communal effort:** Creative cooperation, interaction, communication and collaboration.
- **Civic responsibility:** Assuming responsibility for public welfare in accordance with local, state and federal laws.
- **Leaving no trace:** Respecting the environment, cleaning up and, if possible, leaving places in a better state than they were found.
- **Participation:** Achieve being through doing. Transformative change, whether in the individual or in society, can occur only through personal participation.
- **Immediacy:** Living in the moment to connect with our inner selves and the outside world.

Cruise down the Inside Passage

Bigger than the next three largest US states—Texas, California and Montana—combined, Alaska challenges the American consciousness like an unscratchable itch. It's so massive, so underpopulated and so untamed, it's no wonder it attracts everyone from free spirits and survivalists to hardened criminals hoping to disappear into the snow and fly under the radar. It also attracts cruise ships, which sail the Inside Passage alongside crystal-blue glaciers, snow-capped mountains, deep fjords, icebergs, whales and soaring bald eagles. Before we board the *Coral Princess*, a floating palace of luxe, let's head inland to see the wild for ourselves. It is early September, and the hard sun of summer has lost its shine, but the fall foliage is exploding, as if angels tie-dyed the tundra in honour of a Rastafarian princess.

We trace the Kenai Peninsula, looking for beluga whales at Beluga Point, before making our way along the fjord to the Kenai Princess Wilderness Lodge. Guy, my well-named guide, downloads information about the area, the wildlife, the culture, the abundant natural wonders. He speaks earnestly and could *say anything*, because, well, he looks a lot like John Cusack. The scenery is balm for the dry, cracked heel of the soul. We stop at a couple of roadside attractions—a visitor centre where we learn about the US congressmen who vanished without a trace while flying to Juneau; a conservation centre, where we stare at huge stuffed grizzly bears, elk,

caribou, black bears and a couple of lynx. With 50,000 grizzlies and even more black bears in Alaska, bears are a subject of fascination. Just about every local I meet tells me what to do should I encounter one. Be big! Be small! Run! Don't run! One would think a bear sits in wait behind every tree, waiting to pounce with a bear hug.

We're not on the cruise yet, but the service that has made Princess Cruises such a successful luxury travel brand is on full display at its lodge. Outstanding food, friendly and efficient service, great company. This evening's accommodation is the Denali Princess Wilderness Lodge, one of five

inland lodges Princess owns and operates in Alaska. You can leave an overnight wake-up call with the lodge's front desk if North America's tallest mountain emerges from the cloud, or the northern lights explode in the night sky. Mount McKinley, officially renamed "Denali" in 2015—"the high one"—is the only 6,000-metre-plus peak in North America, and one of the Seven Summits that challenges all serious mountain climbers. Alaskans proudly point out that Denali is taller than Everest, if you account for its elevation from sea level.

Denali National Park and Preserve is the grand attraction for inland bucket listers, and the adjacent town, Denali, opens only during the summer season. During winter, the one traffic light turns off, the Subway and shops close down, and the hotel shutters up for the freeze. Denali is a launch pad for a national park that covers a staggering 24,585 square kilometres, accessed by only one road. To get a sense of the size, we hop aboard a helicopter for a view from above. Fireweed and other foliage erupts with the reds, oranges and yellows of autumn. The taiga, a boreal forest that forms the largest biome on earth, is a palette of colour. The firs, pines and spruce of the taiga grow for only a few weeks a year, appearing stunted compared with their more temperate cousins. The helicopter glides over purple glaciers, grazing Dall sheep, stark grey mountains and untamed valleys too remote for human encounters. The fall colours pop for only a couple of weeks at the end of summer, an advantage of visiting at the tail end of the season, even if the days and nights have become significantly cooler. The Denali Express, which takes passengers from the Princess lodge to their awaiting cruise ship in Whittier, has to be among the world's most beautiful short train routes. Customized cars with pan-oramic windows, full bar, dining service and affable interpreters roll among taiga, rivers, mountains and

fjords. It's a practical means to get passengers from point A to point B but a worthy journey to make just in itself, especially when the sun's rays crack the clouds, beaming a yellow yolk over the luminescence of fall.

Readers might be surprised that I enjoy modern cruise ships. I like that I can travel without moving, that I can actually relax without a million things to do, just like (Oh, the shock! The horror!) a real-life vacation. Admittedly, I view the manicured onshore experiences with a sense of bemusement, but I appreciate the romance of holing up in a stateroom with my wife. It's fun dressing up for formal nights,

where wine can flow, with no car keys in sight. Sure, the excess can be overwhelming. The split levels of passengers indulging in over-abundance and the hard-working crew from developing countries who serve them are a stark contrast. The cruise industry syncs up the wants of its guests (*I want to be treated like a king*) with the wants of its crew (*I want to make enough money in six months that I can go home and buy a house*). The great late David Foster Wallace wrote about it better than I ever could in a brilliant essay titled "A Supposedly Fun Thing I'll Never Do Again." Like all travel, the success of cruising is as much about the people you're experiencing it with as the ship itself. I've been on several cruises, met wonderful people and had a wonderful time. Worth noting is that David Foster Wallace went cruising by himself, spent much of his time alone in his room and made little effort to connect with anyone around him.

On the bridge, we meet the captain, a portly Italian who swings the biggest anchor on board. Below, everything is maximized for space efficiency, but the bridge is spacious, almost minimalist. There is a control panel in the centre, and two identical mini-panels on either side for port docking. Buttons and monitors and gauges and knobs and computers—it looks like something out of *Star Trek*. It must have inspired the USS *Enterprise,* as it did the *Love Boat,* which was based on a Princess Cruises ship in the Caribbean.

The *Coral* creeps up to the Hubbard Glacier in Glacier Bay National Park, where massive glaciers tower over the sea, ice calving, creaking and cracking into the waters below. We grab our robes, cheese and wine, then head to the balcony and enjoy the chill in style.

As with all cruise itineraries, there's a variety of onshore experiences on our journey south to Vancouver. In Skagway, we take a short ferry to the town of Haines and pilot a Kawasaki Mule convoy up a mountainside. In Juneau, we're greeted with a magnificent blue-sky day. The locals in the Alaskan capital, which is accessible only by boat and air, tell us they haven't seen the sun in weeks. Poor weather kills our onshore Zodiac ride in Ketchikan, not that I minded, given that I was tending a nasty hangover from the previous night. A festive dinner culminated in a room party, a late-night dip in the pool area and a real "holy crap, ain't life great" moment starboard at Guy's favourite Deck 8 hangout.

Over just 13 days we have seen outrageous natural beauty and undertaken some unforgettable adventures, all the while being wined and dined like only cruise ship passengers can be. Travellers became colleagues, and colleagues became friends. As every cruise veteran will tell you: there are big ships and there are small ships, but the ships that truly count are friendships.

START HERE:
globalbucketlist.com/alaska

Exotic Bucket List Cruises

Cruising in exotic destinations can remove the headache of logistics (but also some of the adventure). Here are three more options for the bucket list.

The Black Sea: Romania, Bulgaria, Georgia—not the first destinations that come to mind when one thinks of cruises. From spring to early fall, small-ship cruises on the Black Sea draw bucket listers with promises of empty white beaches, baroque old towns, ancient monasteries and fairy-tale castles. In a region notorious for bureaucratic hassles and corruption, cruises here deliver the magic without the hassles and red tape.

The Mekong: I spent two days sailing down the Mekong on a wooden boat. The scenery was spectacular, but I could have done without the smoky engine, rough wooden seat and village stopover where rats ate a hole in my backpack. If you want the temples without the splinters, hop aboard one of the dozen luxury riverboats that typically sail from Vietnam's Ho Chi Minh City (formerly Saigon) to Cambodia's Siem Reap.

The Nile: Cruising down the Nile is an ideal way to discover the temples and other ruins of ancient Egypt. Sure, one can fly directly to Luxor, but three- to seven-day riverboat trips allow you to relax on a floating hotel while still seeing an Egypt beyond the typical tourist attractions. Choose from basic cruisers to five-star palaces, or spend a few days on a felucca, the Nile's traditional sailboat.

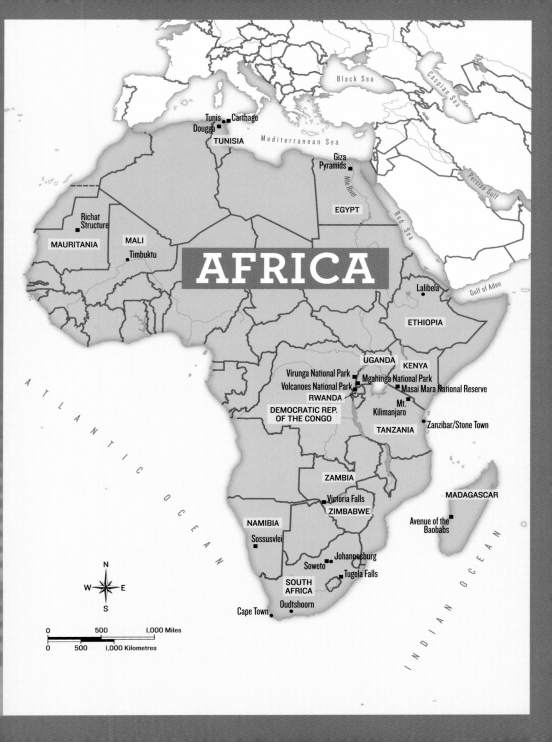

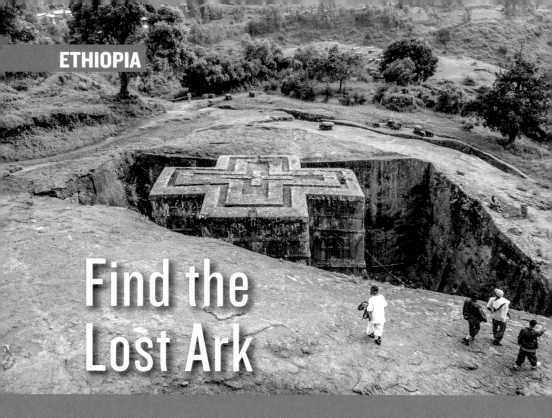

Find the Lost Ark

Bucket listers are drawn to exotic adventures and ancient temples that sit beyond overpriced gift shops and crowded tour-bus parking lots. Destinations like Ethiopia's Lalibela, where ancient monolithic churches have been carved out of solid, red volcanic rock. So what if the plane from Addis Ababa had mid-air mechanical issues, turning a 2-hour flight into a three-plane, 10-hour odyssey? So what if donkeys had blocked the cracked, ass-rattling airport road? Getting around in Africa is seldom uneventful. If it were easy, everybody would be here.

Constructed between the 12th and 13th centuries, Lalibela, with its free-standing columns, carvings and masonry, makes nonsense of the idea that ancient Africa lacked a civilization as advanced as any in Europe. The complex was built to mirror Jerusalem, complete with its own River Jordan, icons and painted frescos, the showcase of an African kingdom far removed from the squalor of the European Dark Ages. Ethiopia adopted Christianity as early as the 4th century, when the Aksumite Empire flourished as a centre of trade between North Africa, the Middle East and Asia. Adhering to the teachings of the Coptic Church, the largely devout country still follows the Julian calendar, observing Christmas in January and New Year's Eve in September. The religious heart of Ethiopia beats in Aksum, believed by Ethiopians (and several historical researchers) to house the original Ark of the Covenant. This is the legendary (and mysteriously missing) ark that housed the 10 Commandments, and gave Indiana Jones his first on-screen adventure. Lalibela may be the country's second-holiest town, but it boasts a richer horde of ancient wonders.

There are 11 rock churches attributed to the reign of one King Lalibela. Legend has it that the daily construction by his subjects was continued by the nightly work of angels. Unlike with the grand churches of Europe, there has been little need for restoration over the years, the solid rock proving to be a durable building material. History here is so thick in the air, I can virtually taste it. Candles light the interiors as they have done for centuries; fleas on the ancient carpets cling to my socks. Paintings, sculptures and frescos are protected in quiet, dark rooms, resulting in some of the best-preserved ancient Christian art found anywhere. Old priests with leathered skin and Coptic bibles guard the churches, still in operation as houses of worship, and most of which contain sections that hold holy relics, access to them forbidden to tourists. Biete Golgotha Mikael (House of Golgotha Mikael), which houses the tomb of the king, is also forbidden to women.

Priests will display their gold crosses, 800-year-old prayer sticks and colourful robes for a small tip. It has become customary throughout Ethiopia to tip locals when taking photos, and here it's worth every penny. I remove my shoes before entering the churches (giving a tip, of course, to someone to watch them). Soon enough, my tennis socks turn red with the iron-rich dust of ages. Flash cameras are not allowed, but a flashlight helps me navigate slippery stairs and spooky passages. My guide explains the significance behind the number of columns, windows and paintings. Symbolism is everywhere. Outside Biete Medhane Alem (House of the Saviour of the World), the largest church, UNESCO has erected a rather ugly scaffolding, as there has been some rain damage. Inside, there are authentic discoveries behind every door as priests continue their day-to-day prayers

much like their forefathers did for centuries.

Biete Giyorgis, the Church of Saint George, is easily the most impressive church. It is a hollow structure carved top down from solid rock in the shape of a Greek cross. Fifteen metres tall, it continues to defy the elements and wow visitors. The mummified corpses of 14th-century pilgrims still protrude from small caves that surround it. This was an afterlife reward for having visited and returned safely from the real Jerusalem.

There are no tour buses or slick gift shops in Lalibela. The roads are rough, and the hotels basic, lacking hot water and regular electricity.

6 Aboriginal Encounters for the Bucket List

Encounters with indigenous cultures take place the world over, typically in the form of a performance or village visit. The ultimate goal is a meaningful connection and responsible exchange of culture. Unfortunately, some encounters veer toward exploitation. Do your research before booking tours or tickets.

Canada: Nunavut Tourism offers homestays with Inuit families for an insider and authentic look at their lifestyle and daily life. You'll eat caribou and Arctic char, meet traditional carvers and seal and whale hunters, and huddle over a hole for some ice fishing. The annual Qimualaniq Quest takes place in March—a 320-kilometre dogsled race that brings the community together for feasting, drum dancing and throat singing.

Ethiopia: There are 52 tribes in Ethiopia's southern Omo Valley, one of the most ethnically diverse regions on the planet. Tours from surrounding towns and cities take you into the Rift Valley, where you can interact with tribes like the Arbore, Ari, Bena, Dorze, Hamer, Konso, Mursi, Tsemay and Turkana. I visited three different tribes during my visit, and had three very different experiences. Reputable guides are a must.

New Zealand: Head to the thermal wonderland of Rotorua for your introduction to Maori culture. Unlike in other Commonwealth countries, where indigenous groups have largely been marginalized, the Maori exert a strong and proud influence on New Zealand culture. In Rotorua, Maori tourist villages have been set up as cultural attractions, explaining and demonstrating Maori history, art and culture.

Papua New Guinea: Each August, tribes from the Papua New Guinea highlands gather for the Mount Hagen *sing-sing* celebration. The cultural show is a world-famous event, with the few hotels in the region booked months in advance. You'd be hard-pressed to find a more diverse, exotic gathering of human beings. Expect elaborate face paint, bones through noses, and headdresses made from the plumes of the endemic bird of paradise.

Thailand: Tourists to northern Thailand usually visit the Padaung, a subgroup of the Karen people. Originally from Burma, they have settled as refugees among other Thai hill tribes. From an early age, girls wear brass rings, which over time distort their collarbones, giving them their distinctive long neck, viewed as attractive in their culture. There are several unscrupulous operators in Chiang Mai, so it's worth looking for tours with an ethical, responsible approach.

A surrounding town, supported largely through tourism, is rife with poverty. As you exit the complex, the transition from Lalibela's glorious past to its challenging present is a shock to the system. Still, these old rock churches will continue to appeal to the more adventurous travellers, those willing to

sacrifice comfort for discovery. In an increasingly roped-off, theme-parked and gift-shop world, Lalibela's rock churches—dust, fleas and all—belong on the Great Global Bucket List.

START HERE:
globalbucketlist.com/lalibela

Great African Empires

Contrary to inherently racist colonial history books, great civilizations illuminated the "Dark Continent" for thousands of years. Great Zimbabwe, whose vast granite ruins gave the country its name, was the capital of a trading empire that boomed between the 11th and 15th centuries. The Kingdom of Ghana governed the rich gold mines of today's Senegal and

Mauritania, with powerful armies and sophisticated taxation and trade policies. The Mali Empire supplanted that of Ghana in the 13th century, dominating trade routes and establishing universities and libraries in Timbuktu. The Songhai Empire, in turn, became the largest state in African history. Benin boasted a powerful kingdom, while Burkina Faso united several into the Mossi Kingdoms. Central Africa's Luba Empire ruled over 1 million people, while the Nok of Nigeria, an ancient culture that used advanced metal and pottery, mysteriously vanished around AD 300. The Zulu Kingdom put up fierce resistance to European settlers in southern Africa, and let's not forget Carthage (page 144), which took on the might of Rome.

See the Great Migration in the Masai Mara

KENYA

Over the years, I've visited dozens of wildlife reserves, but when it comes to the ultimate bucket list safari experience, few can argue with the Great Migration across the Mara-Serengeti ecosystem. Kenya's Masai Mara National Reserve is part of this 25,000-square-kilometre protected natural habitat for Africa's storied wildlife: the big cats, elephant, zebra, giraffe, hippos, antelope, buffalo, hyena and, most of all, wildebeest. The annual migration of approximately 1.5 million wildebeest in search of food—along with hundreds of thousands of accompanying gazelle, zebra and others—is the largest single movement of animals on earth.

As my charter flight approaches the dirt runway, I see shaggy-faced wildebeest scattered all over the savannah, like an invasion of ants on a carrot cake. Warthog are grunting below on the runway, causing our pilot to brake hard and bounce the Cessna 208 Caravan to a stop. Safari rangers and Land Rovers greet us with gourmet snacks and chilled champagne. This is the wild African bush as presented by &Beyond, a company that specializes in luxury safari adventures. Clients may sleep in tents, but these tents have four-poster beds and en suite bathrooms.

On the drive from the landing strip to the camp, I spot giraffe, zebra, wildebeest, buffalo, antelope and a pride of lions. I am hoping to see a kill, or perhaps witness a chase. Many people go on safari with this sort of expectation, and typically it all comes down to patience, timing and luck. During the Great Migration, however, the odds are greatly improved. The Land Rover approaches &Beyond's Bateleur Camp, built into the forest on the edge of the savannah. Overlooking a vast plain, the camp offers luxury tent accommodation, guided safari excursions, a flow of cocktails and some of the best meals I've tasted anywhere. Large leather sofas in the lounge tent provide a comfy midday refuge for reading classic *National Geographic* magazines from the 1960s and 1970s. Dining is outdoors, set just metres from a low electrified fence keeping elephant, hippo and the occasional lion from wandering into camp. An infinity swimming pool allows me to swim and view

wildlife at the same time. Bateleur's staff remember the names of every guest, and offer us our favourite cocktails at every opportunity. The dry African sun calls for Pimm's with ginger ale, frothed with a stick of fresh cucumber. It might be survival of the fittest out there, but inside our camp, guests fatten themselves up in comfort.

On our afternoon's game drive, we encounter another pride of lions, lazing in the shade of an acacia tree. Just a few kilometres away, I see tall, robed figures herding cattle. According to their legends, the Masai people have lived here since the dawn of time. I ask Joseph, my guide, why the lions don't attack the Masai or their cattle. He points to the thousands of wildebeest, and the sheer abundance of food available. He jokingly refers to wildebeest as "lion takeout," and warthog as "lion sausage." Joseph, a member of the Masai tribe, discusses the natural fear lions have of Masai warriors, and how, for generations, Masai boys have come of age by killing a lion. Lions have learned to fear them and vice versa, resulting in a somewhat peaceful coexistence. Still, various beasts hunt in the night, which is why

Bateleur guests may walk to their bungalow only in the presence of an armed guard. Masai villages, meanwhile, protect themselves with a circular defence of thorny scrub.

The Big Five—leopard, lion, elephant, buffalo and rhino—got their collective name from English colonial hunters, not fans of the modern safari. These were the animals that hunters feared most, and subsequently have become a check-list of sorts for tourists. Within an hour into the late-afternoon drive, I see three of the Big Five, and by the next day, I catch a glimpse of the final two. A night safari yields

dozens of hippos, far from a river, silently roaming in the dark like ominous tanks. Every drive can result in the spectacular, the mundane or, most likely, a combination of both.

The following day, we almost catch a kill when the wildebeest roam a little too close to a pride of lions. The tense moment passes when a dozen Land Cruisers pull up, containing tourists chattering too loudly. There is bush etiquette, and these bastards are stomping all over it. During migration, there's a lot of traffic in the Mara, and our camp is by no means the only luxury lodge around. Using radio, guides share information on animal sightings, doing their best to satisfy their clients' desire to be as close as possible to the action. As we wait for a potential chase, a large, muscular lioness walks right past our open-air vehicle, just feet away from my legs. She gazes directly into my eyes. It would be easy for her to leap up and enjoy some Esrock sausage. Fortunately, lions don't attack cars. The wildebeest are being stalked, and they know it. Instinctively they group together, the largest adults on the rim. This is a waiting game, and after an hour and a half, we have waited more than our bladders can stand. We drive off for an anxious pee in the bush, safely guarded by our ranger.

With a never-ending conveyor belt of prey—over 2 million animals—predators can patiently wait, pick out the weak and leave plenty of scraps for the hyenas, vultures and other

5 Bucket List African Safari Destinations

Etosha National Park, Namibia: Almost twice the size of the Serengeti, Etosha's large salt pan creates a striking backdrop to view the Big Five, including the tallest elephants on the continent. Abundant waterholes provide outstanding opportunities for photos.

Kruger National Park, South Africa: This massive park is the size of Wales, and has more mammals than any other African reserve. It is serviced by a 2,600-kilometre road network, with bush camps for all budgets.

The Okavango Delta, Botswana: Slicing through the Kalahari, the Okavango River gathers all your favourite wildlife and birds en masse on the islands, in lagoons and on the plains. The delta boasts outstanding bush camps, some surrounded by water.

The Serengeti, Tanzania: A classic safari destination with abundant wildlife, including the largest population of lions anywhere. The Serengeti shares the annual wildebeest migration with Masai Mara.

The South Luangwa National Park, Zambia: Discovering lions, crocs and elephants outside a vehicle brings a special kind of thrill. Renowned for its walking safaris, the park offers both luxury and budget camps, though it is best suited to experienced safari lovers.

scavengers. We see dozens of skeletons to prove as much. In nature, nothing goes to waste.

A nearby Masai village offers cultural encounters and a craft market. Here I learn about the Masai art of jumping, and how men who can leap the highest are the most attractive to potential wives. After jumping together with a group of warriors, I tell them I'd surely be the only single guy in the village.

On the final evening, we join Masai villagers for a barbecue on the savannah. We drink vodka mixed with honey as the stars glisten above us, and listen to the harmonies of red-robed Masai men singing round the fire. This is the Africa of bucket list dreams, where members of different tribes come together in peace, celebrate good fortune and experience the untamed magnificence of the continent's natural beauty.

START HERE:

globalbucketlist.com/masaimara

Walk down the Avenue of the Baobabs

MADAGASCAR

Bucket listers are suckers for bizarre landscapes, especially when they appear to have been CGId by a Hollywood special effects studio. Such is the case with Madagascar's Avenue of the Baobabs, a channel of freaky trees that straddles a section of the bumpy dirt road between Morondava and Belo Tsiribihina. Locals long ago cleared the dense surrounding forest, but these two dozen towering baobabs survived, largely because of their importance in local traditions. Spirits are said to live at the base, and are offered prayers and wishes. Growing as tall as 30 metres and surviving as long as 800 years, if not longer, baobabs grow a cluster of branches at the top that resemble roots growing beneath the earth. Of the eight known species of baobab, all are endemic to Madagascar, though two species did find their way to the African mainland. Despite its rustic condition, the avenue is part of a national highway, meaning that locals wander between the thick baobabs as frequently as Angelinos might between the palms of Beverly Hills. Substitute ox carts for beemers.

Sunset and sunrise are the most popular times to view the trees—the sheen of the bark dazzles beneath the magnificent Malagasy sky. Prepare to lose your mind capturing the reflections in the adjacent lake. Along with the lemurs, the Avenue of the Baobabs is a star attraction of Madagascar, a somewhat ironic situation given rampant deforestation on the island. Slash-and-burn agriculture and illegal logging have wiped out half of the island's forests. Fortunately, conservation efforts are well under way, helping to ensure this magical spot remains a physical reality and not just a collection of rendered pixels.

START HERE:
globalbucketlist.com/baobab

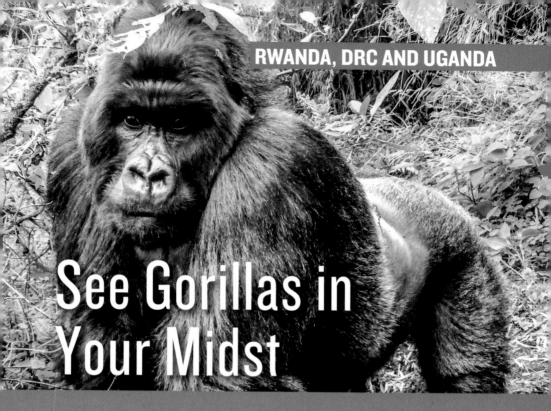

See Gorillas in Your Midst

Trekking to the world's last remaining mountain gorillas draws thousands of bucket listers each year to Uganda, Rwanda and the Democratic Republic of the Congo (DRC). Visitor numbers are limited, logistics are challenging and accommodation and permits are expensive. In 2014, a permit cost US$750 per person in Rwanda; US$600 in Uganda; and US$400 in the Congo. Troops of gorillas inhabit Uganda's Bwindi Impenetrable Forest, as well as a dense massif protected by Uganda's Mgahinga Gorilla National Park; the DRC's Virunga National Park; and Rwanda's Volcanoes National Park. Just 80 visitors per day are allowed into each park, where they are further divided into smaller groups and guided toward particular gorilla families. They call this "gorilla trekking" because trekking is exactly what you will do, hiking through the oft-wet rainforest and stinging nettles, for mere minutes up to several hours, depending on where the gorillas happen to be that day.

On the plus side, sightings are all but guaranteed, since park trackers use GPS to track the individual families.

As with all wildlife encounters, whether the gorillas are sleeping behind trees, quietly chewing bamboo or dancing Gangnam Style just feet away from you is entirely up to them. Guides know the gorillas like they know their own families, and instruct visitors on how to maintain non-threatening verbal and physical cues—keeping your voice down and movements slow. For the most part, the gorillas are nonplussed by us gawking, hairless monkeys. Despite their brute portrayal in bad Hollywood remakes, in reality they are known to be shy and tolerant of other species.

Your visit is limited to just one hour per day, which is ample time to exhaust your camera's memory card. It's an intense hour too, akin to looking in the mirror while playing a fierce game of evolutionary Monopoly. Once the initial thrill subsides, simply observe our beastly cousins in their natural habitat: their hierarchies and politics, the tenderness of the mothers and playfulness of the infants, the appetites of the

one for the bucket list, and there's wildlife aplenty in Uganda's Queen Elizabeth National Park.

All subspecies of gorilla—western and eastern—are critically endangered. As powerful and burly as they may look, these great apes with their barrel chests and superhero muscles are no match for machine guns, bulldozers and human-borne diseases. Ebola has killed thousands, poachers are a constant threat, civil war has sent starving refugees in search of bush meat, and logging, bushfires and agriculture have a devastating impact on the 80 per cent of gorillas still living in unprotected areas. The DRC is rich in both natural resources *and* corruption: 80 per cent is also the amount of land in Virunga National Park that the Congolese government has designated for oil concessions.

Were it not for awareness, conservation efforts, those exorbitantly priced park permits and the power of bucket lists, encountering the biggest primate in a zoo enclosure might tragically be all that's left to us.

upstart adolescent blackbacks and the quiet dominance of the alpha silverback. Whether you choose to make the drive from Kigali, spend a small fortune at a Ugandan luxury mountain lodge or brave the political instability of the Congo, such encounters with gorillas are the magical moments that make it all worthwhile. And no matter which country kicks off your encounter, be aware that each experience will be different depending on the troop you encounter, your trackers and guides, and how eager you are to stay and explore the surrounding region. Virunga's lava lake on the Nyiragongo volcano is arguably

START HERE:

globalbucketlist.com/gorillatrek

Cage Dive with Crocodiles

SOUTH AFRICA

"**U**nderstand, Robin . . . other predators might be curious or scared of you, but these crocs simply see you as food."

Supportive words from Neal Martin, the croc master at the Cango Wildlife Ranch in South Africa's Eastern Cape. He pulls a lever, raising my circular cage into the air and over a pool containing three of the biggest crocodiles I've ever seen. I feel like a large french fry ready to be deep-fried. Tourists are looking at me with an expression I've become accustomed to while researching this bucket list. Their mouths agape, they're thinking I'm one pecan short of a nut pie.

About an hour's drive from South Africa's magnificent eastern coastline, the town of Oudtshoorn draws tourists with two main attractions: the impressive Cango Caves and ostrich farming, of which the region has a long history. It's a fun and quirky detour for those exploring the outer reaches of the country's scenic Garden Route, with various craft markets and roadside attractions taking advantage of passing traffic. But only one of them allows you to enter a steel cage and be lowered into a pool of crocodiles. While the kids cuddle cheetah cubs or look at snakes, birds and other animals, Cango Wildlife Ranch's croc cage diving begs investigation.

The only other place you can do anything remotely similar is in Australia. Not like this, and not with 4-metre-long Nile crocodiles.

My feet touch the water, which is generously warm. I'm wearing goggles for underwater views, supporting myself with interior handles. Immediately, a croc named Ma Baker stirs. Up to this point, she looked like a dark shadow in the water. Another female, Sweet Sue, slowly moves from beneath the viewing bridge, silently drifting toward my cage. Effortlessly, they surround me, no doubt sizing me up for the buffet. The cage begins to look awfully flimsy. From my vantage point underwater, the crocs resemble pure dinosaur. I'm as close to these deadly predators as anyone should ever want to be. Ma Baker, one of the bigger crocs in the park, stares at me with her unblinking gold orb eyeball. I've seen that same sparkle in the eyes of my Brazilian father-in-law, shortly before he devours a slab of meat.

Although they are not the biggest killer in Africa, crocodiles are creatures nobody should mess with. One second you're crossing a river, and in an explosive flash of violence, you find yourself gripped in the jaws of a large croc, spinning you in a death roll. Once you've drowned, it will stash your body under riverbanks and snack away as needed, much like you do with that tub of ice cream in your freezer. I ponder this unfortunate fate when Ma Baker decides to poke her sizeable jaws into my cage, along with her sharp 8-centimetre-long claws.

"Please resist the urge to touch her," says Neal above me.

I'm too focused on resisting the urge to wet my already wet bathing suit. I hold my breath and duck underwater. Unlike her tough, scaly top, Ma Baker's belly seems soft and vulnerable. I can hear Neal's voice in my head telling me to resist the urge to give the tummy a tickle. Sweet Sue is resting almost at my feet when suddenly I lurch around. Hannibal, the biggest croc in the park, is lurking in the shadows, giving me the heebie-jeebies. The crocs are fed well enough, and since the cage enters their pool frequently during high season, they're used to its intrusion. This is not a dangerous activity. Crocodiles just like to play around with their food.

The crane tugs the cage and I'm hoisted up above the water, crocodiles circling my feet. I imagine myself as James Bond in a villain's lair. Few people get this close to a Nile crocodile and live to talk about it. It's a memorable encounter with a fearsome beast but, as with all the wildlife experiences on this bucket list, one that leaves you with a deep respect, and healthy fear, for the creatures that share our planet.

START HERE:
globalbucketlist.com/crocdive

Visit the Home of an Icon

For some of you, it will be Graceland. For others, Mark Twain's house in Connecticut, Frida Kahlo's house in Mexico City, Anne Frank's apartment in Amsterdam, Albert Einstein's apartment in Bern, or Sherlock Holmes's address on Baker Street (although Holmes is fictional, but you knew that, right?). Somewhere on your bucket list is room for a cultural excursion to the home of a person who made a difference in your world. Breathing life into history, such an excursion helps us reconcile the accomplishments of these towering figures with the fact that they were *actually* human. Like us, they had challenges and potential. Like us, they required a bed and a bathroom.

Soweto, the largest township in South Africa, was created during apartheid to house the African workforce that served the white-owned businesses and leafy suburbs hidden beyond view. It was a no-go zone, patrolled by state police looking for any trouble—from black *or* white South Africans—that might disrupt the injustice of the status quo. As a child of apartheid, I grew up with modern shopping malls, smooth paved highways and manicured parks. Beyond the mine dumps on the outskirts of town? Dirt roads, no sanitation services, poverty and desperation.

Fortunately, 1992 saw the beginning of an unprecedented, relatively peaceful transfer of power, ushering in one of the most remarkable political and cultural transformations the world has ever seen. The man largely responsible for this has been lionized as a true political leader, the embodiment of courage, personal sacrifice, integrity and compassion. Although Ngakane Street boasts the home of Desmond Tutu, *another* Nobel Peace Prize winner, I am here to visit a humble brick abode, formerly the home of Nelson Mandela.

Despite its reputation, Johannesburg is worth exploring for a couple of days either before or after your inevitable journey to Cape Town or the game reserves. Sure, check out its vibrant neighbourhoods, flea markets and

megamalls, but it's a visit to the Apartheid Museum that is vital to one's understanding of how this "Rainbow Nation" emerged from a stark, monochrome past. Sombre and powerful, this museum lands an emotional punch; it's a worthy highlight on a Soweto tour. Foreign tourists (and locals too) are picked up at glitzy hotels in Johannesburg's northern suburbs for guided tours into the township. While Johannesburgers might drive with their car doors locked and windows sealed, guests in tour minibuses are reassured that they can leave their doors unlocked and windows down. Much like on *favela* tours in Rio de Janeiro, tourists are safe in Soweto, as if the *tsotsis* (gangsters) have agreed to a cultural ceasefire, perhaps because tourists help Soweto's economy, or perhaps because they've been paid off.

Like the rest of South Africa, much has changed in Soweto since the fall of apartheid. Now incorporated into Johannesburg's municipality, Soweto has seen its dirt roads paved, its dusty markets replaced by shopping malls, its thousands of tin shacks replaced by houses with plumbing and electricity. Soccer City, the calabash-inspired stadium that hosted the 2010 World Cup final, broke through the mine tailings that long separated Johannesburg and Soweto. Green zones with modern playgrounds have kids playing soccer in sight of the renovated mine hostels that once saw heavy political violence.

The Orlando Towers, two chimneys from a decommissioned power plant that once blackened Soweto's air with fumes, have been brightly painted with murals and converted into a tourist attraction, complete with bungee jump. There's a four-star hotel, and a youth hostel offering bicycle tours. We are still in Africa, and there are still large parts of Soweto where people live in squalor. Yet so much has changed since my first visit as a 16-year-old, illegally entering the township with my activist cousin determined to unknot the wool over my eyes. I remember flies and trash and stench, but also beaming smiles and hospitality that I felt, as a white South African, I

hardly deserved. The smiles are still there on the characters I'd met in the illegal shebeens. Now they are legal, and serving beer to busloads of German tourists.

We drive through an area known as Beverly Hills, where the wealthiest citizens of Soweto live. In contrast to the leafy northern suburbs of Johannesburg, the lack of electric fencing and barred windows is noticeable. We visit a few sites famous for their roles in various uprisings, drive past the Chris Hani Baragwanath Hospital—the largest hospital in the southern hemisphere and the third largest in the world. Finally we swing into Ngakane Street toward the Nelson

Mandela National Museum. In the years since my last visit, the road has been paved and sidewalk hawkers now sell souvenirs. From 1946 up to the mid-1990s, Mandela and his family lived on the corner of Ngakane and Vilakazi Streets, in a small brick structure with a tin roof, cement floor, bucket toilet and tiny kitchen and bathroom. In his autobiography *Long Walk to Freedom*, Nelson Mandela wrote: "It was the opposite of grand, but it was my first true home of my own and I was mightily proud. A man is not a man until he has a house of his own."

Because of its size, only 20 visitors at a time can navigate the house, which was renovated before being reopened to the public in 2009. Bullet holes in the walls from several assassination attempts are still present. A display contains a staggering array of Mandela's personal effects, along with illustrious international honours. Given the

Avoid the Horror

Horror movies play off our fear of the unknown, inserting irrational phobias in our fragile imaginations while producers insert box-office cash into their wallets. For your own sake, stay clear of horror films with a travel focus. Explore subterranean wonders without worrying about the monsters of *The Cave* or *The Descent*. Sleep in a friendly hostel without stressing about the organ-mincemeat featured in *Hostel*, and don't worry about a *Psycho* behind the shower curtain at your next motel. Trek in the jungle safe from mutant *Anaconda* or maliciously haunted Mayan ruins, and worry about the radiation, not the zombies, in *Chernobyl Diaries*. There's slim chance you will become an unwitting drug mule like the girls in *Brokedown Palace*; rest assured there's no *Aliens* (or *Predators*) in Antarctica. Don't watch *Avalanche* before visiting mountains, *San Andreas* before checking out San Francisco, *The Poseidon Adventure* before boarding a cruise ship, *Volcano* before climbing one, *Rollercoaster* before taking the kids to a theme park, *Unstoppable* before going on a train journey and *Sharknado* (or its sequels) under any circumstances.

modest setting, they emphasize Mandela's incredible journey, and the hole left by his death, in 2013. Mandela retired from public service after his first term as president—highly unusual in Africa, a continent plagued by crackpot revolutionary dictators. Mandela's integrity and ability to unite South Africans makes me wonder if I'll see another great leader in my lifetime. After 27 years in prison, Nelson Mandela still believed in hope, and worked for a greater good. He rejected revenge for forgiveness, riches for charity. Visiting his home in Soweto and his cell on Robben Island, off the coast of Cape Town, connects us with the humanity beyond the headlines. The humanity we hope to emulate.

Johannesburg is not a city in which to flash your jewellery or get lost in the wrong part of town. You might choose to avoid reading the local newspapers, to keep media fear mongering (and overblown

paranoia) at bay. Why focus on the crime and corruption? With its outstanding restaurants and buzzy neighbourhoods, I prefer to see Johannesburg, the turbulent home of my childhood, for what it now is: the heart of a great nation, just like New York, Hong Kong, Toronto or São Paulo.

Some of you may choose Shakespeare's home in Stratford-upon-Avon. Others, Abraham Lincoln's birthplace in Kentucky, Pablo Neruda's house in Santiago, or Getreidegasse 9 in Vienna—the birthplace of Wolfgang Amadeus Mozart. Restored homes of our personal heroes encourage us to learn about fascinating places as well as inspirational people. A worthy endeavour, therefore, for anyone's Great Global Bucket List.

START HERE:
globalbucketlist.com/soweto

Leave Tunisia in Ruins

TUNISIA

My visit to Tunisia took place mere months before a street vendor set himself on fire as an act of protest against government corruption. Popular discontent for the long-term strongman in power needed just such a spark, and within a month, Tunisia's hard-line government had crumbled under the sustained protest of the masses. Governments in Libya, Egypt and Yemen followed, with further uprisings brutally supressed in Syria and Bahrain. There was a brief moment in early 2011 when the world watched the Arab Spring with hope and optimism, but with civil war in Libya and Syria, the rise of ISIS and ongoing political turmoil, that moment quickly passed. Fortunately, Tunisia has been a success story—at least for now, in my present tense, as opposed to *your* now, that is, the future. In *your* now, Tunisia might be wholly owned by a multinational corporation, Syria might be the name of a moon station and cyborgs might rule Egypt with a well-oiled iron fist.

Regardless of what the future may bring, I can all but guarantee that Tunisia's bucket list entry in this tome will remain relevant, primarily because many of its structures have been standing for millennia.

Tunisia is a country with a historically rich agricultural bounty, and as such it played hot potato in the hands of several great empires. The result is a treasure trove for archaeologists, and a delight for those bucket listers with a fondness for ancient civilizations. What's more, the ruins of Tunisia are plentiful, accessible and relatively safe from the hordes of tourists that invade less impressive sites in Italy or Turkey.

Let's start with Carthage, the seat of the once-mighty Phoenician Empire. Located on the outskirts of the modern capital of Tunis, the remains of Carthage look much as one would expect after a thorough Roman sacking and 3,000 years of neglect. Overlooking the rich hues of the North African Mediterranean, the ruins are not nearly as impressive as their history. Still in Tunis, you'll want to pop into the Bardo, one of the world's great museums. Located in a palace that dates back to the 13th century, the Bardo houses art, statues and dazzling mosaics from the Roman era, as well as a

A Long Time Ago, in a Galaxy Not So Far Away

Tunisia has been the location for just a few Hollywood movies, but an illustrious few they have been. Tunis doubled as Cairo in the Oscar-winning *The English Patient*. More famously, the country doubled for Luke Skywalker's home planet Tatooine in the first *Star Wars* movie. There actually is a place in Tunisia called Tatooine, but the scenes were filmed in Matmata, where people have been living in sandstone caves for centuries. A huge salt flat called Chott el Djerid hosted Skywalker as he gazed longingly at two suns. *Star Wars* fanatics flock to nearby Sidi Bouhlel, now known as Star Wars Canyon, where R2-D2 was captured. The series returned to Tunisia for its Tatooine scenes in *The Phantom Menace*, *Attack of the Clones* and *Revenge of the Sith*. George Lucas sure liked Tunisia, a lot more than anyone liked his three prequels. The "Egyptian" desert scenes in *Raiders of the Lost Ark* were actually filmed around the Tunisian UNESCO World Heritage Site of Kairouan. Scenes from *Monty Python's Life of Brian* were filmed in the Ribat monastery at Monastir. Colin Firth and Ben Kingsley soaked up the Roman ruins during the filming of *The Last Legion*, and the schlocky horror flick *Vampire Diary* was shot here too (though Tunisians are not nearly as proud of that one as they are of the others).

priceless collection of early Islamic and Phoenician artifacts.

As I leave the city, my van is dwarfed by the ruins of Hadrian's Aqueduct, built in AD 130 to supply water to Carthage. Ruins of the Roman Empire are so prolific in Tunisia, I half expect to trip over togas on the sidewalks. I visit the large, tall columns of Thuburbo Majus, the remains of an important trading town that connected Carthage and caravans from the Sahara; next up is the coliseum at El Djem, considered the best-preserved ruin in North Africa and the world's third-largest coliseum. Heading north, I take my time examining the surviving mosaics on the floors of old, subterranean houses in a site known as Bulla Regia. While the best mosaics have been relocated to the Bardo, a few drops of liquid from my water bottle restores a sheen on the colourful floor tiles and it's not hard to imagine how they once brightened the homes of Roman citizens.

It is raining domestic pets when I arrive at the country's rock-star ruin—Dougga. A parking lot's worth of tour buses scram out of there to escape the downfall, but I decide to sit out the storm. Half an hour later,

I have the largest, most impressive Roman city in Tunisia essentially to myself. I walk down boulevards of ancient stone glowing in the pink, post-storm, late-afternoon sun. Dougga's 3,500-seat amphitheatre, imposing columned temples, baths and squares are haunting. As I make my way past crowds of ghosts squeezing plump oranges in their ectoplasmic markets, I realize that this is history that you can *feel*. It reminds me of Chernobyl (page 231): it provides an illuminating glimpse of an abandoned past that will never be again. The Roman Empire, the most civilized and advanced state of its time, thought it would last forever. Time gives three duck quacks and a quart of skunk venom for the grand ambitions of mankind, be they Roman emperors or modern dictators.

Tunisia's political scene might have evolved since I explored its many ancient wonders, and will surely evolve some more. Fortunately, the country's many ancient wonders will survive—oblivious to uprisings, cemented in history and awaiting history-minded bucket listers.

START HERE:
globalbucketlist.com/dougga

Bucket List Man-Made Landmarks

Humanity's most iconic landmarks is a bucket list unto itself, and this list could stretch over pages. Just remember, there's no race, it's not a competition and the journey might well end up being more interesting than the destination. Landmarks not on the list below are discussed in greater detail elsewhere in this book.

- ☐ Acropolis, Athens
- ☐ Alhambra, Granada
- ☐ Big Ben, Buckingham Palace and Westminster Abbey, London
- ☑ Christ the Redeemer and Copacabana, Rio de Janeiro
- ☐ Colosseum, Rome
- ☐ Eiffel Tower, Paris
- ☑ Hagia Sophia and Blue Mosque, Istanbul
- ☐ Imperial Palace, Tokyo
- ☐ Leaning Tower of Pisa, Italy
- ☐ National Mall, Washington
- ☐ Piazza San Marco and Rialto Bridge, Venice
- ☑ Pyramids, Sphinx and ruins of Luxor, Egypt
- ☐ Sagrada Familia, Barcelona
- ☐ Statue of Liberty, Empire State Building and Times Square, New York City
- ☐ Stonehenge, England
- ☑ St. Basil's Cathedral and Red Square, Moscow
- ☐ St. Peter's Basilica, Vatican City
- ☐ Sydney Opera House, Australia
- ☐ Tiananmen Square and Terracotta Warriors, China

Walk the Narrow Streets of Stone Town

ZANZIBAR

It is a muggy afternoon, the sky folding wet towels in its dark, linen-closet clouds. I am enjoying my favourite of all pastimes: scootering about *sans* helmet on a tropical island. Despite the ominous weather, I have few worries on the crackled open island roads, though that can't be said for the village intersections, where people, animals, cars, buses and bikes battle at the same roundabout. This is how I find myself careening toward the trunk of a mango tree, much to the amusement of bored villagers. Somehow I manage to avoid the trunk, crashing into a pile of soft leaves instead. Even bike accidents solicit laughter and clapping on Zanzibar, an island powered by a belief in *hakuna matata*. You might have heard this Swahili phrase in *The Lion King*. It translates loosely as "No worries, mate." As I'm laid out flat beneath the ripe, juicy mangoes, all body and machine parts in working order, *hakuna matata* is entirely accurate.

I'd taken a scenic, adventurous journey to reach this historical island paradise. Sweaty buses, overloaded taxis, 38 hours on the infamous TAZARA Railway through Zambia and Tanzania, and finally, 3 hours on a rolling ferry from Dar es Salaam. By the time I arrive in Stone Town, the movie-set-like capital of Zanzibar, I feel I deserve every cobblestone laid on its narrow, exotic streets. The Gothic churches, ash-blackened mosques, massive carved wooden doors and fragrance of spice are the bonus.

Zanzibar was once the United States' most-favoured trading nation, and not because of clove exports. In the early 1800s, this small island off the coast of East Africa was the centre of the slave trade. Men, women and children, often traded by tribal chiefs for cheap, shiny trinkets, were shipped to Zanzibar from throughout the continent. The Sultan of Oman oversaw this supermarket of slavery and as such enjoyed the kind of wealth that oil bestows on his offspring a few generations later. His House of Wonders, a palace that survives to this day, is four storeys of marble-coated malevolence, located in the heart of Stone Town.

Flush with slave money, Zanzibar was the second country on the planet to get electricity. It was not until slavery ended that the island descended from its lofty, distasteful height. When the British installed their own government, the sultan's nephew attempted a coup, still notable as the shortest war in history (it lasted a mere 45 minutes). The House of Wonders, still bearing the scars from the British naval pounding, is now a museum of a forgotten era that was good to the few and lousy for the many.

Today, Zanzibar is a popular, if somewhat unusual, travel destination. Much like Timbuktu, it conjures images of mysterious adventure, but unlike Timbuktu, it has luxury resorts and a decent tourism infrastructure. Unlike Timbuktu, it has talcum powder beaches; labyrinthine, Jerusalem-like streets; and juicy tropical fruit. Travellers typically fly direct from Nairobi or stop over if they're backpacking between Kenya and South Africa. Most inevitably end up gathering on the patio of Africa House Hotel, drinking not-too-cold beer while traditional wooden dhows sail amid postcard-perfect ocean sunsets. Toothy greetings

The Spice of Life

You can taste the cloves, nutmeg, cinnamon and pepper in the air. Sunsets glow with a saffron-turmeric hue for good reason. Zanzibar once dominated trade routes with its spices, vital for cooking, healing and ceremonial use. Spice tours from Stone Town take you into plantations to discover and taste the various spices, along with exotic fruits. Pop a cardamom seed in your mouth and your taste buds will explode. Spice exporting is still the island's dominant industry, though Asian countries long ago decimated Zanzibar's dominance in the spice trade.

of "*Jambo!*" are to be heard everywhere. Zanzibaris are defiantly friendly, although given the island's economic hardships, you'll want to keep your travel instincts sharp.

Shortly after surviving my Knievel-esque scooter accident, I find myself stuck on a small motorboat, broken down on the Indian Ocean. The rust bucket attempts to putter to an old prison island, creatively named Prison Island. But it putters out. Our smiley skipper believes that pounding the outboard repeatedly with a hammer will remedy the situation. When it does not, he shrugs and sighs the inevitable "*hakuna matata!*" Three hours of baking sun later, his friend arrives in another boat. I trade vessels and continue on to the island, the skipper remaining behind in his open-top raft. He didn't seem too perturbed; in fact, he's probably still out there today. By the time I encounter my first giant tortoise, as prehistorically ugly as one might expect, I have forgotten those three lost hours I'll never see again. My internal clock is slowly adjusting to African time, which follows no logical pattern whatsoever.

If I were a vampire, I'd live in Stone Town. Dark, narrow alleys lie beneath antique architecture, sculpted exteriors and ornamented 3-metre-high wooden doors. Freddy Mercury was born in Stone Town, and I think his teeth vindicate my vampire theory. The government is doing its best to preserve the living museum that is Old Town, but poverty creeps in like an invading jungle. A British expat tells me that Zanzibar is not unlike Tangier in its golden days, when anything went—including, occasionally, your wallet. The island's political situation, together with the antagonism between the Muslim and Christian populations, creates a palpable tension, one that unfortunately is not dismissed with a cursory *hakuna matata*.

Up north in Nungwi, I find the crystal-clear ocean lapping against a stunning sandy beach. There are hotels, but I choose to camp on the beach, not far from the tranquil waves. Cuisine is limited to coconut rice and whatever fish happens to get caught that day. Tuna! Tropical parrotfish! I meet some American environmental students who express grave concern for the destruction of the island's coral and natural resources. Still, mutterings of paradise are on our lips,

sweetened with drops of freshly pressed sugarcane juice.

Arriving back in Stone Town, I find good budget accommodation, exotic street food and great places to hang out just off the tourist track. You learn fast that the quickest way of getting from A to B is the way you won't get lost. A to D to B can save an hour of walking down blind alleys. Day excursions include a spice tour (tasting fruit so foreign to me that it might as well be from another planet), a visit to the sultan's bordello, scooter rentals (mind the mango trees) and an authentic island meal in the home of locals. One night, watching the ocean, I see a dolphin leap out of the water in a runway of moonlight. The moment is over in a heartbeat, and yet I keep rerunning it in my mind.

There may be plenty of things to worry about in Zanzibar: environmental destruction, corruption, food poisoning, tourist scams, road accidents. All of which bucket listers should face squarely, with a big smile, patience, understanding and a joyous *hakuna matata*.

START HERE:
globalbucketlist.com/zanzibar

Swim in the Devil's Pool

ZIMBABWE

Formerly known as South Zambezia, Southern Rhodesia and Rhodesia, Zimbabwe has seen a lot of change. Joining it has been the transformation of old-fashioned travel diaries. Before the advent of blogs and likes and shares and 68 digital photos of something you swear is an aardvark, my own travel journals contained:

- Random thoughts and observations
- Flight stubs and train tickets
- Napkins with names and addresses of people I'd never see again
- Stickers, brochures and handouts
- Printed photographs
- A smattering of ketchup (maybe?) or blood (more likely)

I once travelled with a guy who kept the same journal for almost a decade. He'd tape additional books together and write in tiny script. This impressive travel diary was his bible, an invaluable historical record of his complete life adventures. It was stolen, along with his backpack, off the roof of a bus somewhere between Transylvania and Budapest. What the hell does this have to do with Victoria Falls? Well, I once had a journal, and it contained the most incredible photograph of me jumping off the very lip of the world's largest waterfall.

More water rushes into the chasm dividing Zambia and Zimbabwe than anywhere else. Although it's twice the height and width of Niagara Falls, it's not the world's highest waterfall (that's Angel Falls in Venezuela), nor even the widest (that's Khone Phapheng Falls, Laos). Yet the sheer *volume* of the mighty Zambezi has for centuries attracted bucket listers, drawn to a place the locals call "the smoke that thunders." Traditionally, most tourists to Vic Falls stay in colonial hotels on the Zimbabwean side, but with the country's political and economic collapse, many now prefer the Zambian side. Hotels and tour operators in both countries are known to gouge their guests for the privilege of seeing this natural wonder, including a day visa that allows you to cross borders for the views, at a price of around 40,000 Zambian kwachas, or 10 gazillion Zimbabwe dollars. Actually, Zimbabwe's currency was abandoned altogether, rendering all its notes worthless. Inflation reached 89,700,000,000,000,000,000,000 per cent in 2008. And I didn't even make that number up. In both countries, where the US greenback goes very far, you'll pay up to US$80 just to see Victoria Falls. No more bitching about prices to cruise under Horseshoe Falls in Niagara.

I visited the Zambian side in December, which is the tail end of dry season. With the Zambezi flowing at low volume, you can walk to Livingstone Island, then make your way to the Devil's Pool. Here, a rock barrier creates a pool right at the very edge of the falls. Much to the horror of tourists on the Zimbabwe side, you can even go rock jumping. Across the chasm, tourists can't see the pool and must therefore watch what appear to be tourists committing suicide. This close to the edge, you don't have to worry about crocodiles or strong currents, though

5 Waterfalls on the Bucket List

Angel Falls: With its 979-metre drop, Venezuela's Angel Falls holds the title of the world's highest waterfall. Such is its height that the water turns to mist before hitting the ground. Remote and difficult to access, located as it is in Canaima National Park, it is still one of Venezuela's most popular tourist attractions, and a mecca for BASE jumpers, who leap off the edge with a parachute.

Iguazu Falls (pictured below): Spanning 4 kilometres along the borders of Brazil, Argentina and Paraguay, Iguazu Falls gathers 275 waterfalls into one escarpment, surrounded by lush tropical jungle. The towns of Foz do Iguacu (Brazil) and Puerto Iguazu (Argentina) provide access with metal walkways to the most spectacular viewing points. Hop aboard a boat and get soaked near the mouth of the biggest water mass, the Devil's Throat.

Nachi Falls: A forest of cedar and cypress surrounds Japan's Nachisan region, and cutting through them are dozens of waterfalls. With a height of over 130 metres, Nachi Falls is one of three "divine" waterfalls in the country. Colourful wooden pagodas and temples encircle the airborne stream, and together with the surrounding forest—the waterfall is located in Yoshino-Kumano National Park—it's easy to see how Nachi Falls earned its sacred status.

Niagara Falls: Casinos, resorts and theme parks have cascaded around the world's most visited waterfall, but there's no denying the sheer power and beauty of Niagara Falls. Over 25 million visitors a year are drawn to the spectacle of green water crashing 50 metres below. Hornblower Niagara Cruises boat tours have taken the place of the legendary *Maid of the Mist* on the Canadian side, but feeling the spray beneath Horseshoe Falls remains as iconic as ever.

Tugela Falls: South Africa's Tugela Falls is the world's second-highest waterfall, falling 947 metres between the Drakensberg Mountains. Unlike Angel Falls, however, it is far easier to access and can even be viewed from a major highway. In keeping with the excellent hiking in the region, a series of chain ladders allows you to climb to the summit of Mont-aux-Sources, the source of the falls.

the occasional tourist has been a bit overzealous, missed the pool and found themselves visiting Zimbabwe without a visa, or a heartbeat. If swimming to the edge of the world's largest waterfall isn't enough of a thrill, you can also bungee jump 111 metres off Victoria Falls Bridge, once the highest commercial bungee in the world. Or spend US$500 a night at the Royal Livingstone, for a hotel bill that is sure to give you a heart attack. Zimbabwe is a country with abundant natural resources, and a country that once promised much hope for sub-Saharan Africa. Unfortunately, corrupt, crackpot leaders bled it dry, funnelling cash to private bank accounts overseas. A common joke: Where is the capital of Zimbabwe? Geneva.

I'd love to illustrate this chapter with that epic, once-in-a-lifetime photo of me rock jumping into the Devil's Pool. We set it up so it looks like I'm actually leaping off Victoria Falls itself. Much like Zimbabwe's economy, that travel journal mysteriously vanished, along with the photos, the writing, contacts and splotches of ketchup. It pains me to even think about it. Fortunately, I found a perfect image from another bucket lister that serves as an able substitute. You'll never forget Victoria Falls, even if you do lose your journal. Nor should you forget any of the bucket list adventures in this book, though you might want to keep an online blog and back up your photos all the same.

START HERE:
globalbucketlist.com/victoriafalls

EUROPE

ARCTIC OCEAN

N
W E
S

| 0 | 250 | 500 Miles |
| 0 | 250 | 500 Kilometres |

ATLANTIC OCEAN

Reykjavik •
ICELAND
■ Eyjafjallajökull

Rovaniemi •

FINLAND

NORWAY

Helsinki •   • St. Petersburg

RUSSIA

Preikestolen •

• Moscow

Baltic Sea

Giant's
Causeway ■
SCOTLAND
• Edinburgh

North
Sea

Riga •
LATVIA

NORTHERN
IRELAND

LITHUANIA

Langley
Castle ■

Vilnius •

IRELAND

ENGLAND

Berlin •
POLAND

Glastonbury ■■
Stonehenge   • London

Chernobyl •

GERMANY

Oświęcim • • Kraków
UKRAINE

CZECH
REP.
Kutná Hora •

• Pervomaisk

Azores

Munich •

Budapest •

Terceira →

FRANCE
SWITZERLAND
SLOVENIA
Lake Bled →
Lipica
HUNGARY
ROMANIA
Bran Castle ■

Mont Blanc •
CROATIA
Bucharest •

Black Sea

Venice •

Modena •
• Bologna
Dalmatian Coast

Pisa •

Pamplona •
ITALY
Dubrovnik •

PORTUGAL
• Barcelona
Rome •
VATICAN
CITY

SPAIN

Lisbon •
Buñol •
GREECE

Granada •

Mediterranean Sea

Mt. Etna ■

Athens •
Santorini

Kayak along the Dalmatian Coast

CROATIA

Cradling the turquoise waters of the Adriatic in the shadow of scorched surrounding mountainside, thick stone walls besiege Old Town Dubrovnik. Together with its medieval churches, it could easily be the setting of a fairy tale, an ancient fortress of Tolkien-esque lore. Built by medieval Venetians to protect what would become a major European centre of trade and commerce, these impressive walls saw military action as recently as the 1990s. Although the city by this stage held little strategic value, Serb shells fell on Dubrovnik during the Serbo-Croatian War, an event that mobilized the West to intervene. Somebody should have told Serb commanders that, strategically, it's a terrible idea to bomb any tourist attraction, much less a UNESCO World Heritage Site.

"Surely the Serbs would have kept the city intact for the potential tourism?" I ask my kayak guide, Matko, as we paddle our way across the azure sea.

"You are not thinking like the military," he replies bitterly. "They bombed the Old Town, set fire to the hills, had snipers shooting innocent people walking the streets."

Decades later, the war lingers like a ring around the tub. My rental apartment in the upmarket neighbourhood of Lapad still displays repairs for bullets and shrapnel.

"After seeing what happened in this region, I'm a reborn atheist," jokes Danilo, an American expat who has been living in Dubrovnik since the 1970s. I meet him at a patio bar. He's wearing a fedora and carrying himself with the poise of a jaded CIA agent. I'd been watching too many spy movies.

"The things these people did to each other . . . ," his sentence permanently interrupted by a gulp of martini.

Ethnic fires still burn in the Balkans, but today there are too many superyachts, cruise ships, Lacoste shirts and expensive restaurants to call this a European Middle East. The Dalmatian Coast is spotted with a trove of gorgeous islands, exuding lavender, wealth and a taste of the good life. They call it the new French Riviera, and it's

priced accordingly, but with more medieval ruins. I rent a scooter on the island of Vis, exploring its coastline, drinking its watered-down wine, lazing on its pebble beaches. Hvar is a more popular island, a parkade for mega-yachts berthed alongside one another other every evening in the harbour. Café tables stand on stone streets, beautiful women wear sunglasses at night, an impressive castle on the hill glows each evening with spotlights. It's romantic, it's decadent and it's alluringly lovely. Those of you with buckets of disposable income, rent a staffed yacht and explore the various islands. For the rest of us, we should consider a kayak.

Dubrovnik-based Adria Adventure offers half- and multi-day sea kayaking trips guided by fetching instructors. A couple of Irish girls join me for a paddle to the nearby island of Lokrum to see its stunning coastline. We paddle into coves and nooks, swim in the pool-blue waters, soak up the midsummer sun. Dubrovnik, Split and the islands of the Dalmatian Coast easily live up to their reputation as jewels of the Adriatic. Jewels that come with a price tag during high-season summer. Consider visiting during the shoulder months of May or September, when the armies of foreign tourists have scattered.

START HERE:
globalbucketlist.com/dalmatian

Visit a Church Made with Human Bones

CZECH REPUBLIC

In the 13th century, a monk brought sand from Jerusalem to a small ossuary in Central Europe. Suddenly everyone wanted to be buried there, but soon enough, space ran out. For centuries, monks there collected and stored human remains, until a local woodcarver decided he'd get creative with the surplus of skeletons. Using the remains of some 40,000 people, he created wall art, columns, even a chandelier made with every bone in the human body. Visit the Sedlec Ossuary in the city of Kutná Hora to marvel at the morbid creativity—and the many practical uses of our bones.

START HERE:
globalbucketlist.com/bonechurch

Spend a (K)night in a Castle

L et us hearken back to the age of chivalry, when damsels in distress yearned for gallant knights in shining armour. In reality, King Arthur was likely a grubby, mud-flecked, foul-smelling tribal warlord. In the mythology of our medieval dreams, however, the stares of his hardened knights would spear ladies of the court just as surely as lances penetrated invading barbarians. Ahem. Jousting, feasting, naughty romps behind the ramparts—it's compelling enough to warrant kitschy medieval-themed dinners around the world. Nay, forsake your cheap goblets! Our bucket list is concerned with the authentic, the most splendid of all events. Let us therefore go thither to a restored 14th-century fortified castle in the Northumbrian Valley of the River South Tyne. Nowadays, it is one of the fairest hotels in all the United Kingdom.

Years before I slayed the dragon and rescued the princess, a.k.a. my wife, I pursued, I confess, a fair number of damsels. One of them joined me and my steed (that is, a rickety, cheap rental car), and we rode into the 4 hectares of woodland surrounding Langley Castle. I saw the promise of love flushing her face just as surely as if she'd powdered herself in a coat of ladybug blush. I had reserved the suitably red-hued Greenwich Room, featuring a king-size four-poster bed, a canopied modern bathroom as large as most urban apartments, a dressing room one could park a horse in and a cozy window seat set into 2-metre-thick walls under a glittering chandelier. It is one of five feature rooms, distinguishable from four deluxe rooms and castle-view rooms, which I imagine is strictly for plebs and pages. M'lady was of noble stock and thus demanded the comforts. Ushered into the sweeping entrance hall, I could not help but stiffen straight, talk with honour and reflect on how delightful it was to stay overnight in a castle that looked like it fell off a chessboard.

Admittedly, this was not the first time I'd spent the night in a grand English manor. I'd charmed another damsel in 300-year-old Cliveden House, one of England's poshest hotels, a short drive out of London. (What can I say? Before marriage, I was a busy man of letters.) It

has hosted the likes of Churchill, Chaplin, Roosevelt and guests who regularly show up in sports cars worth more than the GDP of Togo. Individually styled rooms gazed over manicured National Trust–managed gardens, with the dining so formal I found myself constantly choking on the tweed of aristocracy. Cliveden felt like a museum, an expensive glimpse into the upstairs of Downton Abbey, where it was painfully obvious who belonged and who did not. Langley, on the other hand, happily accepted boisterous wedding guests and weekenders from across the kingdom. A quieter, more blissful night of romance could not be asked for. Surrounding areas of interest include Hadrian's Wall, the 117-kilometre Roman fortification that served as a line of defence (inspiration for The Wall in *Game of Thrones*) and building materials for English roads in the 18th century. Perhaps not quite as grand as the Great Wall of China, but rolling English countryside is nothing to scoff at.

There are more surviving castles in Northumberland than anywhere else in England, and you can explore them on your own or through a local tour operator. Unfortunately, you won't be able to spend the night in them, not legally anyway. And so, by my troth, it is for this reason that Langley Castle Hotel looms proud on the Great Global Bucket List: one-of-a-kind accommodation for modern knights and dazzling damsels who wish to relish in the myth of medieval history.

START HERE:
globalbucketlist.com/castle

Medieval Origins of Modern Phrases

Scholars continue to debate the origins of these and other everyday phrases:

Chew the fat: Bacon was often stored above the fireplace. Visiting guests would be offered a piece as a snack during conversation.

Frog in your throat: Medieval doctors believed frog secretions on the throat could treat coughs, an unpleasing scenario for patient and frog alike.

Getting the cold shoulder: If guests overstayed their welcome, they might be fed the worst part of meat (the shoulder), unheated.

Minding your P's and Q's: This one might have originated from modern typesetting (the two letters look similar), though many historians believe it could date back to medieval taverns. Drinkers were charged by the angle of their elbows, determining whether one was drinking a pint or a quart of ale.

Turn the tables: To maintain the quality of the finished side of the table for visitors, families would turn the table upside down and eat on the rough side.

Wet your whistle: Still on the subject of booze, pubs once used ceramic cups with whistles baked into them. If you needed a refill, you simply blew your whistle.

Feel the Spirit of a Finnish Sauna

FINLAND

I'm sitting in a sticky puddle of my own sweat, surrounded by dozens of naked men sprawled on wooden benches in a dark room. In the corner is a large iron furnace, and every few minutes, someone gets up to hurl water onto 1 ton of heated rock. This is greeted by a blast of heat and grunts of approval. A tourist walks in from the showers wearing a bathing suit. He is instantly greeted by moans of disapproval and removes his shorts sheepishly. Finns know the correct manner in which to enjoy a sauna. After all, they invented the word.

a locker room among naked old men reading newspapers. The room smells of time, wood and sweat.

Men and women are separated in public saunas, but a rotund motherly female attendant works in the men's showers, happy to scrub the bejesus out of naked clients with her soap and sponge. In Finland, the heat in

Roller Coaster with a Handbrake

Finnish is one of the few non-Indo-European languages in Europe and therefore difficult to understand on any level. *Vuoristorata* translates as "mountain track," an apt description for a wooden roller coaster inside the Linnanmäki amusement park that has been terrifying Helsinki since 1951. A harnessed manual brake operator can choose just how scary to make the ride, upping the speed, slamming it into corners. He stands at the back of the cars, and looks awfully young to be doing what he does. Like most of the old-time rickety wooden roller coasters still in existence, it's frightening as hell, a lot of fun and a marvel that the brake operator manages to keep everyone alive. There's only one other similar mountain track in operation, in Copenhagen's famed Tivoli Gardens. Modern roller coasters may be technical marvels, but give us the time-honoured safety system of human judgment any day—hasn't failed . . . yet.

Most Finnish apartments and houses have their own sauna, but for those that don't, or for those who prefer to interact with others while soaking in their human juices, community saunas function as they have for centuries. Built in 1928, the Kotiharjun Sauna is the only remaining public wood-burning sauna in Helsinki. I knew I had found the right place when I saw the large neon sign and a dozen half-naked men loitering outside the door. Finns believe the body only looks its best after 30 minutes inside a sauna, but my flabby welcoming party seems to prove otherwise. I pay a 10-euro fee, then disrobe in a sauna is like a spirit, a character who shares your experience. They call this the *löyly*—and respect it, discuss its quality, offer to adjust it if it is too hot or, more often, too cold. Whoever sits on the highest bench has the right to control the *löyly*.

An old man invites me to join him on the topmost shelf. The heat is so intense my ears burn in pain. It is hot enough to fry a flank steak in Satan's ear canal. Finns have another word, *sisu*, which translates as "a combination of strength, spirit and courage." All the *sisu* in the world can't keep me on that upper bench for more than a minute. The temperature is easily above 120°C. How that guy sits in that heat without spontaneously combusting is a mystery, though perhaps it has something to do with the fact that, up to the 1930s, Finnish children were *born* in saunas. Bravado in full force, the *löyly* becomes especially feisty as local men take turns adding bursts of water to the furnace. It increases the steam, the heat and the likelihood of a tourist fainting. Eventually, I crawl out, grab a beer and join the men cooling off outside in the summer rain.

Finns long ago realized the benefits, beyond those of heat and health, of this unusual space, where one is literally stripped of everything—clothes, smartphones and attitudes. Sauna is a time to meditate, catch up with friends, revitalize the body or just debate the news. Culturally, North Americans are not ready to sauna every day, but everyone should embrace the *löyly* at least once in their lives.

START HERE:
globalbucketlist.com/sauna

Explore Berlin in a Trabant

Checkpoint Charlie, the Berlin Wall—it's difficult to imagine that just a few decades ago, European hot spot Berlin was a major Cold War battlefront. Patrolling the front lines were the infamous East German cars known as the Trabant. Built from 1957 to 1990, the Trabant (or Trabi) was a vehicle that epitomized life under Soviet rule. The average East German citizen could wait up to 13 years before being allowed to acquire an ugly yet reliable Trabi. Forget about choosing a colour. With hardly any production changes in its history, the Trabi used a unique gearbox and an engine reliant on gravity to deliver fluids to the right places. Famous for its choking exhaust, it could hit a top speed of 112 km/hr (most likely downhill) and seat four comfortably (provided leg circulation was a non-issue). East Germans would joke that the quickest way to double the value of a Trabant was to fill up the gas tank.

Over 3 million of these cars were produced, of which around 58,000 survive, largely in the possession of collectors. A company named Trabi-Safari offers bucket listers the chance to explore Berlin at the wheel, driving in convoy with a lead car guide as it points out interests via short-range radio. I'm struggling to hear these tidbits because I'm too busy riding the clutch and throttling the gearshift, both of which appear to work on the principle that anyone driving a Trabi will have no need whatsoever to ever operate an actual car. Pull up, pull down, push in, push out— the car lurches forward as Berlin's downtown pedestrians and drivers stare in concerned amusement.

"When you hear people use their horns, it's because they either love Trabis or hate Trabis," explains our guide. Or maybe it's because I almost crashed into them, who knows? Trabi-Safari's cars are painted in bright retro colours (the better for locals to see them and take evasive action), and the company gives ample instruction on how to drive one. It's a very tongue-in-cheek affair, the guide's comments littered with jokes, apt since everyone is driving one.

"All Trabis go to heaven, because they've already had hell on earth," crackles the short-wave radio. My radio picks up random words like *Nazis* and *sexy legs*. It's hard to believe that East German border guards once patrolled the no-go zone in these clown cars. Perhaps their goal was to stop escapees with fits of laughter.

My sky-blue Trabi follows a shocking pink one, and with a yellow convertible Trabi trailing behind, we look like an Eastern European remake of *The Italian Job*. When a new Mini overtakes me, it dwarfs my car. Driving into rush-hour traffic, we pass the Reichstag building, the Bebelplatz Book Burning Memorial, the Brandenburg Gate and more than a few unimpressed drivers who are caught in our wake. Incredibly, Trabi-Safari has had few accidents, since local drivers give the tours plenty of space, assuming tourists have no idea what they're doing or where they're going. Along the Berlin Wall, an iconic piece of graffiti shows former Soviet and East German leaders Leonid Brezhnev and Erich Honecker passionately making out. Seated inside a Trabi, of course.

Dip and Dance

Survived your summer Trabi adventure? Head to the stylish beach bars that have sprouted up alongside the Spree River to celebrate. If you're early enough to beat the crowds, enjoy a swim in a large pool *on* the river at The Badeschiff. Suitably refreshed, dress up for dinner and a dance at the century-old Clärchens Ballhaus, located in Berlin's central district of Mitte. Enjoy old-world dancing in this worn yet lavish ballroom lit by chandeliers and candles. Star in your own Baz Luhrmann movie by sneaking into the Spiegelsaal, a magical room of mirrors.

I am finding it increasingly difficult to put the car into gear, much less believe that this late model is from 1989. A Honda Civic from the same era feels like a rocket ship in comparison. The Trabi's exterior is made from a plastic resin, supported by wool and cotton. I suppose that in the event of a head-on collision, accident victims could wear the trunk on the way to the hospital.

The tour continues toward Alexanderplatz and along Karl Marx-Allee, with its impressive and towering Soviet architecture. Squat, square and stylistically grim, the buildings were designed to be a permanent reminder of the power of the state. For an oppressed population, driving a Trabi must have been an additional form of torture. With the hindsight of history, today we know that the immense and imposing power of the Soviet state was, in reality, a smoky two-stroke engine with a propensity for backfires. As a fun vehicle for discovering Berlin, however, the Trabi is just perfect.

START HERE:
globalbucketlist.com/trabant

Get Squeezed in Budapest

I t's not as straightforward as it looks to squeeze your body through a sliver in a subterranean rock wall. You must employ technique. In my case, I must thrust forward in full stretch, supporting my body on my left arm, twisting my waist toward a sharp bend. After blindly extending my free arm and searching with my right hand for something to grip on to, I pull myself around the corner. If I slip, my butt might become wedged between the rock, joining what my guide refers to as "the Club of Stuckies"—which doesn't sound very fun at all. As I pretzel into position to make my exit, dust glittering in the beam of my headlamp, it's hard to believe I'm just metres below the bustling streets of Budapest.

Millions of years ago, a sea flowed beneath the fabled Hungarian capital, creating a vast network of caves and the underground wells that continue to feed the city's famous thermal baths. In Buda, the part of the city split from Pest by the mighty Danube, bucket listers can explore this underground world with caving tour operators. Adventures are marketed to corporations as unique team-building opportunities, and also to budget travellers, who are usually skinny enough to slip through the cracks. The Matyeshegy Caves are located about 20 minutes by bus from downtown. The system, used as a bomb shelter for citizens during World War II, is closed to the general public.

The soft limestone caves extend for miles beneath the city. My three-hour adventure will cover only a mere 800 metres. My blonde-locked guide, Kata, opens a thick iron door, checks the headlamps of our small group of nine and ushers us in. The door closes with an ominous *thunk*; the resounding darkness and silence is immediate. Here, it's as though the buzz of Budapest's busy boulevards are on a different planet. We descend about 10 metres down a cold, rusted iron ladder, and the challenge begins. Don't get lost, don't get stuck. As we move ahead

in single file, it is crucial we each maintain contact with the person in front, and the person behind. Spelunking is all about teamwork, the

Hungarian Healing

Budapest sits above a sea of natural thermal baths, which Turk conquerors developed into exquisite palaces for pools. Several enormous bathing complexes survive, each with ornate architecture and well-maintained baths. A modest entrance fee grants you access to dozens of baths of various temperatures, along with saunas, spas, whirlpools, showers and, for a few bucks more, perfunctory massages. Think less New Age music and candles, and more Soviet prison camp. Soak up an afternoon inside the Széchenyi Baths sampling the range of cold, warm and hot pools.

leader explaining how to go about negotiating each obstacle ahead. Relaying directions down the chain, a case of "broken telephone line" could result in lost and panicked tourists, or even broken bones.

After a few tight passages, we gather in a large cavern. "Can anyone guess where we go next?" asks Kata. Swivelling my neck, I see five possible exits we could squeeze through. Naturally, she points to a sixth—a fracture beneath her feet. She shows us how to proceed—sliding on her back like a mechanic beneath a car, and pulling herself under so that she disappears beneath the rock. In disbelief, I begin to follow, grunting and groaning as I gyrate, as if in a game of Twister, into the required position. What follows is a series of contortionist challenges, many of which require us to lie flat, sandwiched between moist limestone, as we worm our way through. Now in a room that allows us to sit upright (to the relief of our spinal cords), we decide to see what happens without any light. We all turn off our headlamps. Kata extinguishes her gas-fuelled flame. Instantly we are embraced by an immaculate darkness so thick I can almost taste it. Deep underground, with no light whatsoever, it is natural for your eyes to play tricks on you as they try and repeatedly fail to adjust to the absolute nothingness. I see fractals and kaleidoscopes, demons and angels. Never mind the complicated procedures required to navigate this far—if you get stuck down here without a light, the despair would be overwhelming. Hell doesn't need fire and brimstone, just darkness. We turn our lights back on with a sense of relief and squeeze onward.

At the final challenge, we remove our safety helmets because they cannot fit through the hole. Pushing myself forward inch by inch, my gut sucked in, it feels like I'm working through a contraction in an earthly birth canal. At one point, I become lodged in tight, and curse the consumption of good Hungarian beer and too many damn perogies. Rock grips my hips, and I can't see how I can move forward—or backward, for that matter. Sweat is dripping off my forehead as several of the group behind me decide to take the easy way out, an option with this particular obstacle. But where's the fun in that? Eventually, I start laughing at the absurdity of being stuck in a Hungarian cave—which is just what I needed to jam my way through.

We arrive full circle at the iron ladder. Just three hours have passed, but the sunlight has been a long time coming. Walking into the last hour of daylight is more than a welcome breath of fresh air; the colour of the sky and trees are impossibly vivid, as if God had increased the contrast in his cosmic version of Photoshop. Budapest, slammed with tourists year-round, is one of Europe's most beautiful cities. Why get stuck in traffic when you can get stuck in the ground below?

START HERE:
globalbucketlist.com/budapest

Soak in the Land of Fire and Ice

Destinations often fail to live up to the imagination, especially that of two professional travellers who, between them, have visited just about every country on earth. My buddy Pat and I put a lot of pressure on Iceland to deliver on its reputation, and with active volcanoes, geothermal plants and exploding geysers, Iceland is under enough pressure already.

Still, there are few countries as fabled as Iceland. The second-largest island in Europe and the world's youngest country straddles two continental plates, resulting in constant seismic activity and remarkable scenic beauty. Within minutes of our leaving the capital of Reykjavik, the countryside turns into a wasteland of gnarled volcanic rock carpeted in bright green moss. The land is barren, flat and alien. We hike up to the rim of Eldborg, an extinct volcano, our bright teal tour bus waiting below like a spaceship. At Gerduberg, basalt rocks take the shape of hard-edged symmetrical columns, topped with perfect hexagons. It's easy to see why Icelandic folk tradition is rich with trolls, giants and fairies. The landscape inspires superstition, the intuitive belief that powerful forces are at work, beyond our control. According to one survey, over 50 per cent of the population believes in the existence of invisible elves.

Snaefellsjökull, a challenge in spelling bees the world over, is a volcano that overlooks a spectacular peninsula. Jules Verne set his classic science-fiction novel, *Journey to the Center of the Earth*, inside this very volcano, but we're more drawn to the coastal hikes on the Snaefellsnes coastline, where heaving waves crash against volcanic rock formations, blowholes, bays and beaches. It reminds us somewhat of Newfoundland,

another Atlantic island with a Viking history. The Viking Age lasted from about 790 to 1066, when roving bands of bearded Norsemen terrorized much of Europe. We're sitting inside the replica of a small Viking house built with rocks, the ceiling covered with grass and peat. A room like this would have housed 20 people, sleeping while seated upright, close to a warming hearth.

Incidentally, there is no evidence that Vikings ever wore horns on their helmets. The horns, for

Why Iceland Is Green and Greenland Is Ice

Iceland was named by the first Norseman to deliberately seek out the island, one Floki Vilgerdarson. After an eventful journey that included losing one daughter to the sea and another to marriage on the Faroe Islands, Vilgerdarson settled in for a glorious summer on the island. Then came a hard, freezing, dark and particularly icy winter. Vilgerdarson returned to Norway and told everyone about this horrendous "iceland." That didn't stop others from settling—and discovering that Iceland can be quite lush and green.

The naming of Greenland, on the other hand, is attributed to a ruffian named Erik the Red, banished from Norway and later Iceland for various acts of violence. After his three-year banishment concluded, he returned to Iceland to persuade others to join him in settling a "green land" that he had discovered afar (with Erik as chieftain, of course). Some 500 people signed up, though not everyone survived the crossing. What they discovered on arrival was a land more ice than green, which is why one should never believe a homicidal Viking marauder. Vikings lived on Greenland for 500 years, before abandoning the island for reasons still hotly debated by historians.

which they are so well known, first appeared in 19th-century operas. Still, Iceland's first settlers lived in ornery, harsh times, and their descendants have since put up with one catastrophe after another, from earthquakes and foreign conquerors to the 2008 financial crisis. As our guide tells us about the first Viking settler, I whisper to Pat: "I saw something like this at L'Anse aux Meadows," referring to the reconstructed Viking settlements at Canada's first UNESCO World Heritage Site. By this stage, our references to previous exploits are starting to annoy people on the bus.

Despite a drop in the value of the kroner, we still reckon Iceland is the most expensive country we've been to. When takeout burgers cost US$15; a bowl of soup, US$17; and a beer, US$10, it's no wonder many tour groups picnic for lunch and stay overnight in converted school residences. One such residence's promotional brochure promises "a happy ending every day," which cracks us up. Besides fish, lamb and cheap geothermal energy, the country imports just about everything (barring happy endings). Alcohol is particularly pricey, even at the liquor store. Fortunately, the country's main attraction—incredible scenery—is complimentary.

Our bus has its second blowout in two days, on a rocky sand road that proves too much for the tread. While our driver sets to work rotating spares, the passengers set off into the desert moonscape, finding a welcome

patch of spongy moss to relax on and enjoy the views of the Langjökull ice cap. I'm about to tell Pat that I've never seen *anything* like this but decide to keep the words to myself. Instead, I pop in my earbuds and listen to Sigur Rós, an Icelandic band famous for its haunting, ethereal music. It's the perfect soundtrack.

Once we arrive in the rift valley of Thingvellir, we enter the Golden Circle—the country's most popular tourist route. Crowds flock to the site of Iceland's traditional parliament, located on the Continental Divide, where Europe and North America are literally drifting apart. Our guide sets up a picnic table with lunch. Every day there's something new: herring, caviar, lamb pâté, cold meats, gravlax, sardines,

breads, spreads and cheese. Occasionally, there are Icelandic treats, like candy, dark bread or hákarl, a local delicacy consisting of fermented Greenland shark. This meat is buried for several months underground, where it attains a flavour that can be described, at best, as pickled acidic urine. To wash it down, we swig Brennevín, a strong potato schnapps with an aftertaste of caraway. Trying hard not to gag at the smell, I spear a piece of shark with a toothpick and take a bite. For a moment, I feel I have conquered the latest in a long line of culinary challenges. Then comes the aftertaste. It will stay with me for years.

Local cuisine is unusual. Before the week is out, we will have consumed shark, minke whale sashimi, whale steak, smoked puffin, guille-mot (a type of seabird), *skyr* (a type of yoghurt) and horsemeat. Icelandic horses are beautiful and numerous, so the thought of eating them is a little tough to trot. Iceland is also one of the few countries that still practises whaling. Conservation-ists contend that whale-watching actually brings in more for the econ-omy than hunting, but still, whales remain on the menu. It's odd to track a graceful minke whale in Reykja-vik harbour, in sight of the same whale-hunting vessels that hunt it. As for the fishy taste of whale meat itself, I'll gladly stick to tuna.

All the glaciers and mountains are a recipe for gobsmacking waterfalls. We stop at Skógafoss, Barnafoss and Seljalandsfoss, three gorgeous natural roadside attrac-tions with numerous walking trails to gather views. The highlight is Gullfoss, where torrents of glacier water drop 70 metres into a canyon, resembling a giant white sheet tucked underneath a rocky bed. The Golden Circle continues to Geysir, the site that gave us the word itself. A geyser named Strokkur explodes every 5 to 10 minutes, shooting a steamy stream 30 metres into the air. We arrive just in time to witness

a busload of Spanish tourists get drenched with hot water. As with our pit stops to pee on the side of the road, it's best not to stand downwind.

Eyjafjallajökull is the tongue-twister name of the active volcano that shut down European aerospace in 2010. It looks innocuous enough, much of its ash already absorbed into the surrounding fertile valleys. Not so from above. A helicopter tour gives us a bird's-eye view of the crater. The pilot traces the path of the lava flow, which cracked and melted the glacier, blackening it with ash. Nearby are two other active volcanoes, Hekla and Katla, which promise to cause even *more* havoc than Eyjafjallajökull. It may be a country of only 320,000 people, but Iceland's impact on the world can be devastating.

On our way to the airport, Pat and I make a quick pit stop to soak in the sulphur-rich waters of Blue Lagoon. The strange, milky water is a by-product of a nearby geothermal power plant. With their proximity to the airport, the natural hot springs have become Iceland's biggest tourist attraction. While having a soak, therapeutic white mud on our faces, Pat and I reflect on the week: the hikes on the coasts, deserts and volcanoes; the strange culinary adventures; our wild times in the bars of Reykjavik; the extraordinary geological features we've seen. We decide that Iceland will exceed the expectations of travel virgins and us veterans alike—a country that truly belongs on everyone's bucket list.

START HERE:
globalbucketlist.com/iceland

5 Soaks on the Bucket List

Beppu, Japan: The Pacific Ocean's Ring of Fire may cause havoc, but Japan's public and private baths reap the geothermic benefits. Beppu, located in the Oita Prefecture, is Japan's most famous hot spring destination, generating more spring water than anywhere else in the country, and offering the widest variety of mud, steam, water and sand baths.

Budapest, Hungary: There are 120 hot springs beneath Budapest, servicing opulent bath complexes that still recall Budapest's glory days of the Ottoman Empire. The public baths are as grand as they are efficient (a holdover from Soviet days). The most popular are the Gellért Baths in Buda, and the Széchenyi Baths in Pest.

Hot Water Beach, New Zealand: The only thing better than a hot spring is one you can create yourself. About two hours' drive from Auckland in the Waikato District is Hot Water Beach, a natural phenomenon that allows you to dig out a hot pool between high and low tides. Hot thermal water, reaching as high as 64 °C, swells up through the sand.

Pamukkale, Turkey: For thousands of years, people have bathed in the healing waters of Pamukkale, which literally translates as "cotton castle." Striking white terraces have been formed by hardened calcium, the calcium deposited by the flowing waters. There are 17 hot springs in the area, with temperatures ranging from 35°C to a toasty 100°C.

Thermopolis, USA: Thermopolis literally means "hot city" and is located in Hot Springs County, Wyoming. Here you'll find the world's largest hot springs, accessed by two free park springs, and two commercial operations—Star Plunge and the oddly named Hellie's TePee Pools & Spa.

Rev Up the Engine of Italy

ITALY

I t is known as the "cradle of the engine." Inside a golden circle surrounding the cities of Modena and Bologna is the birthplace of mythical brands whispered on the lips of car lovers everywhere. Maserati. Pagani. Ferrari. Lamborghini. Italian rocket ships that introduced us to speed, design and luxury. The region's most famous sons, Ferrari and Lamborghini, created machines that transcend the metal and bolts within them, commanding religious-like reverence from drivers, dreamers and bucket listers too.

In my small rental car, I enter the municipality of Bologna, soon arriving at the modern headquarters of Automobili Lamborghini. The eponymous bull logo, representing Ferruccio Lamborghini's astrological sign, appears boldly on the walls of the factory. Only 2,000 cars are hand-built here each year, so the factory is smaller than one might imagine. Although Lamborghini has had its fair share of challenges—including several takeovers and bankruptcy—it continues to produce vehicles that define car envy. Vehicles like the Aventador, the Diablo, and its striking predecessor, the Countach. These models, along with one-of-a-kind concept cars, are displayed in the company's onsite museum, open daily to the public. I drool over the Concept S, with adjacent seat booths protected by individual windows, creating the distinct look of a jet fighter. From the mid-1980s, the LM002 looks like a futuristic Humvee, built way before its time. A classic green Countach sits so low on the ground, it barely reaches my thigh. On show is also a Lamborghini police car, donated to the

police force for transporting emergency organ transplants. A car you don't mind being shuttled off to the police station in.

Valentino Balboni, a veteran test driver, pulls up outside in a silver Gallardo LP 560-4 Spyder. He's been driving supercars longer than I have been alive. I've arranged for him to take me into the countryside and demonstrate what Lamborghinis can do. A car journalist might tell you that the Gallardo Spyder has a 5.2-litre V10 engine with an output of 560 horsepower, a power-to-weight ratio of 2.77 kilograms and a top speed of 324 km/hr. I'll tell you that stepping into the Spyder for the first time made me giggle like a schoolgirl. Valentino

presses a button, the engine growls to life and we roar out of the parking lot. There is not a head on this planet that would not swivel the second it sees a Lamborghini.

Valentino races alongside wheat fields, demonstrating the Spyder's ferocious power. Each acceleration jolts me like a roller coaster, lurching my body forward, eyeballs trailing behind. We find a quiet stretch and he invites me to take the wheel. He assures me that I cannot make a mistake given the advanced paddle-shift transmission. This low to the tarmac on a hot summer day, the heat is radiating from the ground, but I'm sweating with nerves, driving a vehicle worth more than I could ever afford to

replace. Fortunately, the Spyder is beautifully forgiving, guiding my gear changes, injecting fuel when needed and sticking firm around corners. I steer us to the factory and pull up in front of a group of jealous tourists. For a brief moment, I imagine I own the half-million-dollar sports car. Then I remember I'm a writer with a job that allows one to sample but not acquire.

It is a short drive from Bologna to Maranello, the home of Lamborghini's nemesis, Ferrari. Maranello is a mecca for racing and car enthusiasts, and is not so much a small town as a Ferrari theme park. I pass Ferrari stores and Ferrari schools, Ferrari-themed restaurants and red-painted hotels. Images of the famous prancing-horse logo are everywhere. It is immediately clear that Ferrari is a much larger enterprise than its stylish competitor, which has been nibbling at its heels since Ferruccio Lamborghini fell out with Enzo Ferrari.

At the Galleria Ferrari, some of the most famous vehicles are on display for the public. Here are the original race cars built by Enzo himself, all the way to Formula 1 triumphs. Upstairs are the road cars: the powerful Testarossa, the F40, Magnum, P.I.'s iconic 308 GTS. I notice a marked difference between these cars and the sleek models at Lamborghini's showcase gallery. Ferraris exude brute strength, more muscle than finesse. A special showcase houses a black 1957 250 Testarossa, which sold at auction for a staggering US$12.1 million. It doesn't even have headlights.

Just about every car at the Museo Ferrari is bright red, a colour that will be forever associated with the company. Yet the 430 Scuderia waiting for me outside is metallic blue, with two racing stripes down the middle. It boasts 508 horsepower at 8,500 rpm, power-to-rate ratio of 2.5kk/hp, an F1-Trac system and E-Diff stability control—to be honest, I have no idea what all that means other than that it is a purebred racing machine built with ample power, for people *in* power. At a top speed of 320 km/hr, it can definitely expect to tear up the smooth Italian *autostrade*.

My test driver's name is Gabriel,

Enzo vs. Ferruccio

How different the vehicle landscape might be if Enzo Ferrari had listened to his customers. Ferruccio Lamborghini was one of the wealthiest men in Italy, having made his fortune manufacturing tractors and appliances. An avid car collector, he loved his Ferraris but found them to be mechanically temperamental. A recurring clutch issue led him to contact

founder Enzo Ferrari. Enzo tolerated the production of road cars as a means to finance his racing initiatives. Blessed with a legendary ego, he had little time or patience for his customers, especially if they were critical of his machines. When Enzo arrogantly dismissed Ferruccio, the spited Lamborghini was forced to repair his own models. Inspired by his success, Automobili Lamborghini was born. Unlike Ferrari, Lamborghini would focus solely on sports cars, shying away from the racetrack. Today, Lamborghini is a name synonymous with the Italian sports car, and a sizable thorn bush in the Ferrari landscape.

and we both agree that a job requiring one to drive a Ferrari all day is a job worth keeping. The vehicle's interior is somewhat basic: bucket seats with belts that fit over the shoulder, like the jump seat on an airplane. A metal footplate supports me as Gabriel screams around the quiet country roads, the engine snarling as he shifts the transmission. I feel like a tiger lurking in the concrete jungle of automobiles, ferociously hunting Toyotas. After screeching past a chicane, I ask Gabriel how fast he was going. With a wry grin, he tells me it was too fast to look at the speedometer. I suppose you'd need a Lamborghini police car to catch us anyway.

It is late afternoon when we drive back to the galleria through Maranello's rush hour, the 430 Scuderia trotting along in traffic at 40 km/hr, all the way back to the stable. I thank Gabriel, awkwardly exit the cockpit and walk over to my blue Peugeot rental. Like most cars in Italy, it is a tiny vehicle capable of squeezing through narrow cobblestone alleys but can still exceed the 130 km/hr speed limit on the highway. It's no supercar, but it's all a bucket lister needs to get to the engine of Italy for the ride of their life.

START HERE:
globalbucketlist.com/supercars

Ogle Buildings in Riga

Seven hundred thousand people live in the Latvian capital of Riga, and seemingly all of them sport stylish leather boots, tight pants and flashy haircuts. It feels like a city of beautiful people with sharp angles for cheekbones and runway-model bodies. In my fleece jacket and hiking boots, I'm a hobbit sneaking among the elves. But if the locals look good, the buildings do too. Riga is the capital of art nouveau, the 19th-century art and architecture movement that aspired to break design conventions. Reacting against Victorian sensibilities, a new wave of architects and designers used flowing lines, futuristic motifs and eclectic artwork to stamp their creative mark. More than a third of the buildings in Riga's Central District, a UNESCO World Heritage Site, are categorized as art nouveau. Although many were damaged during World War II, the city still has over 800 examples, the largest collection of art nouveau buildings you'll find anywhere.

Building watching is one of the city's most popular attractions and demands investigation for our bucket list. Mikhail Eisenstein, father of iconic Russian filmmaker Sergei Eisenstein, contributed some of the most striking examples to Riga's art nouveau. Looking up on the corner of Elizabetes and Antonijas, I am left wondrously baffled by his legacy. What possessed this Victorian-era aristocrat to design a building laden with elaborate masonry, haunting murals, sweeping archways and sculptures time-warped from a sci-fi future? Why did he incorporate the large heads of a king and queen, sitting above an apartment block like bored chess pieces? I've been awed by the modern architectural visions in Hong Kong and Dubai, but they don't compete with the sheer historical wackiness on display in Riga.

On Alberta Street, check out the sphinxes, curvy naked muses and terrifying gargoyles, their faces screaming in agony. With the right lighting, the streets of Riga could be the perfect set for *Lord of the Rings*, *Star Wars*, *Metropolis* and *Batman*—all at the same time. Mikhail Eisenstein's buildings can be found at Elizabetes 10a and 10b,

as well as at Alberta 2, 2a, 4, 8 and 13. Many of these magnificent buildings are mere apartment blocks, with For Rent signs displayed on their windows. Some desperately need maintenance; others are perfectly restored (including the Irish, French and Russian Embassies). Walking maps, available free from local tourist offices, provide routes and further information. More details can be found at the Latvian Museum of Architecture, housed in the Three Brothers, the oldest stone building in the city. Building watching provides a good day out, enhanced by a more familiar passion: people watching.

A perfect place to start is the Freedom Monument, located off a busy pedestrian boulevard in Old Town. An important landmark for the entire country, it was built in 1935 using donations from citizens and nowadays stands as a symbol of the country's survival after four decades behind the Iron Curtain. Locals once called it the "travel agent," since laying flowers at the foot of the monument was an easy ticket to Siberia. Today, flowers are laid daily by locals to honour those deported by the occupying Soviets. Other monuments, like the Monument to the Repressed, the

KGB Victims' Memorial and the excellent Museum of the Occupation of Latvia, recall the turbulent past Latvians experienced under the Soviet regime. On one night alone, nearly 50,000 people were abducted and deported to Siberia. Since regaining their independence in 1990, Latvians are proud of their survival, as symbolized by the shrine.

From the open-air observation platform above St. Peter's Church, I have a lovely 360-degree view of the city and can clearly distinguish the modern city from the old town, with the taut cables of the Vansu Bridge linking two eras across the Daugava River. Riga is on the budget-flight map from just about anywhere in Europe, as more and more bucket listers fly in to appreciate the city's well-earned reputation for beauty—a beauty you can see in the people, and in the buildings too.

START HERE:
globalbucketlist.com/riga

Find Your Ancestral Roots

LITHUANIA

Bucket lists are so much more than places to see and things to do. They can teach us about the world we live in, our place within it, who we are and where we come from. Whatever nationality you're descended from, visiting the country of your ancestors results in rich, emotional travel. Genealogical tourism first exploded in the 1970s, largely credited to the success of Alex Haley's book (and subsequent television series) *Roots*. With the evolution of online genealogy tools—designed to make databasing and research as simple as ever—it has now become one of the busiest traffic segments online. Dedicated and enthusiastic volunteers become private investigators of their familial pasts, looking for unlikely connections, unusual stories and answers to questions of their origins. If you think Facebook is addictive, try looking into your own lineage.

Genealogists advise starting with what you know. I know my grandfather was born in a small village in northern Lithuania called Kupiskis. Before booking a flight to the Baltics, I hit up the All-Seeing Eye of Everything (a.k.a. Google) and found a wealth of knowledge uploaded by an amateur genealogist in Miami. Kupiskis, like all shtetls, has a tragic history. Before World War II, 41 per cent of its population were Jews, *all* of whom were rounded up and brutally murdered by local Nazi collaborators. Over 3,000 men, women and children were massacred, including members of my own family. While many people travel to the countries of their heritage expecting to encounter long-lost relatives, there is no chance of physically discovering a forgotten branch of my family tree. Despite this, I book a flight to Lithuania, eager to see what else I might discover.

Vilnius is a lovely European capital, with big town squares, cobblestone, cheap beer, few tourists, and welcoming locals. It's a three-hour drive from the city to Kupiskis, now a small industrial town. The surrounding countryside explodes in the colours of fall as I pilot an old rental van through it. Each passing kilometre is one more step into the past. A bold sign on the outskirts of the town signals I have arrived in Kupiskis. I feel like a grown turtle washing ashore on the very beach on which I was hatched.

In 2004, a group of 50 Kupiskis descendants from as far away as the United States, United Kingdom, South Africa, Denmark and Australia visited this small town to dedicate a memorial to the Jewish families wiped out in the war. They were greeted by the town mayor and presented with a list, compiled by a local midwife during the war, of the names and ages of the victims—the only such list that exists in the country. These names are now engraved on a memorial plaque on the wall of the old synagogue, which is now the town's library, and my first stop. I run my hand over the names on the memorial, stopping at several with the surname Ezroch. It is exhilarating to meet the names of these ancestors, and depressing to know what happened to them. I've found and lost new family members all at once.

Late afternoon, Kupiskis is half asleep, the streets deserted. Red

Dig Your Roots

··

There are thousands of volunteer genealogical societies worldwide that can help you begin your search. Websites like Cyndis List (cyndislist.com) contain many links to get you started. Talk to the people you know before going to online archives, census records, obituaries, newspaper clippings and other sources of information. It is likely you'll soon encounter a relative or enthusiast on the same path, eager to share and learn from you. Remember when publishing personal information on websites and databases to respect others' privacy. Most of all, have fun determining your six degrees of separation from Kevin Bacon.

and gold leaves cover the roads. Some locals still get around by horse and buggy. There are a few clues that reveal the town's rich Jewish history: the old library, and a street named Sinagogo, still lined with century-old wooden houses. It is cold and damp, and I wonder how my great-grandparents and their children adjusted to the hot, dry veldt when they immigrated to South Africa before World War I. I wonder what might have been if they hadn't. With the help of a local guide named Regina Kopelevich, who specializes in genealogical

tours, I visit several mass graves, some of them with memorials, some of them with vandalized plaques. Who would deface a mass grave? Likely the same kind of person responsible for its existence in the first place.

Jews and Gentiles had coexisted peacefully here since the 16th century. Regina leads me to the ancient, wooden house of a 91-year-old local woman named Veronica. Floating in and out of lucidity, she recalls babysitting Jewish children, even singing me a few Yiddish lullabies from the depth of her memory. Her house overlooks the Freethinkers Cemetery, a site of one of the town's worst massacres. Veronica witnessed the children in her care stripped, lined up and murdered.

"I still see their faces," she says. "I cried and cried."

The room is freezing, as if all the joy in the world has been sucked right out of it. Veronica died a few months after my visit, taking those lullabies and horrors to her own grave.

Back in Vilnius, I spend hours researching life in Kupiskis, reading old reports and the testimonials of survivors. I Skype my grandmother in Johannesburg and ask questions about our family's past, feeling somewhat disappointed in myself that I have never asked her these questions before. In turn, she is fascinated by what Lithuania looks like today, what has become of Kupiskis, a place that always haunted my late grandfather. Lithuania's history did not settle. First the evils of Hitler, then Stalin. It became the first Eastern Bloc country to declare its independence from the Soviet Union in 1991. Although my own roots were dug up, I'm nevertheless drawn to Lithuania, its under-the-skin familiarity. Three of my four grandparents were Lithuanian. It must count for something.

Michael, a distant cousin in New York, was a great resource prior to my visit. An amateur genealogist, he amassed over 3,000 names on my family tree. I ask him how others should begin their personal journey.

"Talk to your parents and the oldest people in your family you can find. Ask them very specific questions. Names of places, birthdates, if they have any newspaper clippings," he tells me. Every time an elder family member passes away, they take with them an important piece of the puzzle.

Genealogical travel brings the rewards of travel you'll find anywhere: beautiful landscapes, interesting new cultures, people, food and history. Yet when you journey into the land of your heritage, it makes those rewards all the more relevant. You don't need plane tickets or hard-earned savings to begin your quest either. If you've ever wondered about where you come from, your bucket list simply wants you to start asking questions.

START HERE:
globalbucketlist.com/lithuania

Say a Prayer on the Pulpit

NORWAY

It's a challenging two-hour hike to Preikestolen, also known as the Pulpit Rock, but expect, once you get there, to fall on your knees in praise of the staggering beauty stretched before you. The cliff's table-flat plateau abruptly ends 600 metres above the glittering Lysefjord. If you're so inclined, you can sit or stand right on the edge, gratefully acknowledging the government's refusal to erect a fence. Hundreds of thousands of tourists visit this attraction each year, and the lack of fatalities proves that fences would only spoil the view and that libel-hungry lawyers don't rule Norway. One day the outcropping will collapse into the fjord below, but legend has it that will only take place when seven brothers marry seven sisters in the Lysefjord area. You can check community announcements in the local paper during the 25-kilometre drive from the nearest city of Stavanger.

START HERE: globalbucketlist/pulpit

Face the Horrors of the Past

HALT!.
STÓJ!

A letter to my grandmother

Dear Bobba, I have finally arrived in Poland.
I thought it would be a grey, bleak, concrete-block kind of country, but summer in Kraków is green and lush, with attractive parkways surrounding the largest medieval town square in Europe. Truthfully, I never harboured any desire to visit Poland. Although you were born here, it is not like we ever had any affiliation with the country. Partly because you moved to South Africa when you were still young. Partly because German-occupied Poland accommodated the Holocaust. There were more Jews in Poland before the war than in any other country in Europe. Over 3 million of them, including our family and relatives. Today there are just holes in the ground where villages once stood. I understand why you have no love or feeling for this country.

You were personally uprooted to a new land, the branches of your family tree cleared away in the old one. Maybe that's why the fields are so green here. No roots, no family trees. Not for us anyway. I understand you are asking yourself: Why revisit the horror? Why go to Poland?

Old Town is an unexpected surprise. It has all the charm and beauty of Prague without the overwhelming hordes of tourists. There is a full moon tonight, the old Market Square buzzing with life, conversation dancing with the clop-clop of horse and carriages circling the cobblestone. Huge banners are strung across the streets advertising a Jewish cultural festival. I visit the Jewish Quarter the following day, and like in Prague, it is now more of a shopping district. While there are few Jews left in Kraków, it appears there are many who visit it. Tourists are being led in large groups by umbrella-carrying women, who stop constantly to inform them about this, that and the other. It has a certain theme-park feel to it all, especially when I come across "Authentic Jewish-Style Restaurants" and "Get Your Jewish Guides Here" stalls. Kraków's Jewish ghetto was created

by the Nazis, then eliminated and occupied by Poles. Now it offers Jewish food to tourists. Such is the world we live in.

I feel some pride in it all, in each Jewish landmark signifying a stern middle finger to the highly efficient machine that tried to eliminate us. It reminds everyone—Poles and visitors—that the Jews may have gone but we're not going away. Do you remember that controversial book called *Hitler's Willing Executioners*? It argued that many Poles and Germans knew what was going on but went along with it. You told me that yourself one afternoon. Something along the lines of Poles always having it in for the Jews. Centuries of pogroms, anti-Semitism and blood libels prove the point, but that was going on everywhere in Europe. Still, the Nazis built their six death camps in Poland, and trucked in Jews from as far away as Norway and Greece. I was speaking to a Polish girl at my hostel about the many young guys walking around with shaved heads. "For the summer heat?" I asked. "If only," she replied. "There are too many skinheads in this town." I have passed several walls in this town with anti-Semitic graffiti. This

town advertising a Jewish cultural festival. This town with no Jews.

I am dreading my visit to Auschwitz. The biggest, most notorious death camp complex, where some 1.5 million people, 90 per cent of them Jews, were massacred with robotic efficiency. And that figure, which is impossible to imagine or make any kind of sense of, includes members of our family. Visiting Auschwitz is something I have to do, something I believe *everyone* has to do. This explains why it is the biggest tourist attraction for visitors to the region. A tourist attraction! The young American frat boys back in my hostel had visited, but all they said was that the guide spoke too fast. Meanwhile, an English backpacker tells me Auschwitz is just one more sight to tick off his list, missing the point entirely. Every item on a bucket list, I argue, should help you learn something of the world, and about yourself. Especially this one.

It is strange, going to the ticket counter at the bus station and asking for two tickets to Auschwitz. As if it is a theme park, or a movie, and not the site of the biggest mass murder in history. The bus does

Travel to Learn

It is not easy visiting any of Europe's former concentration camps, nor Cambodia's Killing Fields, where skulls of victims are piled up in display cases, or Rwanda's Genocide Memorial Centre, which details one of history's more recent mass slaughters. Holocaust museums on six continents are vital to our understanding of this tragic past, and the shocking events that continue to take place. It is a sad fact that Holocaust denial still exists, swirling in a stew of racism, anti-Semitism and ignorance. Bucket lists consist of more than just beaches and thrills. If you have the opportunity, swallow your misgivings and make an effort to visit a genocide museum. Unless we reflect on mankind's atrocities, we will forever be doomed to repeat them.

not say *Auschwitz* on the front, but rather *Oświęcim*, which is the name of the Polish town where one of the camps is located. Forty thousand people live in this town. The bus takes forever, driving through the green countryside, stopping at small villages. Too much time to think. After two hours we enter Oświęcim, and I imagine it will be a while before we get to the abandoned gates of hell. But the bus driver tells me this is my stop. Here, in what feels like the middle of the town. I always imagined Auschwitz to be hidden away and covered up, but I walk 100 metres from a main road and up to the visitor entrance. Locals have always lived within sight of the barracks.

It is 10 a.m. and already there are thousands of tourists here. The museum is free to the public, as it should be. I join the English-language guided tour, which starts with a 12-minute short film, made in the 1940s. In our high-definition age, the fuzziness of this old footage makes it difficult to absorb. As shocking images appear, I overhear some people talk about lunch behind me. Tours are available in several languages, and I soon find myself walking beneath the main gate, alongside the eerie, infamous electric fences. Face to face with the horror of history.

From the Wall of Death to the few ovens that survived the hasty cover-up, I cannot believe what is right before my eyes. But unlike Yad Vashem in Jerusalem, there are few multimedia exhibits. We don't see the complete horror; rather, we are led to the ruins of the gas chambers. As a result, those who have not lived with the Holocaust buried under their skin simply *cannot*

imagine. Perhaps that is why the deniers don't believe. Even with today's beheadings and suicide bombings, the Holocaust appears to fall beyond the scope of my generation.

I didn't know that Auschwitz-Birkenau, just 3 kilometres away, was 100 times bigger than the first Auschwitz camp I visited. Birkenau was where the trains entered, their people sorted like cattle, with men, women and children marched to their deaths. Outrage swells up in our group. "Why didn't they fight back?" asks one tourist. Our guide explains that the Nazis used psychology to pacify the beaten, broken arrivals. Everyone was told they were going to be cleaned before resuming work in a normal labour camp. To avoid panic, they were told to bring their belongings, to hang their possessions by numbered lockers and retrieve them later. Even given the rumours, nobody could have possibly believed what was actually going on.

"One survivor," says our guide, "told me he could see the chimneys of the crematorium and thought it was a heating system for the camp."

This is why there was no panic, and this is why millions went to their deaths like sheep. Inside the surviving barracks, hearing how prisoners lived but mostly died, it is impossible to even imagine. Impossible to believe. And yet I am here. And I believe.

Tucked away at the back of Auschwitz-Birkenau is a small exhibit of a lifetime in pictures—the lives of several Jewish families. It shows just a few human faces beyond the staggering numbers, and it looks very much like the old photos in the breakfast room of your house. They show a legacy that the Nazis, with their hearts more cruel and vicious than any animal,

destroyed; yet here today, the exhibit allows that legacy to live on.

There are places in the world vibrating with such positive energy, your hair stands up like static. Auschwitz is the opposite, the remnants of psychic trauma strangling visitors like a Hessian noose. Pain and suffering and sadness fill the air. Everything is too still. I am breathing air in lumps as I stand by ponds that are still saturated with the ashes of human victims. The Nazis efficiently destroyed most of the evidence, including the main gas chambers and ovens, most documents, the warehouses

of confiscated goods and most of the barracks. The brick barracks that housed political prisoners have been turned into museum exhibits, focusing on life in the camps, extermination, resistance, political prisoners, the Roma and prisoners of war. The most moving for me is a large room of women's hair, literally tons of it. Then shoes, then pots, then hairbrushes. Everyone human on the planet needs to see this. To grapple with its impact, the blow to our belief in decency, the proof of what we're capable of, and why we must never forget, and never allow it to happen again. Incidentally, prisoners nicknamed the warehouses of confiscated goods "Canada"—after a place of wealth and freedom and happiness. A place I now call my home.

The biggest impact of the last few days hits me now as I write you this letter. I don't feel depressed or angry or confused. Just numb, with a fridge-buzz rattling in my head. The hostel is quiet, and I am alone in a room with eight bunks. A different kind of Jew in a different kind of barracks. I ask myself: How could it have happened? Why did it happen? How could the world let

it happen? Will it happen again? Is it happening now? How did the survivors make it? Why would they want to? Who can I blame? Who can I talk to?

There is no one to talk to, except you, Bobba, rocking in your chair on the other side of the world. I am in Poland, where this horror took place. Forgive, but never forget, you would say. I am in Poland because those monsters lost. They lost because of people just like you. Because you raised an amazing family, and that family raised more amazing families. We survived, and we have thrived. I may continue to fly about like a seed, but I have landed where it is safe to grow. I came to Poland, Bobba, because travel teaches us about our dark past in order to brighten our future. My generation is blessed with the opportunity to chase our dreams, even when we explore the site of a nightmare. This is our duty. We will not forget.

START HERE:
globalbucketlist.com/auschwitz

Run with Bulls in the Azores

PORTUGAL

Half a ton of ripped, angry muscle glares into my eyes. Black hide glistening with sweat, a powerful torso primed to trample. A young man suddenly appears at its side, grabbing the monster's horns in a daring act of bravura. As the man darts in small circles with his hand resting on the horns, the bull chases its tail in frustration. The man releases, deftly bolting over a nearby wall. The Beast has been defeated, and a crowd roars its approval. Yesterday, the local news reported from another bullfight that same day. Only this time, the guy slipped during his horn grab, and the bull . . . well, the bull pummelled him to death.

Spain's Pamplona is more often associated with the thrill of bull running, but we're going to run in a different direction. Each summer, the Azorean island of Terceira hosts a unique and festive celebration of its bullfighting tradition. The St. John's Festivals draw tourists and islanders to the historical capital of Angra do Heroísmo for nightly parades, carnivals and a variety of bullfights. Unlike Mexican or Spanish traditions, Portuguese bullfighting does not kill the animal, and it incorporates some interesting twists. *Tourada à corda* (translated literally as "bullfight by rope") takes place every day using temperamental bulls bred specifically for the

event. While Pamplona-style bull running also occurs (along with bullfights on the beach), *tourada à corda* involves several men holding the bull back by a long, thick rope. This tempers the bull's progress as it charges up a street packed with revellers. Theoretically, the rope men can hold the bull back, but that's not always the case. During a rainy afternoon, I watch several bulls race into the crowd, dragging their rope men along, as if they were holding back a Rottweiler with dental floss. Meanwhile, thousands of spectators line a barricaded road cheering young men that taunt the bull by running it in circles, or confusing it with umbrellas and coats.

Usually, these guys dart to safety, although every year, someone inevitably winds up as an item on the evening news.

This Man versus Beast showdown is an integral part of Angra do Heroísmo's notorious history. This UNESCO World Heritage Site dates back to 1534 and over the centuries has seen thrill-seeking buccaneers and bloodthirsty pirates. Located in the North Atlantic, 1,500 kilometres from mainland Europe and roughly 400 kilometres from North America, the Azores has long served as a vital shipping post, fought over by sparring empires. Today, brightly painted churches overlook cobblestone squares, and Terceira's fertile farmland, divided by ancient stone walls, is a checkerboard of rolling green hills. But the bucket list brings us here for the bulls.

With the explosion of a firecracker, the crowd is warned that another Taurus has been released. A feverish excitement ripples up the street and, within moments, men and young boys are racing away from the oncoming beast. Only the brave, the experienced and the lunatics dare get close enough to flaunt their tricks. As for me, I just want a better view. A local

had warned me beforehand to be mindful of the moving rope, which might easily trip me up in the path of the 700-kilogram raging brute. Inching cautiously to the inner circle of men, I see the bull's horns ceremoniously covered in ornaments, the creature bewildered but snorting with indignation.

I can't help but feel pity for it, an innocent victim of a tradition in which men are compelled to prove their courage against a living symbol of strength, power and virility. Then I realize I've trapped myself against a row of large cargo

Meanwhile, in Pamplona

Hemingway immortalized this highlight of Spain's Festival of San Fermín as a true test of manhood, the chance to face down the power of a bull (and quickly run away from it). For nine days each summer, over a million people pack into Pamplona, mostly to observe white-clad *mozos* place themselves daily in the path of six raging bulls. The whole thing is over in 131 seconds, but you can watch replays on television and look forward to another run the following morning. Fatalities are rare, but the drinking and partying cause hundreds of injuries per year.

containers set up as barricades and makeshift stands for the crowds above. The bull turns toward me, snorts, considers his options. If I don't do something quick, I'm hamburger meat. I break into a sprint and the bull snaps its neck in my direction, the long rope coiling toward me. I leap over it, running for my life. I've learned my lesson—and got my thrill.

Animal rights activists condemn bullfighting, on a rope or otherwise. But for the people of Terceira, it's an important and beloved tradition. For bucket listers interested in taking life by the horns, or simply in partaking in an unusual cultural spectacle, a visit to Terceira is a bull's-eye summer adventure.

START HERE:
globalbucketlist.com/bullrunning

Bucket List Arts Festivals

Edinburgh's International Festival and Fringe Festival: Hotels, hostels, B & Bs and converted school dorms are booked months in advance for an international festival that features over 2,000 artists from two dozen countries, in hundreds of performances. Oh, and this doesn't include the Fringe Festival, which runs alongside the main festival and is three times the size. Over half a million people pour into Edinburgh each year for the world's largest arts fest.

England's Glastonbury Festival: With attendance figures hovering around the 200,000 mark, the Glastonbury Festival is the largest open-air music festival in the world. Performing at Glasto is a huge honour, with headliners reserved for the world's best. Glastonbury is also known for its notoriously temperamental weather. When I attended, a torrential downpour ensured the mud was so thick it came up to my knees. In a world of Lollapalooza, Sziget, Coachella, Roskilde and Rock in Rio, Glastonbury continues to hold court.

Germany's Oktoberfest: For 16 days every year, Munich hosts a beer-swigging celebration of Bavarian culture. Specifically: beer, sausages and anything else that millions of visitors can consume. Visitors from around the world drink almost 7 million litres of beer, and there's plenty of singing, dancing and all-round revelling to channel the resulting frenzy. I drank four beers in a famous Munich beer hall, the name of which I've long forgotten (along with almost everything else from the week). The beers came in l-litre jugs, were accompanied by ribald toasts and were washed down with pretzels and pickled cabbage. I vaguely recall hugging locals, tourists and the occasional public toilet.

Montreal's Just for Laughs Comedy Festival and International Jazz Festival: Montreal in summer is glorious. It's also hysterical. The Just for Laughs Comedy Festival has grown into the largest comedy festival in the world, hosting all the big names and plenty of contenders for the title. Besides the stand-up, it's a great opportunity to experience the city at its festive best. If you prefer jazz to laughter, the annual Montreal International Jazz Festival takes place a few weeks prior. Hosting thousands of musicians at venues around the city (including many free stages), it is billed as the largest jazz fest in the world.

Run with the Hash House Harriers

When it comes to social gatherings in foreign countries, think hash. Not the potatoes you have with your eggs, or sticky illegal marijuana resin. Introducing the Hash House Harriers (or H3), an informal, open-to-all quasi-athletic club currently racing in over 178 countries. "Hash House Harriers" might sound like an alliterative joke, but it is a genuine social phenomenon. With nearly 2,000 chapters operating in just about every major city worldwide, hashers come together to run, drink and be merry. Since I know not a soul in the dusty Romanian capital of Bucharest, joining the local hashers seems like the perfect way to explore the city, get some exercise, drink some beer and learn more about this global drinking club with a running problem.

Essentially a twist on the old hare-versus-hound game, each H3 race selects a human "hare" to plan a route that the pack must follow. Using paper, chalk or flour, the hare marks the trail with a series of dots, splits, circles, checks and red herrings, making it challenging for the pack to find its way home. Since most of the Bucharest hashers are here to socialize, winning the race is inconsequential. Anyone of drinking age can join; the only requirement appears to be a jolly good sense of humour.

We meet late afternoon at a park in downtown Bucharest, where a member named Crash Test Dummy welcomes regulars and "virgins." Hashers refer to one another by their hash names, which are assigned to virgins by the group in due course. I quickly realize that hashers have their own unique "mismanagement" titles, as well as distinct vocabulary. Crash Test Dummy, an English engineer who has lived in Bucharest for two years, is the Religious Advisor, charged with blessing the circle of runners. A crusty Scot named Pie-Eyed Piper, the grandmaster, is the ceremonial leader. Materhorny, who works at the Swiss Embassy, is the cash hash in charge of financial affairs. Two things are immediately obvious: hashers are defined by a bawdy schoolyard sense of humour, and they appear to come mostly from expat communities. In these characteristics, little has changed from when the first hashers came together over 70 years ago.

The first hash took place in Kuala Lumpur, Malaysia, in 1938, as a casual exercise for British office workers to run out their weekend hangovers, following a paper trail that would inevitably lead to a pub. The group became popular enough to register as a society, the name arguably chosen to reflect the seriousness of its intention. After World War II, original members spread around the globe, with new clubs (called kennels) starting up in expat communities. Today, there

are family hash events, gender-specific events, large gatherings like the EuroHash and the Inter-Hash, and even a club in Antarctica. With no central leadership, no membership requirements and no chance of taking itself seriously, hashing predates online social networking as a means to instantly make friends and make contacts in a foreign country. "It's a great way to travel and meet people," explains an American agricultural con-sultant. "Wherever you go, you'll always find a hash."

The hare had marked a trail through Bucharest's quiet embassy neighbourhood. Together with the pack, I chase down dots of flour marked with the help of a tennis ball. We chase each dot like we're playing a game of Pac-Man, until we reach a circle and must fan out to find the next trail. A circle indi-cates a change in direction, an X a false trail. The FRB (or front-run-ning bastard) calls out "On, on!" to indicate he or she has found the next dot, and everyone follows. Locals look on curiously, bemused by the eclectic, eccentric group run-ning about shouting and laughing. We dodge traffic and the city's noto-rious stray dogs, and soon enough approach the first beer check. Congregating outside a small neighbourhood shop, we crack open cold beers, share coarse jokes and hash war stories from around the world. Hashers new to Bucharest, like me, are accepted as if old schoolmates. I learn about what the club deems violations, including running with new shoes and pointing with a finger. Each club makes up its own set of violations, and is careful to reiterate that the most important rule is that there are no rules.

"On, on!" We're back on the trail. Hashes take place in forests, parks, streets or wherever the hare chooses, with the length of the course and number of beer checks varying. After running alongside

traffic, we arrive back at the park, where the grandmaster instructs everyone to form a circle, cool down and congratulate the hare for her efforts. With another round of drinks, the running club becomes a drinking club.

We virgins are called into the centre of the circle, handed a cup of beer and roasted like has-been celebrities. We are given the choice between telling a joke, singing a song or flashing a body part. It typically takes a virgin five races before they are named, but I fast-tracked my naming process in a stroke of journalistic exuberance. When I was researching the hashers, I came across the name Big Wanker, which I assumed to be yet

HHH Terminology

Although individual clubs will have their own slang and variants, endear yourself at your first hash with these universal terms:

Are you?: A call for help from a lost hound.

Beer master: Organizer of beer.

Beer near: Indicates the beverages are close.

Bucket: Beer session at the end of the run.

Check back: Backtracking to locate a trail.

Down-down: Chugging a beer as an act of reward or punishment.

FRB: Front-running bastard, the fastest member of the pack.

Grand master: Supreme leader of the chapter.

Hare: Lays the trail.

Hash horn: Used to rally the harriers and harriets.

Hash name: Your nickname, always to be used or face a down-down.

another important H3 title. Earlier, I had asked Crash Test Dummy who the Big Wanker was. "When somebody asks a stupid question like that, they can only, from this day forth, be known as the Big Wanker." I suppose there are worse names, but not too many. "Down down down . . ." and before I know it, I have yet another mug of beer down my throat, my fellow hashers pouring their beers over my head and dousing me in sticky flour. I had been in Bucharest less than 24 hours and already I had made friends with a dozen interesting characters. I had also discovered the parks and streets of Bucharest, although a few beers later, my notes become rather illegible.

You don't have to run with this particular club and, admittedly, the bawdy and physical nature of hashing is not for everybody. However, should you find yourself looking for a human connection at home or especially abroad, search online for the local chapter, show up at its next event, and tell the members that experiencing a hash is on your bucket list. Go on. On, on!

START HERE:
globalbucketlist.com/hhh

Dracula's Castle

Listen to the children of the night . . . counting your tourist dollars. Bran Castle is heavily marketed as the inspiration behind Bram Stoker's *Dracula*, but like a vampire's reflection in the mirror, all is not what it seems. There is little evidence that Stoker even knew this castle existed or that his historical inspiration, Vlad III, ever lived here. The scenic castle nevertheless invites tourists to explore exhibits relating to Dracula, Vlad and Stoker and is the region's most popular attraction. Vampire wannabes will want to check into the Hotel Castle Dracula, located on the exact spot where Stoker set his castle. Do watch out for tax-dodging day walkers or lovesick boy-men who twinkle in the sunlight.

RUSSIA

Rail across Siberia

When you cross one-third of the planet's landmass by rail, the world truly does flash before your eyes. Our bucket list train journey, combining the Trans-Mongolian and Trans-Siberian Railways, begins with a night train from Shanghai to Beijing. From here, I will make my way across Mongolia and all the way to St. Petersburg, discovering that life at 95 km/hr is truly life at a different pace. Some travellers might spend months on such a journey; others, weeks. I'd spend 11 full days on a train, the journey punctuated with stops along the way.

After my first 30 straight hours on the rail, the train gauge changing from Beijing to the Mongolian capital of Ulan Bator, even the most enthusiastic trainspotter would want to stretch their legs. Fortunately, Ulan Bator is full of quirks. Here I discover that the Mongolian barbecue stir-fry concept, so popular in North America, is, in fact, a Western concept. Mongolian cuisine tends to be more challenging on our palate—think horse intestines and fermented camel milk. I spend one night in the capital and one in the countryside soaking up the gorgeous prairie from a traditional ger tent. There's a lot of distance to cross, so it's back to the station for the 48-hour passage from Ulan Bator to Irkutsk, Russia.

My train has no dining car, and no scheduled dining stops along the way either. Train attendants do, however, provide hot water, so meals consist of instant noodles, biscuits, sardines and juice I had bought in Ulan Bator's wonderfully named State Department Store. Given the bland insta-food, my bottle of Tabasco, which I seldom travel without, is worth its weight in gold. International travellers swing by my compartment hoping to score a few precious drops. In return, I ask them for spare books, or something other than noodles, biscuits and sardines. I am happy to share a four-berth compartment with fellow international travellers.

Train Journeys on the Great Global Bucket List

evening, the train crosses 36 bridges (one at over 300 metres) and goes through 87 tunnels. Mexico's most scenic train chugs alongside stunning jungle, mountains, canyons, waterfalls and even high desert.

Blue Train: It's amazing how much comfort you can cram into a carriage rolling along a gauge just over I metre wide. Butler service, en suite soundproofed compartments (with gold tinted windows), double beds with down duvets, marble-tiled bathrooms (many with full bathtubs), panoramic observation lounges, gourmet meals—South Africa's *Blue Train* is known as a moving five-star hotel.

The Canadian: Travel 4,466 kilometres between Vancouver and Toronto, through coastal rainforest, the Rockies, prairies and boreal forests. Roll through four time zones in four days, with panoramic double-storey dome cars, excellent meals, clean bathrooms, fun activities and friendly staff. Recalling the 1950s glory years, VIA Rail's *The Canadian*'s stainless-steel carriages have the feel of another era, especially the rear Park car, with its view of the tracks left behind.

El ChePe: The Chihuahua al Pacifico Railroad, more affectionately known as *El ChePe*, carries locals and tourists some 650 kilometres through the Sierra Madre Occidental and the magnificent Copper Canyon. Departing Los Mochis in the morning and arriving in Chihuahua late in the

The Ghan: With its vast distances and sparse population, Australia is tailor-made for an epic train journey. *The Ghan*, named after the late-19th-century Afghan cameleers who created the route, traverses almost 3,000 kilometres north to south and vice versa from Adelaide through Alice Springs to Darwin.

Maharajas' Express: Recalling an era where India's grand maharajas built their own lines to shepherd them in lavish carriages, the *Express* combines old-world luxury with modern conveniences like a business centre, spa and gym. It offers five itineraries, ranging from the seven-night Heritage of India, Indian Splendor and Indian Panorama to the three-night Treasures of India and Gems of India.

Qinghai-Tibet Railway: China boasts the world's fastest passenger train, the CRH380A, running from Shanghai to Nanjing and Hangzhou at an astonishing 480 km/hr. Think more roller coaster and less leisurely train journey. For less of a blur, the *Qinghai-Tibet* is an engineering marvel that connects the city of Xining to Lhasa, Tibet. Once you cross the Tanggula Pass at 5,072 metres above sea level, you're officially on the world's highest railway, rolling through the world's highest tunnel and stopping at the world's highest railway station.

Rocky Mountaineer: The *Rocky Mountaineer* belongs to North America's largest private rail service, running 1,000 kilometres through some of the world's best scenery. Unlike VIA's *Canadian*, which continues on to Toronto, the *Rocky Mountaineer* is designed to showcase the Rockies in all their glory, with guests seated in two-level glass-domed panoramic cars while interpreters point out wildlife and sites of interest.

Royal Scotsman: 36 guests are pampered in absolute luxury aboard the *Royal Scotsman*. The train offers two- to seven-night itineraries that take in the majestic Highlands, along with themed trips like the four-night Whisky Journey, offered in association with the Scotch Malt Whisky Society. Enjoy gourmet bliss in the mahogany-panelled dining car. Pack a kilt for alternating formal nights (or rent one on board).

Venice-Simplon Orient Express/Eastern and Oriental Express: Two separate train journeys on different continents, run by one company. The original *Orient Express*, running between Strasbourg and Vienna, ceased operation in 2009. The *Venice-Simplon* is a luxury train operating from London to Venice, with vintage carriages dating back to the 1920s. Swap Europe for lush jungles and exotic temples aboard the more modern *Eastern and Oriental Express*, which journeys between Malaysia, Singapore, Thailand and Laos.

On long train rides, camaraderie forms between cabin mates eager to share their tales of transit hell. Some of that hell includes navigating the labyrinth that is the Chinese, Mongolian and Russian rail network.

Russian border crossings are seldom uneventful. For reasons undisclosed to the passengers, all train toilets are locked 20 minutes on either side of the border, which would be bearable if this were a 40-minute process. After nine hours, the sun bakes our stalled compartments. Having received no sympathy from the train attendants, several international passengers stage a mutiny. Stone-faced Russian guards relent and allow us to urinate behind a wall—men and women together—under armed supervision. Our bladders are too full for us to worry about machine-gun stage fright. Turns out the train's delay is due to the discovery that our hard pillows, supplied by Mongolia's rail network, contain smuggled clothes as stuffing. Eventually, a bribe makes its way to the right authority, and we continue the journey, our pillows still intact with knock-off Lee denims. Not pointing any fingers, but I can tell you the train attendants looked especially relieved.

Peering out the window, I see traditional Mongolian ger tents become grey, Russian wooden houses. Old Soviet iconography wilts on the facades of passing stations; Asian faces on the platforms become Caucasian. Travelling such a vast distance overland, you see geography and culture morph before your eyes. It is clear we are leaving Asia and on our way to Europe, our minds full of wonder, bellies full of instant noodles.

I interrupt Siberia's 4,800-kilometre stretch with a much-needed break in the town of Irkutsk, overlooking Lake Baikal. By volume, it is the world's largest freshwater lake, and at over 1,500 metres, the world's deepest

too. Frozen over during the long winter months, the lake becomes in summer a popular tourist region, with colourful markets and festive boat cruises. Aboard such a vessel, I join booze-infused locals for a dip in the bracing 6°C water. Aided by the courage induced by cheap vodka, I visit a traditional Siberian *banya* smoke sauna, where an attendant whips me with birch branches. A barrel of ice-cold lake water is dumped over my head when I exit. Suitably invigorated for the long stretch ahead, and happy in the knowledge that Siberia is so much more than a Soviet prison

sentence, I return to the station. There are posters advertising an upcoming concert featuring '80s one-hit wonder Dr. Alban, no doubt in the throes of his own artistic Siberia.

Since the Trans-Siberia Railway crosses five time zones, authorities decided that all trains in Russia must run on Moscow time. Local time and train time are perilously different, of particular importance for those daring to explore platforms during short stops along the way. Rather than risk getting stranded searching for sardines, it's easier to just stay onboard for the 72-hour train journey to Moscow and buy food through the window. Fortunately, the latest train has a dining car, albeit one with tremendously overpriced food and famously dour Russian service. Instant noodles, procured from platform stalls, once again feature prominently on my menu. I waste away the long hours reading, sleeping, playing cards and gazing out the window at the soporific Siberian countryside. Endless rolling green hills and forests, punctuated by small villages and industrial towns, become a constant blur of motion. It's great backdrop for deep thought. As for the scenic beauty of the Ural Mountains, we cross them under the frustrating cover of night.

Eventually, we roll into Moscow, where I spend a few days exploring the city before hopping on the final overnight leg to St. Petersburg. By this stage, I am a hardened train veteran. My journey had started in China—exploring Tiananmen Square, the Forbidden City and the Great Wall (page 263). In Mongolia, I had enjoyed the big sky and kindness of soft-spoken locals, if not the fatty boiled lamb. I had swum in the icy waters of Lake Baikal, bought Russian nesting dolls, explored Moscow's Red Square and St. Petersburg's Hermitage. But it is the trains that linked all these experiences together. They might not always be on schedule, but bucket list memories like the Trans-Siberia Railway are conveniently timeless.

START HERE:
globalbucketlist.com/tsr

Discover the Reality of Space Travel

Just a couple of hours' drive outside Moscow, reality and science fiction breach each other's orbit. The tree-lined entrance to the space-age-sounding Star City looks decidedly low-tech, but like other space tourists before me, I am thrilled just to approach the formerly top-secret Yuri A. Gagarin State Scientific Research-and-Testing Cosmonaut Training Center. When the Soviet Union crumbled and Russia transformed, so did its once-hallowed space program. Administration was begrudgingly handed over by the military to a civic scientific organization called Roscosmos, the Russian Federal Space Agency. Since budgets were slashed for more earthly concerns, alternative revenue streams were vital to keep the program in orbit. Thus, the last frontier became available to adventurous tourists, and by tourists, I refer to billionaires who can afford a US$20–30 million entrance ticket.

The first was American businessman Dennis Tito; among the most recent is Cirque du Soleil founder Guy Laliberté. Like a half-dozen other *touronauts* before him, Mr. Laliberté trained in Star City for a once-in-a-lifetime opportunity to be strapped to 40 metric tons of rocket fuel and blasted into space.

Star City's squat, brick buildings have seen better days. Weeds crack through concrete pavement, the paint is chipped and the shrubs, overgrown. My guide, Marina, is one of the few hundred personnel left in a facility that once housed thousands. She seems slightly embarrassed, as if she personally should have cleaned up. Inside the main building, I look at proud photographs of famous cosmonauts, old Soviet heroes with thick moustaches and fading hairlines. I'm led toward a hall housing an exact replica of the Soyuz spacecraft, designed in the 1960s and still the most reliable method of sending humans to space. Seven metres high with a small circular entrance, the three-man passenger module is a cramped, dark cubicle that pierces space like a bullet. A far cry from *Star Trek*'s *Enterprise*, the Soyuz buttons and knobs look like something you might find on an old fax machine. Despite it being tiny, Sandra Bullock did make it look cozy during her orbital escape in the Oscar-winning film *Gravity*.

Mission control is a bunch of old PCs on a desk, with some well-worn sofas nearby, separated by green plants. The real mission control, located nearby in the city of Korolyov, is a lot more serious, but this is still the official training centre, and that couch still looks like something you might find in an alley. It costs a staggering US$400 million for a single successful launch; Marina explains that US$30 million barely covers the price of the seat. But space

tourists are hardly joyriders. They must spend up to a year at the facility, honing their bodies into peak condition, learning science and engineering—and how to withstand incredible physical and psychological pressure. One Japanese millionaire didn't make the cut. Cosmonauts must have space in their blood.

"In America, they just give them pills," says Marina, suggesting US astronauts skirt the challenge. The competitiveness of the Space Race is still alive in her voice.

Day visitors are not allowed to use any of the facilities, including the legendary "vomit comet"—a zero-gravity simulator in the form of a big plane spiralling out of control. If I had a couple of thousand dollars and had done the required paperwork, it would be possible to pay for a spin in the world's largest and most powerful centrifuge. I move on to the Hydrolab, a massive pool filled with 12 metric tons of water, where budding cosmonauts can accustom themselves to movement in space. I notice a display cabinet holding various cosmonaut utilities: toiletries, foil-wrapped food and, of course, fine Russian caviar. Eating is not something

You Spin Me Round

With a radius of 18 metres and 300 metric tons of rotating elements, Star City boasts the world's largest and most powerful centrifuge. The human body begins to deteriorate at sustained G-forces above 10G, with G-force being the energy of acceleration. This monster machine can generate up to 30G, which is enough to crush every bone in the body. As the G-force increases, pressure can result in injuries or blackouts. Space tourists learn how to contract their chest muscles and breathe with their lower abdomen while dealing with the intense pressure of the capsule as it re-enters the atmosphere.

encouraged before strapping into another training chair, which spins at such radical speed it is guaranteed to make the occupant blow their borscht. Given the challenges, I wonder if those billionaires knew what they were getting into. Goodbye designer clothing, which has been swapped for a 100-kilogram spacesuit (though the helmet is gold-plated to protect the wearer from solar heat).

Marina enthusiastically explains everything, and she's used to visitors expecting something more ... Trekkie. Rocket science may attract the best and brightest minds, but the mechanics are still rooted in the nuts and bolts, not stun guns and tractor beams. The next hall houses a life-size replica of the legendary Mir Space Station and is still used for various training purposes. Lego-like in structure, Mir housed a rotating crew of three people for 12 years in orbit, before being crashed into the Pacific to make way for the International Space Station. Walking around, one sees printer ports and duct tape, loose wires and circuit switches—all accentuating the *fiction* in *science fiction*. Budding bucket list space tourists can break their piggy banks and contact Space Adventures, a tour operator that puts everything together, somehow navigating the mountain of Russian red tape. It's even planning a strip to the moon, but that costs extra. Alternatively, you can drop US$200,000 for a ticket on Virgin Galactic's VSS *Enterprise*, as hundreds of people have reportedly done. Richard Branson believes ticket prices will one day come down to just US$20,000, which I suppose is a bargain for a suborbital space flight. Meanwhile, Hilton Worldwide has announced plans to connect space shuttle fuel tanks to create an orbiting hotel,

while Bigelow Aerospace, founded by a motel tycoon, is developing expandable space station modules. Elon Musk's SpaceX is developing technologies to enable the colonization of Mars.

Far from a theme park, Star City is a very serious endeavour at the forefront of science, and the futuristic era of space tourism. Shown around the training facility,

I wonder if this is what it must have felt like walking the early-20th-century assembly line of a Ford Model T factory. Could all these strange, clunky machines actually get us anywhere? Check back a century from now and the answer might be: "To infinity, and beyond."

START HERE:
globalbucketlist.com/starcity

Run with Unicorns

SLOVENIA

One of the traumatic cinematic experiences of my childhood was watching *The NeverEnding Story*, in which a white horse drowns in the Swamps of Sadness. Our boy-hero Atreyu desperately tries to save his white steed, Artax, screaming his name repeatedly, but Artax slowly disappears into the blackness. It was my first real confrontation with the concept of death, and I wasn't the only one. Search online and you'll find plenty of blog posts with titles like "We Need to Talk about Artax" and "How a Boy, His Horse and a Swamp Basically Screwed Up a Generation." As a direct result, I was never attracted to horses. All that changed in Slovenia.

The noble Lipizzaner breed of horses has long captured the human imagination. Associated primarily with the Spanish Riding School of Vienna, Lipizzaners were bred by the Austrian-Hungarian Royal Court as early as 1580, when the Lipica Stud Farm in modern-day Slovenia was founded. Known for their elegance, strength, intelligence and longevity, purebred Lipizzaners can be traced back to just six stallions. Wartime Europe almost wiped them out, but the breed has since rebounded, with several thousand registered worldwide. In Slovenia, the horses remain a proud symbol of the country. Offering demonstrations, courses, tours and competitions, the Lipica Stud Farm has become a mecca for horse lovers from around the world, drawn as they are to the original "cradle of the race."

A narrow road leading to the farm is lined with lime trees and a picturesque white picket fence. Legend has it that three limes were planted for every Lipizzaner stallion sent to Vienna, and centuries later, the abundant trees would seem to verify this. Although the Spanish Riding School of Vienna currently breeds its Lipizzaners in Austria,

Wedding Bells Are Ringing

While in Slovenia, head over to the gem-green waters of Lake Bled and hire one of the locals to paddle you across to Bled Island, where you'll find the Church of the Assumption. The church has been on the island since the 11th century, though the current steeple dates back only to the 1400s. It's popular for both local and destination nuptials—legend has it that the groom who can carry his bride from the water's edge up the 99 stone steps to the sanctuary ensures a prosperous marriage. Seal the deal by tolling the wishing bell, which has echoed around the lake for 600 years.

Lipica still has some 400 horses and continues to operate according to strict tradition. These horses are known best in the sport of dressage, in which riders and horse demonstrate control and skill in a number of disciplines. Originating in the royal courts of European empires, dressage today takes place at events worldwide, including the Summer Olympic Games. During a demonstration, I watch an elegantly dressed rider direct his groomed Lipizzaner to leap in the air; it does, tucking in its forelegs while kicking its hind legs at the peak of the jump—a movement known as *capriole*. A horse fan from Australia explains to me that this is not a circus. Classical riding is approached with the utmost respect. I've galloped on the plains of Mongolia and the deserts of Jordan, but I am about to learn that Western-style and classical-style riding breed two very different types of riders. "Western style" refers to North American cowboy or rodeo-influenced riding, a style I am familiar with. Riding Western is like playing power chords on a guitar. Riding classical, a concerto on the violin.

I'm hoping to make music with my stallion, Maestoso Slovena. Since a horse's first name indicates its father, its last name, the mother, a horse as noble as the Lipizzaner does not receive a cute pet name. Tall, regal and powerful, Slovena is as far from your drowsy trail horse as a Porsche is from a go-kart. Classical riding is deeply technical. The horse interprets each of the rider's subtle movements, such as weight shift or knee pressure, as a specific instruction. Certainly this proved to be the case with M. Slovena. My patient Italian instructor, Fabrizia, keeps reminding me, "Back straight, hands down, reins loose, squeeze your legs!" Large, old mirrors in Lipica's indoor training hall reflect my poor efforts, but eventually I am able to make Slovena gently trot along the walls of the Big Circle, or diagonally across the Little Circle. Fabrizia explains that many Western riders who visit Lipica struggle with the intricacies of classical riding, not to mention the strong personalities of the Lipizzaners. Once we move into the outer training facility, I feel like Slovena is riding me. Occasionally, she goes where I want, if only to avoid hurting my feelings.

Fabrizia guides me into the surrounding meadows, where 40 mares are grazing. The mares have mowed the lawn of the Slovenian countryside, the rolling green meadows now as fine-tuned as fairways. Autumn is approaching, blowing a cool tang in the morning air. I hear them first, a dull thud of hooves stamping the soft pasture. There is a moment of suspense, and then they appear, three dozen white horses galloping with the grace of ghosts. Their white coats are ripped with muscle, and frame noble jaws, wise eyes, long necks and fine tails that capture rays of morning sun. For a moment, the imaginative line dividing fantasy from reality shatters, and I enter the mystical world of unicorns.

The horses stop to graze in a protective circle. I ask Fabrizia if it's okay for me to approach the horses.

"Ask them yourself," she replies.

As I approach the herd, their heads snap up with curiosity. I walk

slowly, an amateur horse whisperer treading lightly. After a few minutes they visibly relax, and a lone mare gracefully wanders over to investigate. Her eyes are wide as orbs, black as tar. She breathes heavy, takes in my scent and allows me to stroke her head, as perfectly shaped as the knight on a chessboard. I walk toward the accepting herd and soon find myself alone in its circle. Sure, these are domesticated horses, but this is as special a wildlife encounter as any I've had. When they take off, I decide to run alongside them. You don't have to be a horse lover to appreciate the moment, and you don't need to believe in mythical creatures either. In Lipica, the reins that connect human and horse have been held tightly for centuries, a never-ending story for passionate horse fans and bucket listers, present and future.

START HERE:
globalbucketlist.com/lipizzaner

Join the World's Biggest Food Fight

SPAIN

et us celebrate the mighty tomato! Plump as the baker's wife, moist as a summer downpour, the tomato tastes of carnal culinary pleasure. What is a pizza without its red saucy base? What would become of spaghetti bolognaise, the BLT, lasagna, the good ol' fashioned all-dressed hamburger? As for French fries, they are the yin to ketchup's yang. Thinking about the joys of *Solanum lycopersicum* is enough to make me pick up a ripe tomato, squeeze it in my fist and let its fluids drip down my arm. And if I feel like throwing a tomato in a spontaneous celebration of gastronomic joy, I know just where to go.

Each year, the small Spanish town of Buñol is invaded for La Tomatina, an annual food fight that incorporates an estimated 150,000, or 40 metric tons of, tomatoes. With its proximity to nearby Valencia, you might think oranges would be the fruit of choice for a local food celebration, but it's far more fun to hurl the sweet acidic tomato, shipped in from another region for the occasion. It is important to note that one must follow the rules at the world's largest food fight. First, the event has become so popular that the number of participants has been capped at 50,000, all of whom must purchase a ticket to help pay for the cleanup. No bottles or objects that can cause injury are allowed at the event, and it is not permissible to rip the shirts of fellow revellers (good luck with that one); tomatoes must be squashed before you throw them, and all throwing must stop immediately at the sound of the second canon. Traditionally, the fight begins only when someone manages to scale a soaped wooden pole to obtain a ham at the top; however, nobody actually manages to do this before the tomatoes start flying. La Tomatina quickly descends into a full-blown blizzard of red chaos. Everything you're wearing, including your skin, will stain red. Closed-toe shoes are strongly advised so your digits don't get trampled, and goggles will prevent seeds stinging the eyeballs.

The tradition takes place the last Wednesday of August, and locals aren't exactly sure how it started. What is known is that the first tomato fight took place in 1945, and it might have had something to do with locals pelting politicians: tomatoes—pelting the unpopular for centuries. There are theories that La Tomatina's origins lie in the manifestation of a class war, a practical joke or the messy result of an overturned truck. Franco, a fascist dictator who undoubtedly deserved a good tomato pelting, banned the event for its lack of religious significance. A spirited tomato fight overcomes politics, which is why today you'll find similar events in the United States, China and Colombia. Any tomato fight must, however, pay homage to Spain's original La Tomatina, and so does our bucket list.

START HERE:
globalbucketlist.com/tomatino

Visit a Ghost City

UKRAINE

T he site of the world's largest nuclear meltdown was never intended for tour buses, and given the risk, the Ukrainian government would prefer to keep them away. Nevertheless, a handful of tour operators offer sightseeing trips to Chernobyl. Before you get your glow on, we should ask, isn't it dangerous? Why would we want to visit a nuclear disaster, much less put it on our bucket list? Valid questions, the answers to which I intend to find out.

On April 26, 1986, reactor number four of the Chernobyl Nuclear Power Plant exploded, releasing a deadly radiation plume that blanketed parts of Europe. The official cause of the explosion is still a mystery and the overall consequences are still hotly debated. The death toll ranges from 40,000 to 100,000 depending on your sources, and competing studies analyze spikes in cancer, animal mutations and the disastrous effect on the environment. Once you cross the barrier at the 30-kilometre zone (also known as the Zone of Alienation), you've entered the world's largest toxic waste site. *Everything* is contaminated, though harmful isotopes in the atmosphere have now been reduced to levels of relative safety. Several hundred people—security, scientists, fire fighters and support personnel—still live around Chernobyl. An estimated 300 more are resettlers, an aging population who returned to their surrounding farms after the disaster and refuse to leave. When the adjacent city of Pripyat was evacuated, authorities had to convince over 50,000 people their lives were in danger. After all, one can feel an earthquake or smell a fire, but radiation is a silent killer.

Armed guards and large signs warn visitors they are entering a restricted area with high levels of radiation. My tour guide, Sergey, hands over to security the passports

and permits for our group. Ushered through, I expect to be greeted by a post-apocalyptic nightmare, but the countryside appears benign: thick bushes, leafy trees, a cloud of dust in the late summer heat. We drive up to the barracks to meet our assigned government official. His job is to shadow our group during our visit and make sure we follow the rules: no alcohol; no wandering into restricted zones; no souvenirs, no touching anything, not even a stone. You'll sign many waivers pursuing this Great Global Bucket List item. Few are as ominous as this one.

Our minibus stops to view the six reactors, squatting like large post-industrial corpses in the distance. Chernobyl's other reactors continued to operate until as late as 2000, when the entire plant was shut down. Sergey hands me a Geiger counter, a device that measures radiation. A dull ticking sounds as the counter registers 0.220. In the Ukrainian capital of Kiev, just over 100 kilometres away, it read 0.011. Sergey calmly explains that radiation only becomes deadly in short doses at around 6,000. Somewhere between the numbers and gadgets I realize that the air I'm breathing contains around 20 times the normal level of radiation. My Geiger counter is just warming up.

Disaster Tourism

Massacres, devastating storms, battles, earthquakes, eruptions, prisons—places with a dark past form the basis of a new genre of travel known as disaster tourism. Considering that Pompeii is one of the most popular tourist attractions in Italy, it's not exactly a small genre either. One can walk the beaches of Normandy or the fields of Gettysburg, explore the S-21 Prison in Phnom Penh, boat to the site of the *Exxon Valdez* spill, cycle on a Hurricane Katrina bike tour in New Orleans or visit the crash site of United Airlines Flight 93, a concentration camp in Poland (see page 195) or Japan's Hiroshima Peace Memorial Park. Often criticized for objectifying and profiteering on the misery of others, disaster tourism, when done right, can be an educational and emotional interaction with history's darkest chapters.

Within view of reactor four, an iron bridge crosses a river of radioactive water. Below, I see large catfish, their bodies thick as sharks. Nature has proved to be incredibly resilient. Moose, deer, boar, wolves and bears live in the area, breeding in large numbers, now unthreatened by humans. Scientists have been unable to prove any large-scale mutations, as if indigenous animals have adapted their diets to include a higher level of radiation. Swimming in toxic water without fish hooks to worry about, the catfish grow and multiply.

My Geiger counter now reads 0.530 as I stand in front of the guilty reactor. Pointing the device in the direction of ground zero, or to the grass that lines the asphalt road, that number increases. Today, a massive cement sarcophagus encloses the reactor, a makeshift solution designed to keep radioactive lava and uranium isotopes from entering the atmosphere. Chernobyl remains a time bomb, capable of another explosion, leak or fire that will expel even more radiation into the atmosphere. It may be from the hot afternoon sun, but my skin feels unnaturally warm. Workers are pottering about up ahead. Surely it can't be that dangerous?

Firefighters rushing to the scene of the disaster had no idea what the dangers were. They reported tasting something like metal as their bodies were pummelled with deadly yet silent radiation. The reactor fire continued for nearly two weeks, finally being put out by helicopters dropping 5,000 metric tons of sand and lead. By this time, several firefighters had died from acute radiation sickness. Levels were so high that measuring devices at the time couldn't read them. Workers in some areas were limited to just 40 seconds per shift to avoid deadly exposure. Every truck, crane, shovel and protective outfit became instantly toxic, buried in contaminated soil. A memorial now honours the dozens of firefighters who subsequently lost their lives—some within days, others within months.

"This is the hottest zone of our visit," explains Sergey as we exit the bus not far from the reactor. The Geiger clock spikes radically: 1.200, 1.600, 1.900, 2.000. The very thought of how much radiation I am exposing my body to is unnerving. Fortunately for the inhabitants of Pripyat, wind blew the radiation in a *V*-shaped pattern, saving the city from the full brunt of exposure. Within two days, however, a proud Soviet city, covered in iconography and built as a symbol of national pride, was permanently abandoned. Residents were allowed to pack only suitcases, and forced to desert most of their belongings, even their pets. This ghost city is the true attraction for post-disaster tourists. In the eerie quiet, the trees, brush and weeds are returning concrete-block buildings to nature. It is a haunting snapshot of a modern world without us—deserted, disturbing, deceased.

Next we visit an old school where hundreds of textbooks lie scattered on the floor. Broken windows, smashed by vandals or birds, shatter any youthful joy that might have remained from the children who once roamed these halls. Light fittings rust, chalkboards split, paint peels, the wooden desks sprout radioactive green moss. I hear my voice echo through the corridors, out the buildings and through the abandoned apartments across the street.

Next we visit a fairground that was due to open just two days after the disaster struck. A corroded Ferris wheel never took a single paying customer. Sergey reminds us to stick to the asphalt and avoid stepping on the moss, which concentrates radiation, for fear of contaminating our shoes. I explore an old theatre, dark and musky, seats torn out, the stage collapsing. A kindergarten contains

the blackened faces of dead-eyed dolls, a scene so frightening you can choke on the dread. In 2,000 years, will archaeologists discover similar ruins in New York, London or Tokyo? What will they make of our cracked, flat-screen televisions, our memory-foam mattresses and smartphones, rotting with time?

An archaic machine straight out of *Dr. Who* sits against a wall. It is our first line of defence for radiation poisoning, measuring levels of particles on my shoes and hands. It takes a few seconds before I see the reassuring glow of green light, indicating I have passed. A second piece of equipment that is able to gather a more thorough reading of our contamination levels greets us as we exit the Zone of Alienation. If you fail this test, authorities might quarantine you for a couple of days. Although I have been exposed to high levels of radiation, it is still considered harmless given how little time I spent in the area. That Sergey runs a dozen tours a month and the complex has permanent residents answers my first question. It is safe to visit Chernobyl? Yes, providing you stick to the rules.

As for the second, why would anyone want to visit in the first

place? Walking among the ruins of Pripyat is an emotional journey into a terrifying past, and into a future that unfortunately may manifest. Japan's Fukushima disaster is a case in point, even as stockpiles of nuclear weapons continue to threaten every living creature on the planet. Recall the ruins in Mexico, Cambodia, Peru and Tunisia, the remains of once powerful nations that ruled for centuries. History washed these civilizations away. Visiting Chernobyl is a fascinating yet chilling reminder that it might yet reclaim our own.

START HERE:
globalbucketlist.com/chernobyl

Open the Toolbox of Armageddon

UKRAINE

In a tiny control room crammed with gadgets and monitors sits a small button. Twenty-four hours a day an officer monitors the panel, awaiting a single phone call. On orders, he would place a key into a slot and turn it clockwise. Punching in an access code, he might take a breath before pushing a small white knob. In just over half an hour, a missile carrying a payload of 10 thermonuclear warheads would hit multiple targets in the United States. Each warhead would vaporize an area of 200 square kilometres, along with every living creature inside it. Millions would die instantly; millions more would perish from the effects of deadly radiation. As thousands of missiles proceed to criss-cross the sky seeking targets, the world as we know it would cease to exist. All it takes is one push of a button, located in a control room 30 metres below the Ukrainian countryside. My finger draws near. My hand starts to shake.

ASIA

ARCTIC OCEAN

RUSSIA

Lake Baikal

Irkutsk

Ulan Bator

MONGOLIA

Jinshanling

Gobi Desert

Beijing

Sea of Japan (East Sea)

JAPAN

Tokyo

Black Sea

Istanbul

Aral Sea

TURKEY

Göreme

Mt. Nemrut

Ölüdeniz

Gobekli Tepe

Caspian Sea

Derweze

TURKMENISTAN

Seoul

Nachi Falls

Yellow Sea

Sakurajima

SOUTH KOREA

ISRAEL

Tel Aviv

Xi'an

Dead Sea

Jerusalem

CHINA

Wuhan

Yellow Mountains

Wadi Rum

JORDAN

Persian Gulf

Huashan

Chongqing

Yangtze River

Taipei

TAIWAN

Red Sea

New Delhi

Mt. Everest

Agra

MYANMAR (BURMA)

Mekong River

HONG KONG

INDIA

Bagan

LAOS

MACAU

Chiang Mai

Vang Vieng

THE PHILIPPINES

Goa

Arambol

Arabian Sea

Bay of Bengal

Siem Reap/Angkor Wat

THAILAND

Mount Mayon

El Nido

Cebu

Chocolate Hills

Anjuna

CAMBODIA

South China Sea

Palawan

Kota Kinabalu

Colombo

SRI LANKA

MALAYSIA

MALDIVES

Borneo

INDONESIA

PACIFIC OCEAN

N
W E
S

Komodo Island

0   500   1,000 Miles
0   500   1,000 Kilometres

INDIAN OCEAN

Balloon over Bagan

BURMA/MYANMAR

After decades of rule by an oppressive military regime, the spotlight of global tourism is once again shining on Burma a.k.a. Myanmar. Nobel Peace Prize winner Aung San Suu Kyi has led her own Mandelarized charge to freedom, winning the country's first true democratic elections in late 2015. Building a future requires a forgiveness of the past and, among other things, we'll have to forgive the military regime for restoring the ancient temple complex of Bagan with all the sensitivity of the Hulk in a China shop.

Bagan includes the remains of 2,200 temples, pagodas, stupas and monasteries from an ancient Buddhist empire, their bell-shaped ceilings piercing the sky like an army of pawns on a sprawling dusty chessboard. It has obvious comparisons to Angkor (page 248), and temple fatigue is inevitable. That is why we are going to get up very early, amid the sound of tropical birds whooping and roosters doing the whoop-de-do, to hop on a 1940s-era Canadian-made bus for the short drive to the awaiting airborne chariots of Balloons over Bagan.

Ballooning is the Merlot of soft adventures: definitely quaffable, largely inoffensive, always good in a pinch but not entirely as memorable as one would hope. Granted, a hot-air balloon is romantic—a spinning top canvas elevating a picnic basket of passengers feeling bursts of heat on their necks in the cold early morning. The lack of memorability comes down to the fact that balloon virgins imagine the flight will elicit a distinct thrill, like an uncouth joke in polite company. Expecting a roller coaster, they are met by an airborne ferry. Prodded by a gentle breeze, the basket is safe from turbulence, neither rocking nor swaying. Even those afraid of heights find the sensation calming.

Fact is, ballooning is considered to be the safest form of air transport. After the initial buzz of elevation has died down, the location of your flight quickly becomes crucial. A quiet float over grazing animals in the Serengeti is gobsmacking. Drifting above the red rocks of Turkey's Cappadocia is certainly bucket list–worthy. Ballooning on our bucket list, however, is reserved for the splendid sunrise in Bagan.

Over 10,000 religious sites once spread across these plains, commissioned by kings during the boom of the Pagan Empire. Kublai Khan and his Mongol hordes had other ideas, galloping in from China during the 13th century to pretty much raze everything in their path. The city of Bagan survived as a small settlement, its structures atrophying with time, with only the relics of its abundant temples remaining as cultural fossils in a bed of sandstone. Earthquakes and tropical weather have done their best, but despite all this (and the clumsy efforts of misguided restoration), Bagan still has the world's largest concentration of religious landmarks.

Ballooning for the Bucket List

Ballooning is the oldest human flight technology and one of the most magical ways to take in a view. So hop in the basket and fire up the burner over:

- The migration of animals in the Masai Mara or Serengeti, in Kenya and Tanzania.
- The outback in Alice Springs, Australia.
- The rock formations of Göreme, Turkey.
- The monoliths and mesas of Monument Valley, USA.
- The Alps in Gstaad, Switzerland.
- The temple complex of Angkor Wat at sunset, in Cambodia.
- The Nile and the ruins of Luxor, in Egypt.
- The icebergs in the Canadian Arctic.

The ballooning briefing takes place before sunrise, accompanied by French-pressed coffee and shortbread biscuits. Pilots enthusiastically explain balloon basics as envelopes are stretched out on the ground, awaiting propane-heated air. Morning quiet is punctured by blasts of heat. The wicker basket, weighing over 400 kilograms, is tipped on its side until the rising envelope positions it upright but still held down by ropes so passengers can slide into their separated, padded compartments. Once everyone is on board, the ropes are released, and the balloons ascend without much drama. The high walls of the basket all but force you to look ahead as opposed to straight down. This is fine, especially when the orb of light breaks over the horizon, coating the temples with a fresh layer of golden paint. Since Bagan's temples span over 100 square kilometres, a hot-air balloon is the ideal vehicle from which to take it all in.

As for the politics of Burma a.k.a. Myanmar, I can only hope that by the time you read this, its citizens enjoy the political freedom they so deserve. If not, solace can be found in Bagan's ancient temples, which have seen them come, and seen them go, many times before.

START HERE:
globalbucketlist.com/bagan

Find Your Own Temple

I've climbed inside the pyramids in Cairo, seen the sunrise over Machu Picchu, walked the marble boulevards of Ephesus and witnessed the sunset on the Taj Mahal. As for the sprawling complex of temples in Cambodia, it beats them all. Spend three days exploring ruins that cover 1,000 square kilometres and the history, architecture and exotic adventure will seduce you too.

The Angkor Archaeology Park is what remains of the once powerful Khmer Empire that ruled Cambodia, Thailand, Laos and Vietnam from the 9th to 14th century. The cities were primarily built with wood, so it's the vast stone temples that have survived to this day. That Angkor remained intact after decades of civil war, genocide and a blood-thirsty dictator is a miracle in itself.

Siem Reap is the service town, located just a few kilometres from the complex gates. Although Cambodia might seem like an exotic destination, it packs in plenty of foreign tourists, who fly directly into Siem Reap's slick new international airport. The dusty town is sprinkled with its own temples, "same-same but different" markets and busy parks, but Angkor is the draw. Authorities offer one- and three-day passes, perhaps knowing that two days would be ideal for most of us. Unless you're historically inclined, in which case you can easily spend a week exploring the many ruins before the inevitable temple fatigue sets in. The scale of Angkor is what sets it apart—it's like cramming many ancient wonders into one theme park. Constructed over a 500-year period, the temples vary in

design, with the bas-reliefs and carvings revealing both Hindu and Buddhist influences. Crossing a stone bridge lined with the carvings of angels and demons and seeing the enormous heads of Angkor Thom's South Gate pointing in the four cardinal directions of the compass makes you feel like you've made it—made it to a place you've seen in documentaries, Hollywood movies and magazine pages. Made it somewhere special. A short tuk-tuk ride away, Angkor Wat, with its 60-metre-high spiral towers, is the largest and most famous temple. Like the set of some fantasy movie, it is lined with

stunning carvings and surrounded by an enormous moat. Orange-robed monks and white-robed nuns walk among thousands of daily tourists, adding their own colour to our vivid photographs.

Back in Siem Reap, busy Pub Street is lined with century-old French colonial buildings that have been converted into lush, modern bars and dishy restaurants. Foreign-owned boutiques, bookstores and bars cater to the crowded foot traffic. Political stability, and the fact that tourism is largely conducted in US dollars, has created a tourism boom. Five years after my first visit, the airport road is now lined with dozens of new hotels, built for a steady influx of Japanese, Korean and Chinese visitors. Rock-bottom prices, however, have remained relatively intact. A couple of bucks for meals, tuk-tuk rides, Thai massages.

My guesthouse, located just off the main road, is a steal at under US$15 a night.

There are various methods to get to the temples and, given the jungle heat, walking should not be one of them. Hire a driver or tuk-tuk,

Phnom Penh's Temples, Tortures and Triggers

Cambodia's capital typically soaks up just a day or two of a visitor's itinerary. Guesthouses, hotels and tour operators arrange a full day with a tuk-tuk, so you can visit everything right, wrong and in between. You'll probably start with the impressive temples and Silver Pagoda inside the Royal Palace. If you're

by popping a cap in its ass. For some bizarre reason, especially given the nearby massacres, visiting a firing range in Phnom Penh is something one does. Choose from an AK-47, MI6, M60, K57 and a half-dozen other weapons and let off some steam, no experience necessary.

coming from Thailand, you might be tempered by temple fatigue, but it's well worth the visit. Next up is a deeply disturbing yet vital look inside the Tuol Sleng Genocide Museum, and at the adjacent Killing Fields. With the bloody scars of the Khmer Rouge still visible, it's not easy to stomach, but if you do one thing in Phnom Penh, do this. Finally, send off the day

MASS GRAVE
86 MASS GRAVES
8985 VICTIMS

rent an electric bicycle or a scooter. Guesthouses are happy to arrange everything for you. Whatever you choose, you'll see lush green fields where coconut trees spring from the rice paddies. Local children smile and wave, monkeys chatter cheekily, elephants stand in the shade, their masters ready to take tourists for a literal—and figurative—ride.

Inside the temple complex of Angkor Thom, I ride past the Terrace of the Elephants, with its intricately carved sculptures, and putter toward Ta Prohm, a jungle temple straight out of an Indiana Jones movie (or more accurately, *Tomb Raider*, which used the temple as part of its set). Another, less crowded "root" temple is Ta Som, which has an impressive entrance. Archaeologists have left these temples much as they found them: with enormous fig trees cracking into the stone. It is an eerie, incredible sight, like walking through a modern city in a thousand years from now to find roots growing out of a department store. No matter how important we think we are, or how important the Khmer

thought they were, the jungle waits patiently to reclaim its land.

Visitors gravitate to their own favourite temples, the places where they might forget where they are or feel like they alone are discovering a lost world. Some temples are easily accessible along a popular circuit route. Others, such as the pink sandstone masterpiece of Banteay Srei, are located many miles away. Sometimes it's not about the temples at all but the scenic countryside and waving locals you encounter along the way.

While most historical wonders are safely protected behind ropes, the fact that you can clamber over the steps, pyramid-shaped towers and temples of Angkor lets you literally touch the past. Sure, some of the rock-star temples can get crowded, but there's enough space to make you feel like you're front and centre. Breathe the air in dark, forgotten passages and see candlelight flicker in rooms where dusty statues of Buddha still sit.

START HERE:
globalbucketlist.com/angkor

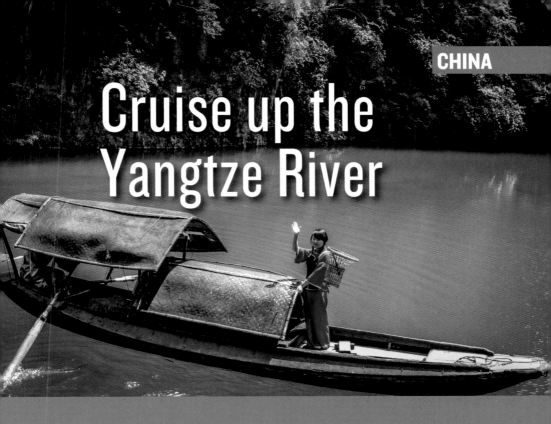

Cruise up the Yangtze River

The boat trackers pull us forward, strain visible from their furrowed brows to their grass sandals. For millennia, men like these helped small boats navigate the narrow channels that splinter off the mighty Yangtze River, using rough ropes to heave wooden vessels along the shallow waters. Today, they perform this arduous task strictly for tourists. With the river now raised 175 metres to accommodate the Three Gorges Dam, modernity has sunk the boat trackers, along with entire towns and villages. Damming the Yangtze River, which the Chinese government called the single greatest engineering feat of all time, displaced over 1 million people above the water line, relocating them to futuristic-sounding "new immigrant cities." The Three Gorges Dam is a hydroelectric project so vast in scale that it generates the equivalent energy of 15 nuclear power plants, supplying 15 per cent of China's hydroelectric power. You can't actually see the Great Wall of China from space, but you *can* see the refashioned Yangtze.

On board one of the dozens of luxury riverboats that explore the world's third-longest river, I am soaking up the river adventure, and the breakneck transformation under way in modern China.

You may not have heard of Wuhan, despite its neon-covered buildings and upscale fashion malls. Yet the departure point for my four-day Yangtze adventure has a population of over 10 million people. Ten. Million. Its downtown core gives me the sense of capitalism run amok; it is an overwhelming sprawl of shopping and advertising and neon and industry, linked by a chain of impressive bridges choking with traffic. Considering the amount of product manufactured in China, I find the selection available in malls and markets surprisingly limited. But I didn't come here to shop. I came for the 6,400-kilometre river with an ancient history that has divided and inspired China through the ages.

Luxury river cruises cater to Chinese nationals and Western clientele, ships like my M.S. *Yangtze Star* offering sumptuous meals, spotless cabins, nightly entertainment, excursions and two staff for every passenger. The idea of floating between the imposing three gorges—Qutang, Wuxia and Xiling—has long attracted travellers. Fears that this might change because of the dam have proved unfounded. Certainly, some towns no longer exist but, at

The Three Gorges Dam, by the Numbers

- To create the world's largest hydropower project, 13 cities, 140 towns and 1,600 villages were flooded, displacing an estimated 1.3 million people.
- When all 32 generators are functioning, the dam generates the equivalent power of 15 nuclear reactors.

- There have been reports of ecological deterioration and cracks. Environmentalists have long warned that the dam will result in catastrophe. It draws water across five major fault lines.
- The dam is 185 metres high and 1,983 metres wide.

the same time, the increased water level now allows riverboats to travel where before they could not. A hot white sky above us, we putter beneath ancient hanging wooden coffins belonging to the Ba people, inhabitants of this region 2,000 years ago. The scenery is lush, the canyons rocky and steep. In the late-afternoon mugginess, we float under the steep peaks of the giant Wuxia Gorge, all the more remarkable considering we are so much higher today than boats were pre-2009.

A cargo boat overflowing with coal narrowly passes us on the right.

"See," says an Italian tourist. "One day this river will be black." China has transformed since Chairman Mao swam in the cleansing waters of the Yangtze. Years of unchecked industrialization have polluted the river yellow-brown (golden, if you listen to Chinese authorities), impacting fish populations and threatening its native river dolphin with extinction. Since the Yangtze no longer flows its natural course, the risks of an environmental disaster like flooding are ever-present.

At the Three Gorges Dam visitors' centre, in the hazy early hours, the scale of the project is clear. The planet's largest locks transfer cargo and cruise ships from one side of the dam to the other. It's a four-hour journey through five massive gates dropping us metres at a time. Controlling the Yangtze has been a dream of China's since the early 1900s, as a means to prevent flooding, harness the power of the river currents and facilitate transport along the river. Since ground breaking in 1994, the project has been both a source of national pride and a global controversy. Environmentalists rue the consequences, archaeologists can only guess at the wealth of history that has been submerged and understandably perplexed locals argue about the impact and methods of displacing so many people. In the end, a commercially exploding country, which is dependent on coal and holds one of every six people on the planet, desperately needs a source of sustainable energy.

Impressive attractions have been built above the waterline to provide more incentive for tourists to visit the region. The Three Gorges Tribe is a postcard vision of life from China's past. Walking along an emerald green tributary, visitors see beautiful, red-robed girls singing on old wooden boats, young boys playing the flute, re-enactors playing nobility and

peasants going about their daily lives. There are musical performances and even a traditional wedding, in which I somehow end up playing the groom. My stand-in mother, a *male* actor, gives me away to a fetching bride, toasting us with firewater (rice wine), and before I know it, I am throwing sweets into the crowd. Beautiful pagodas, temples and music—here is the China that tourists expect to see, and despite it being a manicured imitation, it is quite lovely. On the final stretch to Chongqing, the world's largest municipality with a population of over 28 million, I once again see China's past buried beneath neon streets, shopping malls, markets and towering skyscrapers. More people reside in Chongqing than in Australia and New Zealand combined. Twenty-eight. Million.

The dramatic change along the Yangtze reveals a country embracing the future with such gusto, it appears the traditions of the past might survive only for the pleasure of tourists. Whether this makes you argue, mourn or celebrate, sailing the three gorges of the Yangtze remains, reassuringly, on the Great Global Bucket List.

START HERE:

globalbucketlist.com/yangtze

Track Down an Online Legend

Ever receive a forwarded email containing a dubious photo? An image that solicits a raised eyebrow of disbelief, a vocal "Where the *hell* is that?" It's quite possible you received this one, under the banner of "The World's Most Dangerous Hike" or maybe "Sunday Walks for the Clinically Insane." Beneath a chain-link handrail, you see three narrow wooden planks floating against a wall of solid rock. Snow-capped mountains appear in the distance, and while you can't determine just how high these planks are, you know they're teetering on the edge, much like the nerves of whoever must have put them there.

An uncredited photo of these two-by-four planks stapled against a mysterious mountain haunted my imagination. After a few hours of online sleuthing, I discovered the photo is real, the path does, in fact, exist, and it's located just 120 kilometres from China's historical capital of Xi'an. The city is already a popular destination for bucket listers drawn to its 3,000-year-old history and the nearby Terracotta Warriors. Some foreigners might make the 90-minute drive to Mount Hua, one of China's five sacred mountains, to enjoy the wild views and serene temples. Few know about the Cliffside Plank Path. Accessing it requires no climbing experience, and since I have none to give it anyway, I decide to investigate. Some Internet legends are born to be busted.

I arrive at the base of the mountain Hua Shan to find a parking lot full of domestic tour buses, and cable cars ferrying people to the base peak. Every year, millions of Chinese make a pilgrimage to the five great Taoist mountains, which have long featured in legends, history and art. The West Great "Splendid" Mountain, Hua Shan, attracts thousands of people every day. Besides the visually striking mountains, there are temples, teahouses, trails, viewpoints and opportunities for meditation and reflection. Everything seems harmless enough, though the optional insurance to purchase with your entrance ticket suggests something scary this way comes.

Once atop the base peak, you can visit the various temples and teahouses open to the public, accessed by long concrete paths that snake to the four peaks of the mountain. Steep, slippery steps

are carved directly into rock. Their proximity to 1,000-metre drops does not seem to rattle the cheery Chinese of all shapes, sizes and ages. "We don't encourage foreign tourists to visit Hua Shan," one of them explains to me. "Too dangerous."

There are no hiking boots in sight, though most visitors wear thin white cotton gloves to hold on to the cold, heavy iron chains that bracket the paths. Thousands of engraved locks are clamped to the chains to seal their rusted wishes to the fate of the mountain. My bones,

meanwhile, are starting to rust from the chill.

When I left Xi'an that morning, it was hot and humid. I simply did not expect Mount Hua's 2,160-metre elevation to freeze the air and dust the trees with snow. My thin sweater is suddenly woefully inappropriate for the challenge at hand. But a little cold never killed any . . . well, too many people, right? I follow the helpful signs in broken English toward the "No. 1 Steep Road on Mount Hua." The path in question sits 2,100 metres high, between the south and east peaks. After I've

Holy Mountains in China

China's five sacred Taoist mountains are named according to the Chinese cardinal points: centre, east, west, north and south—and each year, millions of Chinese make the pilgrimage. All have long featured in legends, history and art. The East Great "Tranquil" Mountain, located just north of the city of Tai'an, in Shandong Province, has 22 temples and over 1,000 cliff and stone inscriptions. The South Great "Balancing" Mountain is located in Hunan Province, part of a 150-kilometre mountain range, at the foot of which stands the largest temple in South China. The North Great "Permanent" Mountain is one of the tallest peaks in the country, but its difficult location in Shanxi Province has made it the least accessible of the five. The Center Great "Lofty" Mountain is on the banks of the Yellow River in Henan Province and is home to the famous Shaolin Temple. East China's stunning Yellow Mountains—although not considered one of the five sacred peaks but fabled nonetheless—receive more visitors than any of the others.

walked for an hour, the heavy tourist traffic has petered out to nothing. I exit a beautiful temple, walk around a boulder and spew my pistachio snack right off the sheer rock face. An extraordinary view to be sure, but the mountain path is now only centimetres wide and blasted by strong wind. A sign indicates it will cost 30 RMB (less than five bucks) to continue. I hand over the cash to a bored attendant and receive a harness and set of carabiners. Without gloves, my hands are ice blocks, and in an act of compassion, the attendant takes off his thin white pair and gives them to me. He's likely thinking I'm an idiot who's in way over my head, and rightly so.

Iron bars are hammered into a crevice, and I scale down them slowly. A few feet below, I reach the thin, cracked planks on the rock face. They match those in the photo perfectly. Clipping on to the safety chain above, I shuffle along the wood, overwhelmed by the silence, the mountains, the beauty, the cold, the fear. A 5-centimetre-thick plank of wood is all that separates my feet from the void.

After a few minutes, I hear a fit of giggles from the crevice above. A half-dozen Chinese students

students making their way from the other side. Detaching our safety harnesses, we squeeze over one another, hugging bodies, vulnerable to balance, strong wind, creaky wood and shattered nerves. Over the years, many people have fallen to their deaths. Hence the introduction of the safety harnesses—you know, the ones we have to unclip to pass one another.

I return the gloves to the attendant, stroll back along the cement trail and buy some tea to warm my chilled bones. Is this the world's most dangerous hike? No. Wherever that is, I hope it's not open to the general public. Yet there's plenty of awe and wonder to be experienced exploring China's holy mountains, along with the deep satisfaction of getting one of those emails and being able to say "Yep, I've been there!"

emerge, thrilled to find a foreigner on the path. We take some pictures together, and I walk carefully to the end of the planks, to a small temple in a cave. I presume this is where one offers thanks for making it across alive. To return, I must once again brave the planks, but this time there are more Chinese

START HERE:
globalbucketlist.com/hua

Zipline off the Great Wall of China

CHINA

hina has an incredible 1,300 million people, and it feels like every one of them is lined up this morning in Tiananmen Square to see the stuffed corpse of Chairman Mao. Having already lined up to see Lenin's cadaver in Moscow's Red Square, I reckon one embalmed Communist icon is enough. After walking around Mao's mausoleum (his *Mao*soleum?) and the Monument to the People's Heroes, I veto standing in the lengthy line to see Mao himself—partly because of the oppressive heat, partly because queues drive me crazy and partly because I don't appreciate the crowd police yelling at me with a loudspeaker in a foreign language. A detached female voice also booms "No bags, no cameras, please stand in line" straight out of an Orwellian nightmare. Giving up the corpse, I make my way toward the lively portrait of the chairman at the far end of the square signalling the entrance to the Forbidden City.

Long the seat of emperors, the Forbidden City was so named because the unwashed masses were not allowed inside it for some 500 years. Majestic in scale and vision, it is today open to anyone who can pay the modest entry fee, that is, just about everyone in China. Overwhelming crowds shuffle along the paths, robbing the temples, squares and gardens of their famous tranquillity. I rent a taped walking guide, the voice recording as monotonous as a creaking ceiling fan. And so, as I make my way through the Palace Museum complex, including the Hall of Supreme Harmony, the Palace of Heavenly Purity and the Palace of Earthly Tranquillity, I rue the fact that the closest I will come to their intended purpose is listening to their beautiful names. I choose to avoid the Hall of Literary Brilliance, in a stunning lack of self-confidence.

Relieved to escape the square, I'm promised by a rickshaw driver a "natural air-conditioned" ride back to the hotel but he immediately pedals in the wrong direction. He clearly meant it when he told me he would take me for a ride. I eject, jump in a cab and spend the next hour going nowhere. Picture a python around the neck of a Barbie doll and you'll get a sense of Beijing's choking traffic. At this point, my decision to visit China's capital needs vindication the way

As Not Seen from Space

Blame Ripley's, and don't believe it. In 1932, Ripley's Believe It or Not published a cartoon that claimed the Great Wall of China is visible with the naked eye from the moon. It was quite the statement, since at the time, humans had yet to leave our atmosphere. Nevertheless, the cartoon evolved into an oft-cited factoid, so that many a schoolkid, myself included, grew up *knowing* that the Great Wall of China is the only man-made structure that can be viewed from space. Then people actually went into space, and to the moon, and guess what? No wall. A Chinese astronaut did manage to capture a photograph of the wall with a high-powered camera under ideal conditions, but that doesn't count, as there are other man-made structures that can be captured equally as well. Despite the myth, the public often ask returning astronauts whether they saw the Great Wall of China. NASA's website quotes Apollo 12 astronaut Alan Bean in an article about the ongoing misconception: "The only thing you can see from the moon is a beautiful sphere, mostly white, some blue and patches of yellow, and every once in a while some green vegetation. No man-made object is visible at this scale."

chopsticks need a bowl of noodles. Fortunately, when you hit the wall in Beijing, all you have to do is go for a walk on it.

Visitors to the Great Wall—that awe-inspiring stretch of brick that stretches over 20,000 kilometres across China—usually go to a completely restored section about an hour's drive from Beijing. Here you will find too many tourists and, ultimately, not much of the wall itself. Fortunately, if you're prepared for a six-hour return drive (budgeting for the traffic, of course), you can access the Great Wall at Jinshanling, widely viewed as the best-preserved section of the wall. Scramble up to the walkway and hike across 67 watchtowers surrounded by green valleys and distant mountains you can actually see (most of Beijing is fogged in a cloud of pollution). From Jinshanling, it's a 10-kilometre stroll to the exit and pickup point at Simatai.

The hike's length, together with strenuous climbs to each watchtower and the crumbling condition of certain sections, tend to scare away the crowds. Consequently, I find the rolling wall lanes empty save for enterprising touts selling water, refreshingly cold beer and postcards flaking with the humidity. I cannot help but marvel at the almost incomprehensible scale of the wall, which snakes along the ridges of mountains as far as my eyes can see. No wonder over 1 million people are believed to have died during construction (legends have it that bodies are buried in the wall, or were mixed into the building materials). Sure, it's hot and sticky and thoroughly exhausting, but who wouldn't get a buzz hiking the Great Wall of China, especially when there's someone to sell you a cold beer at the next watchtower? Each tower offers a new view and a chance to rest in the shade as people have for millennia. Some sections are little more than collapsed rock; others, a testament to lasting Chinese ingenuity.

After four hours I reach a long swing bridge that indicates the end of the hike. Authorities have closed the wall up ahead because of dangerous cliffs. A combination of sore legs, heat and thrill-seeking encourages many hikers to cough up a small fee to ride a handy zipline, zapping them to the bottom of the valley in 20 seconds (while eliminating an additional kilometre of walking). Ziplining off the Great Wall of China caps off a remarkable day of history, natural beauty and cold beer. If only one could zipline over the traffic on the return trip to Beijing.

START HERE:
globalbucketlist.com/greatwall

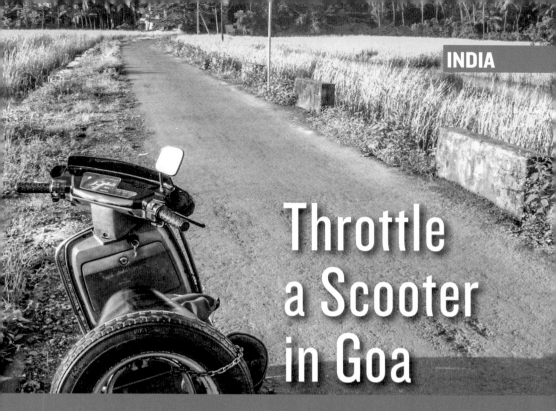

Throttle a Scooter in Goa

Full power! It's a phrase that trance-music freaks scream in Goa when they peak in the absolute bliss of partying nirvana. Some Israeli guys are wearing black T-shirts with *Full Power!* stencilled on them in bright orange. Two travellers are talking at an adjacent table in a beach shack. Like most of the clientele, they wear India's traveller uniform: thin linen pants with loose cotton shirts. "I can't go full power tonight," says one of them. "Not feeling well."

Goa is India's coastal paradise, once a legendary stop on the hippie trail, nowadays enormously popular with tie-dyed techno freaks and UK family tour packages. A Portuguese colony until as late as 1960, Goa consists of several beach towns (see sidebar, page 270), each drawing its own clientele. All are accessible by scooter or bus, so I follow my nose to sleepy Arambol, finding a quiet rustic room for a few bucks a night and perfectly grilled slabs of kingfish for the same. The price is *always* right in India. Sun-dried, grey-haired hippies smoke in the beach cafés. These are the folks who are still tuned in but never made it back from dropping out.

Loose herds of sacred cows roam the beach, dogs yapping at their feet. Some kite-boarders zip over heavy waves, while fishermen tend their lines on the shore. As I walk each evening under coconut trees illuminated by pricks of starlight, the diversity of India continues to amaze me. Manhole-size raindrops fall the following morning and continue to plummet for an entire week. It is the tail end of the monsoon season, with rain lashing out like an injured tiger, slashing the coast with high winds that bend the palm trees into yoga poses. I hole up reading books about religion, the page ends curled with humidity. In the beach restaurants I meet an intriguing cast of international travellers and friendly locals. We play backgammon and plan day trips for sunnier days.

At last, the monsoon concludes and, somehow, the red dirt roads of Arambol are dry within hours. Tarps are removed, stalls reopen, tourism high season has officially begun. Groups of new travellers arrive by the hour. Originally, I planned to stay in Arambol for a couple of days, but it feels like home now. I know the spots with

the best curries, and the stories behind the odd assortment of travellers I share tables with. Aimee and Hayley from Adelaide have been here for seven months, having been stranded by a Thai skipper on a boat trip from Malaysia to Turkey. They've adopted a puppy named Puja and don't look to be leaving anytime soon. Ashi, who arrived three years ago, is a singing Spaniard with bulging eyes. A true cast of characters.

I decide to rent a scooter and bullet along the rice paddies and coconut groves, swerving around cows and buses, stopping in at temples. Although it's not always the safest idea, I love exploring anywhere by scooter *sans* helmet,

Beach Villages in Goa: A Primer

Goa has hundreds of villages, and sniffing out "the next Anjuna" is part of the fun. Here's a quick look at some of the popular options:

Anjuna: Once the epicentre of the hippie trail, Anjuna draws backpackers and holidaymakers with pricier options than Arambol. Visit the hugely popular Wednesday flea market, where the eclectic diversity of visitors will be on full display.

Arambol (pictured above): The village has grown and now has ample accommodation, hundreds of restaurants and market stalls. With a long beach safe for swimming, Arambol has become increasingly family-friendly.

Calangute/Baga: Calangute and the nearby resort town of Baga are the likely destination for European sun-and-sand holiday packages.

All-inclusive resorts line the beach, serviced by shops, restaurants and bars. It is less India, more *anywhere*.

Mandrem: Close to Arambol, Mandrem is a world away from the bustle of Calangute. Quiet beachfront bungalows and resorts attract those interested in yoga, reiki courses, Ayurvedic massages and epic sunsets.

Morjim: The village to check out if you're craving borscht. Russian tourists love this beachfront village, which has nightlife and restaurants straight out of Moscow. Located at the mouth of a river, it's a good location for kitesurfing.

Palolem: The crescent beach of Palolem, once a mellow village for those in the know, has exploded in popularity and become increasingly crowded. Development has notably brought higher prices but also good restaurants and accommodation options.

wind in the hair, sun on the neck. Scooters tickle my heart, and lest I forget, it was a scooter accident that kick-started my travels in the first place. In India, I quickly learn that using my horn is essential, primarily to alert everything else on the road that I exist—and would like to continue to do so. At one point I almost hit a mischievous monkey and can't resist giving it the finger (my opposable thumb, of course). Colourful Hindu temples alternate with small, spooky Portuguese-style churches, and through the green jungle-like thicket I see crumbling old-style villas from another era. I pilot my 125cc Honda rocket ship to Anjuna, ground zero for the trance-hippie scene. Like Arambol, it has a great beach and dozens of restaurants and guesthouses, but prices are significantly higher here. It did not take long for me to start calling a $6 meal in India expensive.

Old Goa rivalled Lisbon as a trading centre during the height of the Portuguese empire. Centuries of fire, corruption and plague have left just a few buildings standing, mainly in the form of enormous European-style cathedrals. I feel like I've scootered through a wormhole and emerged in northern Brazil. With its gold-flaked ornaments and blackened statues of Christ, Old Goa is far removed from the ashrams and temples on the Ganges. I speak to a local named Carlos Gracias, and another named Angela Fernandez. When Pope John Paul II died, India declared a day of mourning. Just over 2 per cent of India's population is Christian, but that adds up to 24 million people, which is more than the population of Portugal, Ireland and Norway combined. Goa's Portuguese roots support Christian family trees, which make this state vastly different from others in the country.

From Old Goa, I explore the state capital Panjam before returning to the embrace of Arambol. Each evening, I lounge at my favourite restaurant, where beer is cheap and old-timers strum songs on their chipped guitars. Mothers are cradling babies, a light drum or flute adds to the rhythm. It's the kind of place where time dissolves like sugar in hot masala tea. The monsoon that spring cleans the beaches is a distant memory; now, a warm evening breeze dances between my fingertips. More and more travellers are discovering Goa, and some of them, understandably, are reluctant to leave. In the film *The Bourne Supremacy*, superspy Jason Bourne (played by Matt Damon) and his girlfriend disappear under the radar in a bucket list tropical paradise. We see him jogging on the beach, his bikini-clad girlfriend loving life in a beach bar. Unfortunately, pursuing Russian assassins had Goa on their bucket list too.

START HERE:
globalbucketlist.com/goa

Witness the Taj Mahal at Sunset

"You can't visit India and not see the Taj Mahal!" proposes someone, seconded by someone else and agreed to by the majority of the bucket list strata. I'd just spent a month exploring India, discovering less-known but just as impressive structures like New Delhi's Jama Masjid, built in 1656 by the same bloke behind the Taj Mahal. I loved the Red Fort, as well as Mumbai's Gothic Chhatrapati Shivaji Terminus (the former Victorian Terminus). In Rishikesh, I participated in a traditional *puja* on the Ganges, and saw the Dalai Lama inside his inner sanctuary located in the mountains of Dharamsala. Would India's most famous tourist attraction be the cherry on the cheesecake or a disappointing mousetrap?

Europe's holiday season is almost at an end, bringing thousands of backpackers to Delhi, who await their return flights home. Subsequently, accommodation is scarce, and the only place I can find at seven in the morning after a bone-shaking night bus from the north is a ground-floor prison cell with boarded up windows and bathroom muck so thick I can build a mountain with it. Close Encounters of the Third Grime. A stained Hello Kitty bedspread is a pleasant, if somewhat disturbing, touch. I dump my bags, abandon sleep altogether and hail a taxi for Delhi's train station. Before I can pay my driver, a charming fellow rushes up to convince me I can avoid long lineups and buy a train ticket inside an office across the street. Here I find a desk beneath a sign that reads: OFFICIAL GOVERNMENT BOOKING OFICE. If you're going to scam tourists, it pays to use spellcheck.

It takes me three hours to buy an authentic return ticket to Agra, the city that services and surrounds the Taj Mahal. First I must get a number, speak to official number one, who refers me to official number two, who tells me I have to go to the office downstairs, number 203, where I'm told I have to go to the office upstairs, number 301. I have two hours to kill before the train leaves, so at least all this gives me something to do. The key to travelling in India is to never be in a hurry to get anywhere. Ever. You're only going to drive yourself crazy, and there's no point complaining, because everyone around you is crazy already.

On the train platform, I ask some elderly Europeans if they are going to Agra. They avoid eye contact and brush past me. When I finally see what I look like in a cracked mirror, I understand why. I am wearing my one month in India. Eyes red and shifty, like the front of the Trans Am in *Knight Rider*; arms and neck covered in bug bites. Having not showered for a while, I smell like a burnt pakora. All this helps me blend in with a platoon of friendly Indian army soldiers, who ask me questions and offer me curries in tin cups. The train takes an interminable age to reach Agra, where tourists are led like sheep to the marble slaughterhouse. By the time I negotiate a taxi, stop off to get some overpriced lunch and arrive at the main gate, my

expectations are sky-high. Also sky-high is the special tourist price, 40 times more than the local's price. Relative to other costs in India, it's like paying $300 to visit the Eiffel Tower. How could the Taj Mahal possibly be worth all this?

Several thousand domestic tourists are lined up at the Western Gate, but for a 50-rupee tip, a young boy directs me to the Southern Gate, where the lineup is a fraction of the length. Money well spent. As for the entrance fee, I agree that locals should pay less than foreigners, especially in India, but one can't help but feel violated. Concurring, the guards actually light a cigarette after taking my money. I am searched and have a calculator and MP3 player confiscated—I can collect them at the conclusion of my visit. I have no idea what threat either presents to the ivory tower of romance, but having not slept in 36 hours, I decide it's best to adhere to one of the principles of Islam: submission. Almost there, just one more archway and . . .

Oh my! Burning through the haze of Agra, the late-afternoon sun sparkles on the white marble. Even with thousands of people about, the Taj Mahal hovers like a fairy-tale palace, a real-life manifestation of wild imagination. I take a memory card worth of pictures, scoping out the angles, kicking off my shoes to look inside (there's not much to see). Mogul emperor Shah Jahan commissioned the building to house the body of his second wife, who tragically died during childbirth. Unveiled after 20 years of construction, in 1653, it is a remarkable and timeless send-off. Without doubt, this is one of the planet's most magnificent structures.

Shortly after sunset, I begin the long journey home: the three, make that four—oh look, it's a five-hour train ride to the wrong station.

A little girl pees in the middle of the crowded carriage passageway, her yellow stream dribbling slowly to either end with the pulsating motion of the train. A young boy falls asleep next to me, resting his head against my arm. His mom looks at me with a strange mixture of embarrassment and pride. The train finally arrives and I return to the backpacker neighbourhood of Paharganj in Central Delhi for sleep so deep a freight train could not wake me up.

Perhaps you too harbour dreams of visiting India but are afraid of all the madness that writers like me seem to go on about. Don't be. There is nowhere else on earth like India, and it evokes emotions that few countries will. My eventful journey to the Taj Mahal was not unlike my month-long journey: frustrating, uncertain, sweaty, smiley and, finally, full of the undeniable magic that makes it all worthwhile.

START HERE:
globalbucketlist.com/tajmahal

How to Not Get Sick in India

It is possible to travel extensively in India and not get a case of Delhi Belly. What's more, you'll be sampling some of the best food on the planet.

- **Don't drink tap water:** Obviously, enough said. Keep a bottle of drinking water handy for brushing your teeth. Importantly, watch out for ice in drinks.

- **Don't eat meat:** A significant number of Indians are vegetarians, and the cooking of vegetables has been elevated to an art. You won't miss meat.

- **Don't eat uncooked cheese:** Cheese is heaven for nasty microbes. Paneer is fine—it's an Indian cheese cooked in many amazing curries.

- **Don't eat eggs:** Leave the sunny-side-up treats back home. An undercooked egg will tie your intestine into a sailor's knot.

- **Don't drink milk:** Most travellers do well with lassi, a delicious yoghurt-based drink. Ask beforehand if it is mixed with tap water or ice.

- **Don't eat fish unless you see it caught and cooked:** On the coast, fish doesn't come fresher, though you may want to make sure that's the case first.

- **Don't eat uncooked vegetables, and peel your fruit:** Most vegetables are cooked in curries so delicious your taste buds will dance a Bollywood musical.

- **Always wash or sanitize your hands, especially before eating:** Just like your mom taught you.

Look Out for Dragons

If squirrels are rats with good marketing, what can we say about the feared Komodo dragon? The world's biggest lizard recalls an evil force of destruction (the Hobbit), a lovable pet (*How to Train Your Dragon*), a fearless steed (*Avatar*), wise warriors (*DragonHeart*), musical stoners (Puff the Magic Dragon), a breathing weapon (*Game of Thrones*) and a lacrosse team's mascot (San Francisco Dragons). Bruce Lee chop-sueyed opponents in *Enter the Dragon*. A moody goth-hacker with a large dragon tattoo took on corrupt Swedish officials. Marvel's Fantastic Four battled a humanoid android named Dragon Man (whatever the hell that is). Every week, an entire subculture of gamers who barely know sunlight enter imaginary dungeons to battle their dragons, while the first commercial spacecraft to deliver cargo to the International Space Station and return safely to earth is called . . . *The Monitor*. Just kidding, it's the SpaceX *Dragon*.

The Komodo dragon, however, a freakishly overgrown type of monitor lizard, dominates its ecosystem just as surely as it does our imagination. A real live dragon! Imagine how different our conception of it would be if the species hadn't picked up its nickname from adventurer W. Douglas Burden.

Burden's 1926 expedition to the remote islands of Indonesia captured two live beasts and brought them to New York, a wonderful tale of old-world adventure that inspired the movie *King Kong.* Your own adventure to the islands of Komodo National Park is unlikely to be as thrilling. Reptiles, particularly those at the top of the food chain, are prone to lazing in the sun all day, especially when they have an ever-present food source in the form of garbage. Meanwhile, tour operators, especially those in certain parts of Asia, are prone to milking every dollar they can sniff from international tourists hoping to see a rare creature with the coolest name in the animal kingdom.

Visiting the islands of Rinca and Komodo is typically an overnight trip for tourists flying in from Bali or taking a boat tour from the port city of Labuan Bajo on the island of Flores. Depending on the season, tours may be quite busy, and everyone must pay the entrance fee, park tax, and photo and video fee, while enduring all the paperwork that comes with it. Once you're through the bureaucracy, rest assured, there will be dragons, and not exactly slouches either.

Komodos grow up to 3 metres in length, weigh up to 70 kilograms,

A Fine Cup (of Crappy Coffee)

Indonesia produces the world's most expensive cup of coffee. Kopi luwak sells retail between US$100 and US$600 a pound in North America (around $50 a cup). Supplies are extremely limited because, well, there's only so much crap a poor civet can take. Kopi luwak are coffee beans that have passed through the digestive tract of a civet, a weasel-like creature that consumes beans along with berries. The digestive process removes the bitterness of the bean and gives it a distinctive, sought-after flavour in the process. From Java, Sumatra, Bali and elsewhere in Indonesia, the coffee makes its way to the finest kitchens in the world. If you find yourself paying too much for a cup of coffee that tastes like ripe turd, take solace in the luxury. The rest of us will sip on plain old arabica instead.

bite with toxic venom, eat up to 80 per cent of their body weight in a single meal and are known to ruthlessly ambush their prey. This includes deer, water buffalo and the occasional human being. Not too long ago, a group of stranded scuba divers washed up on Rinca and had to fight off attacking dragons for two long days and two longer nights. Islanders who share their living space with the vicious carnivore occasionally, although surprisingly rarely, end up in the belly of the beast. Dragons can smell blood from nearly 10 kilometres away, so if you cut your finger in your hut, make sure that your door is closed. Fortunately, most of the lizards are well fed and experienced guides keep encounters incident-free.

There are an estimated 4,000 dragons left in the wild, and seeing them in their natural habitat is undoubtedly a thrill. One might argue an encounter with marine iguanas in Galapagos, crocodiles in the Zambezi or large sea turtles in Borneo is just as significant. Give those guys a little PR spin, nickname them "unicorn iguanas," "ghost crocodiles" and "monster turtles"; soon enough, our fearsome dragon may have additional reptilian company on the bucket list.

START HERE:
globalbucketlist.com/komodo

Explore the Holy Land

Passengers clap and cheer when the plane's wheels touch down at Ben Gurion Airport. Israel inspires that sort of emotion. It's been 16 years since my last visit, and in that time, the country has evolved through a tech boom, the Second Intifada, various political crises and several tense years of peace. For all the news Israel gets, it's still just a sliver of land in the Middle East, and for all its cosmopolitan edge—including a nightlife rated among the world's best—Tel Aviv is only the size of a small American city. I wouldn't think 400,000 people can sustain a 24/7 city, with cracking bars, clubs and all-night restaurants.

Jet-lagged, I drop my bags and find my way to a drinking hole called The Minzar. In this bar that never closes, I find an eclectic clientele chatting, drinking and smoking, the big issues being hashed out with raised voices and plenty of hand movement. Classic rock bounces off the walls. It's 2 a.m. on a weeknight. I wonder when people sleep.

The Dan Tel Aviv has seen its share of politicians, pop and movie stars: the Clintons, Madonna, Leonardo DiCaprio. My room faces the beach, and it's the beach that surprises me most: big, clean and brown-sugar sandy, with an attractive Copacabana-like promenade. A white heron watches men fish, while surfers run about looking for the best breaks. Removed from hot-spot borders and settlements, locals tell me Tel Aviv is its own world within a country. Old parts of the city have been renewed into entertainment districts like the Old Tel Aviv Port, or turned into trendy neighbourhoods, like arty Neve Tzedek. The city has the world's largest collection of Bauhaus buildings, now a UNESCO World Heritage Site, running up leafy Rothschild Boulevard. I pop into Shampina, a hipster champagne

lounge; then enjoy the wild art at Nanuchka, a Georgian bar; and wind up at an underground speakeasy, where I chat with a beautiful girl who is half Czech, half Yemeni. Jews from 125 countries have made Israel their home. In Tel Aviv, the melting pot runneth over.

Up north, the Sea of Galilee is casting a purple glow across the sky, its calm waters reflecting the Golan Heights. During a college break in 1993, I spent two months volunteering at a kibbutz nearby. Then, as now, kibbutz represented a cheap escape to an unusual, meaningful lifestyle. The sleepy lakeside resort town of Tiberias looks much now

as it did then, a destination for tourists and pilgrims following in the footsteps of Jesus. The church at the Mount of Beatitudes looks over the site where Jesus is said to have preached his sermon and walked on water. It often feels as if the entire country is a biblical theme park, full of names and places mentioned in the bible, laced with Roman and Crusader ruins—like those found at Caesarea, Acre and Beit She'an. At the Scots Hotel in Tiberias, Christian bible groups, Jewish tourists, students and hikers make for an interesting mix in the hotel restaurant. We gather in the hotel's bar, where a Russian bartender serves us excellent single malts. Prices are not cheap, but the pour is generous, and the blend of clientele is definitely interesting.

Jerusalem syndrome is an unusual mental condition that strikes hundreds of visitors to the holiest city in the Holy Land each year. Victims get swept up in a delusional messianic rapture, inspired by the names and places so familiar from the bible. Jerusalem's ancient yellow stone resonates, no matter your beliefs. Jews around the world pray in its direction, and in Jerusalem, they pray toward the Temple

Mount. Islam's third most holy site, the Dome of the Rock, gleams above it in the late-afternoon sun. The Dome sits on the exact site of the Holy of Holies, the most important site of the first and second Jewish temples, and is therefore a powder keg for fundamentalists of both religions. Heavy rain has cleared away the plaza where Jews gather to pray at the famous Western Wall—all that remains of their holy temple. Small notes containing prayers and wishes have been stuffed into the wall's ancient cracks. I see a fragile, skinny man rocking back and forth. The following day, I spot the same man swaying at the exact same location. I wonder if he's especially devout, or if he's coming down with the syndrome.

It's a short walk from Temple Mount to the Church of the Holy Sepulchre. I pass Christian tourists carrying a large wooden cross to the 14 Stations of the Cross, retracing the final steps of Jesus Christ. It takes them through the narrow streets of the Arab Quarter, lined with souvenir shops. The Church of the Holy Sepulchre holds the site of Golgotha (also known as Calvary), the place where Jesus was crucified. Just steps away is the Stone of Anointing, where Jesus' body was laid

Big Facts, Small Country

For all the attention it gets in the news, we often forget how small Israel actually is. This is one of the reasons land ownership is so controversial. Israel is smaller than Wales. It is smaller than Vancouver Island. It would occupy a mere sliver of California, and be drowned by the waters of Lake Michigan. Tel Aviv's beachfront is as long as the country is wide at its narrowest point. Yet Israel produces 93 per cent of its own food, has the highest university-degrees–to-population and museums-to-population ratios in the world, and has more companies listed on the NASDAQ than any other country save the United States and Canada. Israeli technology has given the world voicemail, the cell phone, antivirus software, instant messaging, smart cards, Pentium microprocessors and ingestible video cameras for medical diagnosis. It welcomes homosexuals, boasts the most Bauhaus buildings in the world, publishes more translated books than any other nation and is the only country in the world to have revived an unspoken language (Hebrew) into a national tongue, shared with Arabic as its official language. Nine out of 10 homes use solar power to heat water, and yes, there is a store in Jaffa that sells hummus-flavoured ice cream.

down, rubbed with oil and prepared for burial. Visitors place their foreheads on the stone, along with bags containing souvenirs to be blessed. A few steps away is the Tomb of Jesus, where I light a candle in respect. Around me, many devoted Christians break down in tears. It doesn't matter what religion you follow, or even if you believe in God. Walk aimlessly through the quarters and history of Old Jerusalem simply to savour its ambiance. There is nowhere in the world quite like it.

Not far from the Knesset, where fragmented political parties scrap together ruling coalitions, lie two defining sites of the nation: the Israel Museum, which houses the Dead Sea Scrolls, displays the earliest bible texts ever discovered and acts as a physical link to a past stretching back 2,000 years. On Mount Herzl, the Mount of Remembrance, is Yad Vashem, the Holocaust Museum. I walk through a maze of cement rooms as the guide explains the rise of Hitler, the rot of anti-Semitism, the ghettos, the death camps.

"We have to personify what happened," explains the guide, now somewhere in another room, her voice a whisper in my wireless headset. "Only then can we begin to understand the numbers." With the tour concluding inside the haunting Hall of Names beneath a spiral of photos and tragedy, Yad Vashem is not an easy visit but an essential one.

How does one pick up the pieces after the Holocaust? You look around, and see miracles. Jews somehow moved on, rebuilt their lives and created a future in their Promised Land. Modern Israel, a prosperous nation, is a testament to what dreams and hard work can accomplish. It is a young nation, sometimes prone to impetuous and hotheaded behaviour, just like its citizens, also full of accomplishments, challenges, threats. No other democracy has foreign presidents and even its own voting citizens— fundamentalist Arabs and Jews— openly calling for its complete annihilation. But for all the sour news stamped onto international newsprint, Israel is an essential destination on our bucket list. As for the politics? The moderates I meet, of every faith, simply want to live in peace. Israel and its Palestinian neighbours deserve a future. When that day finally comes—*Baruch HaShem*, *In sha' Allah* and Please God—there will be clapping and cheering around the world.

START HERE:
globalbucketlist.com/israel

283

Float in the Dead Sea

ISRAEL/JORDAN

One doesn't swim in the lifeless waters of the Dead Sea. One experiences them. With water 9.6 times saltier than that of the ocean, the lowest point on earth is not a sea at all. Much like Saskatchewan's Little Manitou Lake, Djibouti's Lake Assal and Lake Vanda in Antarctica, it is merely a saltwater lake. When it comes to bucket list soaks, however, one should live by the popular real estate mantra: Location, location, location. The Dead Sea separates Israel and Jordan, two exceptional countries divided by faith. Both Israel and Jordan are rife with hotels and cosmetics factories that capitalize on visiting tourists, and the mud they will inevitably buy when they do. Rich in minerals and with qualities that treat acne, psoriasis, dry skin, hives and dandruff, the mud of the Dead Sea is processed and sold in small tubes at prices far beyond the going rate for backyard dirt.

One of the many benefits of actually visiting the Dead Sea is that you can slather your body with as much of this storm-cloud-coloured mud as it can bear. You can feel it pull the toxins right out of your skin as it begins to dry. You can build mud sculptures, or even have mud fights, though you definitely do not want to get it in your eyes. Not even Rambo can rub away the pain of Dead Sea in the eyeballs. Apparently Sylvester Stallone was in the area filming *Rambo III* and disregarded sound advice to keep his head above water. He dived in headfirst and ended up in hospital.

Fittingly, given its name, the Dead Sea is actually dying. As waters continue to evaporate, it is receding at a rate of 1 metre each year. The waterline during my first visit in 1987 is marked some distance from the current one. Many

The Dead Sea Scrolls

In 1947, a young Bedouin shepherd went looking for his goat, and instead found the greatest historical manuscripts of all time. Hidden in clay pots inside a series of caves for almost 2,000 years, over 800 scrolls contain the oldest known copies of the Old Testament and reams of additional writing from a Jewish sect called the Essenes. Academics, historians and theologians have been in a tizzy analyzing the fragments ever since. Visit the Hershey Bar–shaped Shrine of the Book at Jerusalem's Israel Museum to see many of the scrolls for yourself.

The Treasury at Petra

You saw it in *Indiana Jones*, and it's tough to stop whistling Indy's theme song walking down the rock channel to this 2,000-year-old Nabataean ruin. Jordan's most popular attraction, Petra's Treasury, is actually a tomb (misnamed by treasure hunters) that glows red in the late-afternoon sun. It's the highlight of a vast ancient city with much to explore (don't miss the Urn Tomb). Good hotels nearby, fresh hummus, the musky smell of camel—it's not exactly Indiana Jones's last crusade but deservedly takes its place on the bucket list.

tourist beaches are no longer safe due to the emergence of deep sinkholes as water continues to drain from underground caverns.

Rather encouragingly, marketing agencies from Israel, Jordan and the Palestinian Authority cooperated to enter the Dead Sea in one cohesive bid for a "New7Wonders of Nature" marketing promotion. In a region with so much turmoil, this singular fact is far more interesting than the competition itself.

Just off the beach in Jordan's luxury Mövenpick hotel, I'm floating in cool waters at sunset, watching the lights of Jerusalem twinkle 35 kilometres away. To my right, the Palestinian village of Jericho greets the evening stars. Relaxing in a silky saltwater embrace, I feel the travel tingle one gets ticking off any bucket list experience, the buzz of living life to its fullest, even when floating in a lifeless sea.

START HERE:
globalbucketlist.com/deadsea

Camp Overnight in Wadi Rum

JORDAN

Wadi is an Arabic term for valley or dry riverbed. *Rum*, in this particular case, is the name of a 720-square-kilometre desert in southern Jordan, populated by seven Bedouin tribes. It is unlikely you will ever camp with nomadic Bedouins in a valley of alcohol, but this other-worldly landscape is certainly rich in spirit. Wadi Rum, a UNESCO World Heritage Site, is one of the most popular destinations in Jordan, and for good reason. Three-and-a-half-hours' drive from the capital of Amman, the scenic valley and archaeological sites can be explored by camel, horse, foot or Jeep. The adventurous will be drawn to the stellar rock climbing (surely a highlight for any climber's bucket list). This time, however, the Great Global Bucket List prefers a more cultural adventure. Local Bedouins have run the protected habitat's tourism services with great success. While some tribes have relocated to permanent villages, others still roam the wadi as they have done for millennia.

At the visitor centre, I am welcomed with a red kaffiyeh, which is wrapped tightly around my head, Bedouin style, and led to a dromedary—a single-humped camel. Hold your horses! Since we're going to be riding one for a while, it's worth learning more about these even-toed ungulates:

- The camel originated in North America, migrating to Asia across the Bering land bridge.
- They do not store water in their humps, but rather in body fat.

- Most mammals will die if they lose 15 per cent of their body weight in water. Camels can lose 30 per cent without harm.
- They can live up to 60 years, carry 200 kilograms, drink 100 litres of water in 10 minutes and fight off predators with their teeth.
- They smell something awful—especially if you happen to be downwind of one in Jordan.

After clumsily hopping aboard the beast (there's no unclumsy way to get on a camel), I am guided by a leather-skinned Bedouin man into the wadi. Hardcore travellers swear one should always use local transport, and in this case, I agree. Traditionally robed, I feel like Robin of Arabia, perhaps because director David Lean filmed *Lawrence of Arabia* in this very location. More recently, Wadi Rum was used as the location for the filming of *The Martian*. It isn't hard to see why. Lifeless sand, red rocks and melted-chocolate cliffs inspire visions of Mars (confirmed by another sci-fi flick filmed here, *Red Planet*). Of all the ecosystems on my bucket list—jungles, beaches, mountains, plains—exploring a desert evokes the deepest emotion for me. I've been lost in two deserts, albeit briefly, and both memories are accompanied by inspiration, as opposed to fear. There is something about the sand, the splendour of the rocks, the comforting warmth of the wind. Now I'm steering my camel under archways glowing in the late afternoon, ripples in the sand kidnapping shades of the blood orange sunset.

We arrive at our camp, consisting of a half-dozen goat-haired Bedouin tents. Guests can choose to sleep inside or outside, but the promise of exceptional stargazing typically makes the decision for them. Grateful to be back on my own feet, my butt reeling with the rolling motion that characterizes a camel's gait, I explore the surrounding area, scrambling up a cliff facing east. My *abaya*, a traditional Arab cloak, dances like Batman's cape in the strong wind. I remove my kaffiyeh, hold it by two corners

for a moment and let it go, watching it float in the breeze like a wonderful impression of that plastic bag in *American Beauty*. Shades of peach fuzz pop in the dusk sky, a moment of certified bucket list travel buzz.

Reclaiming my garment below, I return to the camp to find a feast being buried in the sand. It will take three hours for lamb, chicken and vegetables to be cooked by the hot desert sand in traditional Bedouin style. It is served with all manner of breads, dips and delights, along with sweet sage tea to soothe my dry throat. Huddled under blankets by the fire, I scan the night sky for shooting stars. I count 23 before my lids close and everything goes black. It has been as memorable a day as any you'll find on this bucket list, a mezze of culture, natural beauty and unforgettable desert adventure.

START HERE:
globalbucketlist.com/wadirum

Float down the Mekong

I first heard about Vang Vieng from three British backpackers in northern Brazil. To be honest, I thought they were six sips short of a pint. There are many travel legends and myths in the world, but this one sounded just a little too good to be true. Apparently—and you'll need to read this using a British accent—"There is this village in central Laos, right, and what you do, right, is get yourself a rubber tube, right, and float down this bloody fantastic Mekong River, I mean for hours, right, and stop all along the way to enjoy these *cheeky* river bars, right, and it's just crawling with beautiful people, right, and 50-pence bottles of the world's best cheap beer!" Right on.

Half a year later, I decide to see if this particular legend is true. To get there, I will spend two days floating down the Mekong River inside a coffin-shaped boat, have large rats eat a hole in my backpack, live through an all-night ritual pig slaughter and survive a harrowing minibus ride with countless blind corners, blind hills and, possibly, blind drivers. Within a few hours of arriving in Vang Vieng, I decide that it was all worth it. My right-o British friends *had* been right on the money.

The village is bustling with travellers from around the world, lounging in bars and cafés, all to a reggae soundtrack. Now, there are a fair number of inexplicable cultural phenomena on our planet—David Hasselhoff's fame in Germany, sumo wrestling rock stars in Mongolia, Justin Bieber— and one of them is the *Friends* TV show in Laos. It's played non-stop on pirated DVDs in the town's restaurants and bars, so I sit back and let the mindless banter of Rachel and Monica and Joey and Ross and oh-God-I'm-going-to-be-sick wash over me until I achieve sitcom Zen and start getting into it. On the plus side, it does provide

Kip to Be Square

In Laos, everyone's a millionaire. That's because the local currency, the kip, typically trades at about ₭8,000 to US$1. Convert US$124 and voilà, you're a millionaire too. Denominations range from ₭500 to ₭100,000 notes. Since bank machines are costly to use and few and far between, you'll likely find yourself doing the kip fandango: overloading your pockets and backpack with thick wads of bills. You might be tempted to empty notes on the bed and roll around in them but, unfortunately, kip bills are about as fresh and crisp as week-old Caesar salad. Don't be caught kipping with too much kip either, since once you leave Laos they are basically useless.

something to do when the rain starts to pour.

Picture fresh fruit shakes, yoga, pillows and blankets draped in little pits of bohemian paradise. Delicious Thai-influenced food abounds at ridiculously low prices. Then there is Beerlao, undoubtedly the finest brew in Southeast Asia. You see people wearing Beerlao T-shirts all over the subcontinent—hell, I've seen a couple around North America too. Somewhat malty, well-balanced, crisp yet refreshing and less than $1 a bottle. Beerlao (sounds like "Beer-owl") is the

final ingredient we need to create a budget-travel paradise. Drum roll, please, for the star attraction: the bucket list–worthy Vang Vieng tubing experience.

You rent a black tire inner tube, the rental of which includes a ride on the back of a truck for about 10 kilometres upstream. Once there, plop in the warm water, sit on your tube and begin to float along with the gentle current of the Mekong. Within minutes, you'll hear the music of Bob Marley or Jack Johnson or Manu Chao. Soon enough, a local with a long stick will offer to pull you toward your first river bar. As a means of attracting clientele, the bars offer music, water slides, platforms and swings, which are usually included in the price of a bottle of beer. Float on, enjoying the lush riverside scenery in the shade of tall jagged mountains, perhaps having a meaningful conversation with your fellow spirited floaters, buoyed by the warm sun and cold beer. Suitably refreshed, mount your rubber doughnut and continue on your merrier way, forming new communities with your friends, foot-connected on your floating rubber bagels.

It can take anywhere from two hours to an entire day to get back to Vang Vieng, depending on how long you choose to stay at the bars. After six hours, the sun slowly setting behind the mountains, I

waft back into town, drop off my tube and have an early-evening nap before hitting nearby cafés to reconnect with new tubing buddies from around the world.

Dozens of guesthouses and hotels have sprung up to capitalize on increasing tourist traffic to the region. It's the kind of place travellers plan to visit for one day and end up staying for a week, visit for one week and stay for a month. A local tells me that Vang Vieng was a fraction of the size just a few years ago and is growing too big for its own inner tube. Perhaps it is too big already. But if you do find yourself in Laos, I wouldn't worry. Vang Vieng will be there for you.

START HERE:
globalbucketlist.com/vangvieng

Bungee off a TV Tower

MACAU

Given that I once wrote a column called "Thrillseeker," you might think I'd enjoy jumping headfirst off the edge of a 233-metre-tall TV tower. To be honest, the world's highest commercial bungee jump held as much appeal as did playing Russian roulette with a fully loaded revolver. There is a distinct difference between gung-ho base-jumping adrenalin junkies, and us bucket listers who simply do these things because, as Sir Edmund Hillary attested, they are there to do. On seeing Macau Tower, I can already feel my knees jackhammering away at each other, but life is too short for *shoulda-coulda-woulda*. Here in the world's biggest gambling centre, I am eager to take the leap and risk it all.

Along with Hong Kong, Macau is a special administrative region (SAR) of China. What this means is that both SARs belong to the same quasi-Communist country club but follow a different set of rules. While the Chinese love to gamble, it is illegal to do so on the mainland. Not so on the island of Macau. A 45-minute ferry ride from Hong Kong, Macau has now surpassed Las Vegas in gambling receipts. With billions of dollars of foreign investment—largely Vegas-style casino developments—the former Portuguese (and once quiet) colony is booming. Macau's old town still maintains some European charm (complete with 17th-century fortresses and churches) and is a UNESCO World Heritage Site. But scattered throughout the island are the main draw: glitzy casinos beaming neon into the sticky night sky.

Wynn Macau is a spectacular riot of colour. Glowing Grand Lisboa is straight out of a science-fiction movie, while the Venetian battles it out with the nearby City of Dreams to be the world's biggest casino. With over a billion people on the mainland to support the boom, gambling moguls are dreaming big. Hong Kong real estate tycoon

Stanley Ho is one such mogul. Inspired by Auckland's Sky Tower, he felt Macau needed a sky-scraping landmark of its own. Built over four years and opened in 2001, the Macau Tower is one of the world's tallest free-standing structures: 338 metres at its highest point, with a visitor deck at the top where you can gaze out over the construction bubble.

I'm not here to admire the view. There's a bungee cord with my name on it. New Zealander A.J. Hackett is widely credited as having introduced bungee jumping to the masses in the late 1980s, both as a pioneer jumper and entrepreneur. His operation is the brain behind turning a TV tower into a sky-high urban playground. For now, Hackett's Macau Tower is listed in the Guinness book of records as the world's highest commercial bungee jump. It claims to use the most bungee-advanced technology, but as I'm tugged toward the edge of the platform by a heavy, 50-metre-long elastic, this fact does little to assure my nerves. At this point, my sphincter can pretty much make diamonds from coal. There is no gentle way to hurl headfirst toward concrete at 193 kilometres an hour, swallowing

a five-second free fall, and then rebound to do much of it all over again.

The dreaded countdown begins, and then . . . everything is a blur. There's too much stimulation and fear to bother with screaming. I'd say life rushes before my eyes, except I can see the ground rushing toward my eyeballs. Just as I brace for death, the bungee recoils, shooting me back up toward the platform. It takes the mind a few seconds to gather its wits, and the last place you want that to happen is suspended during the recoil of the world's highest bungee jump. I plunge once more. This time I scar my throat with screaming, until finally, at last, the bounce settles and I find myself upside down, talking to a camcorder duct-taped to my hand. I use the word *insane*. A lot.

Kept in position by pilot cords (to avoid wrapping around the tower's trunk), the bungee is slowly lowered onto a giant air mattress on the ground. All the blood in my body has rushed to my head, and I can't quite decide if I feel horror, relief or adrenalin-soaked happiness. No matter how many chips the casinos rake in, ticking off this fearsome bucket list adventure is like winning the jackpot.

START HERE:
globalbucketlist.com/macau

Bungee Jumps on the Bucket List

Thrill-seekers will jump off just about anything. Below are listed commercial operations where normal folks can take their own leap of faith.

Bloukrans Bridge, South Africa: Bloukrans used to be the highest commercial jump at 216 metres. It still gets bonus points for the comely bridge, the surrounding scenery, the location on the Garden Route and the traffic-stopping action.

The Nevis, New Zealand: 134 metres above the Nevis Gorge is a tiny suspended cabin blowing in the wind. To reach it, you must brave an open-air cable car, and only *then* can you take on the upsettingly scary eight-second bungee free fall.

Verzasca Dam, Switzerland: Oh, James! Remember that scene in *GoldenEye* when James Bond bungees off a 220-metre-high dam wall? It's known as one of the best stunts in movie history. Well, strap in, 008, you can do it too, and at the exact same location.

Victoria Falls Bridge, Zimbabwe: On the plus side, the crocodiles swimming 111 metres below in the Zambezi River might distract you from the remote chance your bungee might snap. Which actually happened in 2011. And it's on YouTube.

Monkey Around in Borneo

MALAYSIA

Although it is technically dry season, Kota Kinabalu is still so wet, the atmosphere has turned to water to save rain the trouble of falling. Parts of the town, located on the north coast, are flooded. Locals appear more bothered about the FIFA World Cup, which screens live at three in the morning. Malays are notoriously nuts about their soccer, and there is speculation that the guy who jumped off a nearby building yesterday—making the *Borneo Times'* front page and, I imagine, a rather unpleasant mess on the sidewalk—did it because of his team's poor performance. "People kill themselves whenever it's the World Cup," explains a taxi driver, as if that explains everything.

Borneo, the world's third-largest island, is terrifically exotic. I expect to find dense jungle, strange wildlife and hairy bugs—and I am not disappointed. The island is split between three countries: Indonesia, Malaysia and the wealthy sliver of oil-rich Brunei, where the sultan owns 5,000 cars and locals don't pay taxes. It's a lot to cover, so I'm focusing on the Malaysian state of Sabah, which includes the bonus of Malay cooking. I am itching to feast on those rich sauces, much like mosquitoes are feasting on me.

"Mr. Esrock, please, a rest! I need some oxygen replenishment," says my guide, Dell. He pauses and promptly lights up a cigarette. It is raining on the steep, muddy steps of Mount Kinabalu, the tallest peak in Southeast Asia. The summit towers above at over 4,000 metres, making the hike to the top a knee-cruncher. I had decided on the spur of the moment to give it a shot, even though I lacked the proper permits, equipment and anything resembling fitness. Dell and I made it to the halfway point before turning back because thick sheets of water began to descend from the sky. It's a good thing I came in *dry*

season. Sabah is populated with Muslim Malays, Buddhist Chinese and indigenous tribes largely converted to Christianity. Like the rest of Malaysia, the state is politically stable, everyone seemingly united by bad American wrestling on TV and England's poor performance in yet another World Cup. Locals assure me that 50 years after this book is published, that last sentence will still hold up.

Further north near the town of Sandakan, I am determined to find cinema's best-ever sidekick. Any which way you look at it, and every which way but loose, there is little doubt that an orangutan out-acted Clint Eastwood in those classic 1970s buddy-ape movies. Orangutans, expressive and red-headed, are native only to Borneo and Sumatra. *Orangutan* literally means "man of the forest" in Malay, and since the apes share 96.4 per cent of our DNA, you can see where the *man* comes from. With the encroachment of palm plantations, poaching and the illegal pet trade, the primates are endangered. According to the Orangutan Conservancy, their numbers have dropped from 60,000 to 40,000 in the past decade alone.

The Sepilok Orangutan Rehabilitation Centre covers a protected jungle of 43 square kilometres. Many of the great apes calling it home have been rescued or rehabilitated, including orphaned babies reintroduced into the wild. Today there are between 60 and 80 apes swinging free in Sepilok's forest canopy. Tourists are allowed to view a feeding platform twice a day, which has something of a zoo-like flavour to it. One would think in the jungles of Borneo you'd get a little closer to animals than the nearest

Sweet and Spicy

It takes a while to get used to, but you'll soon enjoy eating like the locals, spooning curry-soaked coconut rice into your mouth by hand. Malaysians like their dishes sweet and spicy, and who can blame them? My favourite is *nasi kandar*, a chicken, beef or lamb stew served with three types of savoury curry sauces. From buffet style to fine dining, food is served with little fuss and is consistently excellent around the country. Malaysia's culinary delights benefit from a large Indian population. The result: Indian favourites with a distinctive Malay touch. Malaysia topped my World's Best Cuisine list for many years, until repeated visits to Thailand gave it pole position.

zoo. Since orangutans are susceptible to human diseases, one needs a special permit *and* a blood test before rangers will let you near an ape. Some visitors might leave disappointed, but the orangutans are happy, and that's the point.

Other than the sandflies, there are few complaints at our next Borneo wildlife sanctuary. In my hand is a tiny turtle hatchling, flapping away with surprising strength considering it is just minutes old. Along with several hundred siblings, it will be released into the South China Sea from the beaches at Turtles Island National Park. The island is one of several in a marine park where century-old turtles, weighing up to 150 kilograms each, gather to lay their eggs. To ensure the turtles' survival, rangers collect these eggs, incubate them in protected nests and release the hatchlings. It is just past midnight, a warm sea breeze enveloping my rudimentary thatch cabin, when a ranger yells "Turtle time!" A giant female, ancient and majestic, shuffles up the beach and lays 84 Ping-Pong-ball eggs. Even with the help of rangers, only 1 per cent of the hatchlings will survive to adulthood. The rest feed a food chain of sharks, lizards, birds and people. I bless my little flippered friend and watch her shuffle into the sea. Should she survive, she will return to this same beach in about 40 years to continue the cycle of life. I'd love to be here when she does, but I'm afraid I'll be devastated if she doesn't show up.

Back in Sabah, I'm puttering on a narrow boat looking for horny monkeys. Only later do I realize that the native "promiscuous monkey," when not misheard, is actually called a "proboscis monkey." Catering to all budgets, several wildlife lodges line the massive Kinabatangan River. It flows through a protected jungle that is home to monkeys, exotic birds, bush pigs, crocodiles and a rare species of pygmy elephant. Eventually, I do spot a proboscis monkey, with its distinctive fat nose and pot-belly. Living proof that the animal kingdom has a sense of humour.

Jet-lagged to hell, I follow the sound of cheering in the early-morning hours to find lodge staff glued to the satellite TV. They hand me a cold beer, and I join them for the latest World Cup match, viewed from the last place any of those players on the pitch could possibly imagine. Regardless of the score, I attained my goal. And although I merely scratched the surface, Borneo's bucket list–worthy natural attractions are well worth exploring before life blows its final whistle.

START HERE:
globalbucketlist.com/borneo

Stay in an Ocean Villa in the Maldives

How blue and warm is the seawater of the Maldives? It is as blue as a Smurf holding his breath. It is as warm as pee in a wetsuit, and as clear as the skin on a factory-fresh Barbie doll. Throughout the year, the wind blows a warm breeze, and the Indian Ocean gently laps against squeaky white beaches like a kitten at a bowl of milk. In winter, you are advised to bring a jacket because the temperature can plummet to a low +23°C. *Brrrr.* Seaplanes, many of them piloted by maverick Canadians, park at the airport near the capital island of Malé, ready to whisk well-off tourists away to one of almost one hundred remote island resorts.

Our bucket list destination is Gili Lankanfushi, on the island of Fushi. It is one of the most luxurious resorts in a country full of luxurious resorts. I chose this resort because a TV network is footing the bill, and after one glance at the photographs, well, one doesn't need any more reasons. A powerboat picks up guests upon their arrival in the capital. I am handed a bag for my shoes. At the Gili Lankanfushi, nobody wears shoes. Ever. The sand is soft and swept free of anything sharp or bothersome. The only things you have to worry about tripping over are cute hermit crabs as you marvel at the exorbitant delight of paradise.

From the base of the island, wooden jetties stretch out in several directions, connected to dozens of individual luxury villas. Each villa, every one about the size of a townhouse, has several private decks, luxury bathrooms, four-poster beds, wet bars and satellite TV. Each guest receives a bicycle with padded pedals for riding along the jetty, should the act of walking seem too strenuous. Glass bottoms in the villa reveal stingrays, tropical fish and small, harmless reef sharks swimming beneath your feet. On the upper deck, a double bed is made up by your butler, should you decide to sleep under the stars (with wheels to gently roll it under a thatch roof if the shooting stars distract you from your slumber). With no expense spared, the villas are designed to be tranquil and uncluttered—and to *look* like no expense has been spared. I hop onto the wireless connection to see that it's snowing in Toronto. Then I gaze out at a lone palm tree on a small neighbouring atoll and toast the fact that life is magical, and the timing is perfect.

At dinnertime, guests gather along the beach for candlelight cocktails beneath the manicured coconut trees. "We prune the trees; after all, we can't have coconuts falling on our heads," says Kurt, the affable manager. The resort even sets its own time so that guests can enjoy more sunlight. Despite alcohol being illegal in Malé, the resort has a fully stocked wine cellar. I ask the sommelier which is the cheapest bottle of wine. "We don't stock any cheap bottles of wine, sir," he tells me.

For those seeking absolute privacy, there are also the Crusoe

6 Overwater Villas on the Bucket List

Captain James Cook, on discovering Bora Bora: "Scarcely a spot on the universe affords a more luxurious prospect." The island is not alone. Here's a list of more spots that will make your jaw drop with delight, your romance sparkle and your wallet tremble with fear:

☑ Four Seasons, InterContinental, Hilton or St. Regis, Bora Bora

☑ Likuliku Lagoon Resort, Fiji

☑ Pangkor Laut Resort, Malaysia

☐ Rosewood Mayakoba, Mexico

☐ Song Saa Private Island, Cambodia

☐ Vahine Island, Tahiti

Residences, which can be reached only by boat (on call 24 hours a day). Russian oligarchs have been known to frequent such residences with female national volleyball teams in tow, as well as celebrities like Paul McCartney, impressed with the resort's commitment to protecting its environment.

The Maldives is the smallest country in Asia and the flattest country on the planet. It is also strictly Muslim, which is why the crowded capital of Malé has no bars, clubs or cinemas (and thus no tourists either). On the private island resorts, however, all major credit cards are accepted, and you can use them to buy whatever

pickles your liver. Of the country's 1,200 islands, only 200 are actually inhabited, and word on the Indian Ocean is that rising sea levels will vanquish this tiny nation during this century. One nation. Under water. In fact, Maldivians are expected to be the world's first "environmental refugees," 200,000 people forced to swim to higher shores. A tragedy for them and a tragedy for us too. Even if most of us never get the chance to grace such a luxurious destination, just knowing that it exists gives us something to dream about.

START HERE:
globalbucketlist.com/maldives

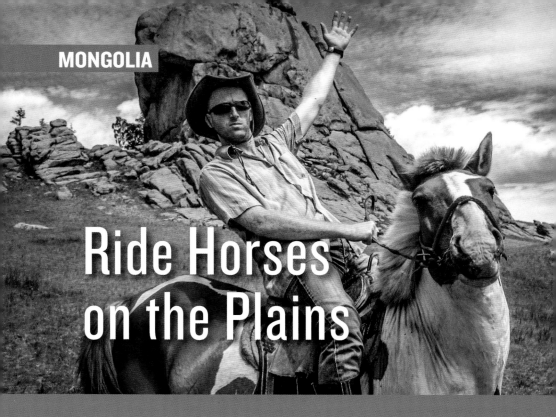

Ride Horses on the Plains

On the green plains of north-central Mongolia, the local horses are renowned for their speed. Since I've never really galloped before, I'm a little nervous lining up my steed for an impromptu race. I call my horse Landbiscuit, tighten the reins and race off at the sound of a yell.

"Choo choo!" screams the kid on my left as I pass him, which I assume is Mongolian for "Giddy-up!"

The countryside looks like an oil painting beneath an over-sized sunny sky. Tethered to my neck, my hat flies back as Landbiscuit bolts forward. I may not be a traditional nomad, but dammit, I can pretend to race like one.

From the dry Gobi Desert in the south to the fairway-green northern plains, Mongolia is rife with history. In the 1200s, the Mongols were a fierce nation under the leadership of Genghis (pronounced "Chingiss") Khan, a man who built the largest land empire in history, one stretching from China to Europe. By the 1400s, the empire had collapsed. Nevertheless, Genghis Khan remains Mongolia's most famous and celebrated figure. The Chinese conquered Mongolia for a few hundred years, splitting the country into Inner and Outer Mongolia. Inner Mongolia is today still part of China, whereas Outer Mongolia was more or less taken over by the Russians, becoming a Communist country backed heavily by Moscow. When the Iron Curtain was cut off its hooks, Mongolia was thrown into turmoil until the present democracy was established. Although the economy has improved thanks to oil and gas discoveries, some locals miss those stable glory days as they struggle with the complications of a market-based democracy. Over half of the country's 2.6 million people live in

the capital of Ulan Bator—or, if you like, the vowel-heavy Ulaanbaatar—and about 40 per cent of the population live the traditional nomadic lifestyle as Mongolians have for centuries. The language is full of *shhh*s and *tsitsi*s, and when spoken softly, sounds almost magical, like elfin.

Nomadic Mongolians live in traditional ger tents—easily assembled circular wooden structures with an iron stove in the middle. There are several ger camps where visitors can enjoy this nomadic lifestyle just a few hours' drive from Ulan Bator. While the accommodation is simple, and a field mole keeps

sneaking in to poop on my bed, the surrounding scenery is mythically beautiful. Outcrops of marble look like boulders on a golf course, the scattered forests almost manicured into position. In three days, I do not hear or see a plane, and take every opportunity to rent horses for rides into the surrounding hills. I chance upon a traditional archery competition in which young men on horses take aim at a target made of lamb's skin. But wrestling is Mongolia's biggest sport. Men dressed in loincloths try to tip each other over, much like Japanese sumo (also very popular in Mongolia).

Considering that traditional hats are topped with a metal phallus, watching the exhibition match proves to be a pointed spectacle.

With the help of a local guide, I am invited into a nomadic family's tent. Twice a year, they pack up and move to a different area, together with their horses and camels. In many parts of the country, land has no ownership. Nomads are free to camp according to their own agreements. The father offers me a cup of fermented horse's milk, and I accept it. It smells acidic, like urine, but I gulp it down, faking a smile even as it strips the enamel off my teeth. Mistaking my smile for pleasure, he tops up my cup for another round. Now my head is spinning more than my stomach. Fortunately, I couldn't stay for the boiled sheep's head. Mongolian-style barbecues have become popular in the West, but this stir-fry type of cuisine is not common within the country itself. Inspired by Mongolian history, the Mongolian barbecue is actually a Western invention. The most popular Mongolian barbecue restaurant in the capital is part of an American chain. That's the kind of global feedback loop that makes my stomach spin even more. As for

the Mongolians themselves, they're happy to eat boiled lamb, sheep and delightful entrees such as horse intestines.

Because they find themselves at the crossroads between China and Russia, Mongolians take their vodka seriously. Locals order vodka by the bottle at the bars that sit off Ulan Bator's sooty streets. It didn't

Go Go Gobi

In 2014, Bill Clinton was asked what's at the top of his bucket list. His reply: "Ride a horse across the Gobi Desert to the place where people think Genghis Khan is buried." Mongolia is your gateway to the Gobi, with all its incredible landscapes and history. Scale the Khongoryn Els sand dunes, hike in the canyons of Gobi Gurvansaikhan National Park, interact with nomads, discover dinosaur digs in the Flaming Cliffs and walk the ruins of Karakorum, the capital of the Mongolian empire in the 13th century. Travel by old Russian van, two-humped camel or horse (no word on which is most comfortable). Incidentally, Genghis Khan was buried in a secret location near the Burkhan Khaldun mountains 800 years ago. Scientists have analyzed satellite photos, and 10,000 volunteers have covered over 6,000 square kilometres searching for it, so far to no avail.

take long before I found myself in a loud, kitschy nightclub talking to some local men. They were angry that Chinese men were coming to Mongolia to "shop" for wives. Their English was as dicey as the cheap vodka, but I tagged along for a ride that included a fracas involving the army, an armed shirtless taxi driver and a policeman holding a Taser to my face. It seems serious in retrospect, but at the time, it was hard to take any of it too seriously, especially with everyone talking like Legolas.

As the country finds its feet in the modern age, Mongolia still has an exciting untamed edge to it. Of course, I ended up losing the horse race, and so what if my competitors were only nine years old. Every now and then, a memory pops into my head. Galloping at full speed in a green meadow, wind in my hair, hooves thundering around me, *choo choo!* A memory I will always cherish, from a fascinating destination that belongs on everyone's bucket list.

START HERE:
globalbucketlist.com/mongolia

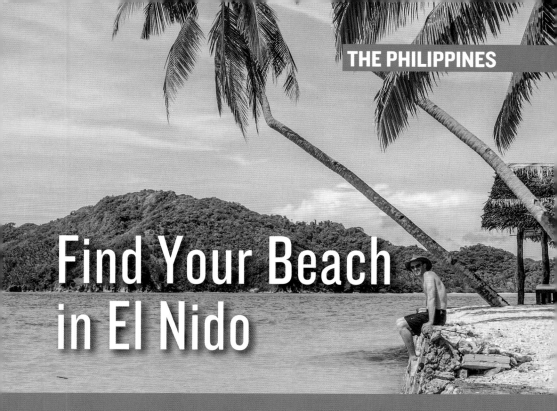

Find Your Beach in El Nido

*T*he Beach, a novel written by Alex Garland, became a smash hit in the 1990s. Although it was adapted as an overwrought Hollywood movie starring a miscast Leonardo DiCaprio, the book wonderfully captures the idea of the traveller's last great, unknown paradise. The plot centres on a young British backpacker who hears about a secret beach in Thailand, free of the *Lonely Planet*–clutching hordes. After swimming across the sea to find this island sanctuary, things go pear-shaped with the onset of armed smugglers, hungry sharks, hipster politics and, of course, sex with scantily clad beach babes. The movie was filmed on one of South Thailand's Phi Phi Islands, but here's a little-known fact about both movie and book: Thailand did not inspire Garland's mythical, secluded island paradise. In fact, it was based on El Nido.

The Great Global Bucket List has taken us to some extraordinary places, so when I say that Bacuit Bay in southwest El Nido is on the podium of paradise, it's worth taking note. There are 45 isles around El Nido, located at the northern tip of Palawan, known in the Philippines as the "Last Ecological Frontier." In 1967, the entire province was declared a fish and wildlife sanctuary, somewhat at odds with the fact that its capital, Puerto Princesa, is the country's fastest-growing city. El Nido's islands are mostly deserted, protected by law and harbouring beaches as private as they are attractive. Serviced by a small town (also named El Nido) are several high-class luxury resorts on the bay. I get the chance to visit the Miniloc Island Resort. Warm, crystal seawater washes against limestone cliffs and white powdery beaches; emerald lagoons are dotted with coconut trees. Toss in five-star service and how could we not go goo-goo at the possibilities? Especially if we're staying in overwater cabins, partaking in snorkelling and sea kayaking, and have a homemade condiment table that stretches all the way to the

Kingdom of Culinary Heaven. It doesn't matter that we get here in rainy season. From the moment we arrive, all we can think about is how we are going to return here once we leave.

Sunlight reflects off the turquoise waters of the South China Sea as I paddle my sea kayak through the limestone channel of Big Lagoon. There's a reason Jacques Cousteau said this region was the most beautiful place he'd ever explored. The rainbow colours of fish and coral beneath me are extraordinary. Guests putt-putt about on wooden *bangkas*—small, motorized outriggers typical of the region. Resorts will drop you off

on an island for the day, along with a picnic lunch and bottle of wine. It is essentially yours—to laze on the beach, snorkel or explore the rainforest. I recognize this place from the pages of *The Beach*—my own hidden island paradise (thankfully devoid of Hollywood drama). Gazing over the deserted islands, I notice dark clouds approaching, soon to unleash heavy tropical rains. Not for the first time, I acknowledge that I am in one of those places most only ever read about, and wonder how I got so lucky (yet again). Then I raid the picnic basket for another fresh piña colada.

El Nido is renowned for some

of the world's best diving and snorkelling. I stare into the eyes of intimidatingly large jackfish, luminous flighty parrotfish, fish that look like dogs, fish that look like raccoons, fish that look like Republicans, fish that look like anarchists. Clean fish, dirty fish, spiky fish, smooth fish, naughty fish, nice fish, scary, sporty, posh, ginger and baby fish. Those inclined will want to spend as much time as they can underwater. Above water, well, that's just fine too.

It's a bumpy prop flight back to reality. The small plane, flying direct from El Nido to Manila, hits a thunderstorm and bounces erratically around in the sky. On arrival, I get on my knees and kiss the landing strip. Driving from the airport, inching forward in Manila's loud, choking traffic, I already long for the shade of a coconut tree. No man or woman is an island, but that doesn't mean we can't aspire to live on one.

START HERE:
globalbucketlist.com/elnido

The World's Longest Underground River

Palawan is home to the world's longest navigable underground river, an 8.2-kilometre-long waterway that creeps into a limestone cave. Inside the Puerto Princesa Subterranean River National Park, don a hard hat and flashlight as you row, row, row the first kilometre deep into the cave, between bats and cave formations. As light from the mouth slowly disappears, the acrid smell of guano gives the impression that a beast, complete with rows of stalagmite teeth, is swallowing you. Thank goodness there's always light at the end of the tunnel.

Meet Yoda near the Chocolate Hills

THE PHILIPPINES

I'm not sure if the world's second-smallest primate inspired George Lucas to create Yoda, but the resemblance is uncanny. However, unlike Yoda, tarsiers can fit into your hand, and I doubt they can handle a Jedi. What's more, tarsiers actually exist, and Yoda doesn't. Strong with reality, it is.

Tarsiers are protected on only one little stretch of jungle, on one little island in the Philippines. It is called Bohol, accessible from the gateway of Cebu City. Beyond the monkeys, Bohol has some of the best beaches in the country, bizarre landscapes and an interesting history.

Let us begin with a cocktail at the infinity pool at the Panglao Island Nature Resort, overlooking a white sandy beach, the smell of hibiscus in the air. Warm air blankets us like a comforter, coconut trees whistle in the wind. Seeing the region's highlights can all be accomplished on a day trip from the hotel: taking in historical landmarks like the Baclayon Church, having lunch on a floating restaurant and visiting communities on the Loboc River. The Philippines is a riot of colour, and you don't need to look further than the jeepneys. Decorated by kitsch connoisseurs, jeepneys are the most popular form of transportation in the Philippines and worth seeing for their own sake.

Bohol's biggest attraction is the 1,700 unusual geological formations known as the Chocolate Hills. Credited to erosion (or the teardrops of a giant, if you prefer to believe local mythology), the hills look like various sizes of upside-down tea cups scattered across the landscape. Their name refers to their appearance during the dry season, when they

turn milk-chocolate brown. My visit coincides with the wet season, when "Chocolate Mint Hills" might be a more accurate name. Sheets of rain force me to take shelter in a nearby restaurant. Steam rises off the formations when the rain relents. I climb the stairs to the top of a viewpoint. It's a truly unique landscape, more so for being so off the radar.

Bohol's second-most-popular attraction is much, much smaller. The tarsier might not actually be a primate—some experts believe it's closely related to the lemur. That doesn't make it look any less weird. The tarsier has a rat's tail, creepy webbed feet and the look of a gremlin who stayed up past midnight. Its eyes are bigger than its brain, and 150 times larger than our own in

relation to its body. These creatures are threatened with extinction, and Bohol has the only protected tarsier habitat in the world. I walk along a pathway through a lush rainforest, hoping to spot the elusive creature. There it is! Frozen to a branch, looking so nervous, my sneeze might give it a heart attack. As birdwatchers already know, there's a great sense of satisfaction in encountering something rare. This chapter could easily feature the common spotted cuscus of Papua New Guinea, or the phallic mushroom rocks in Taiwan's Yehliu Geopark (page 319). I liked the juxtaposition of a huge geological wonder residing so close to a tiny, fragile creature so vulnerable even its classification is in dispute. The beaches of Bohol aren't too bad either. Regardless, any bucket list should include a healthy collection of bizarre natural encounters, wherever we're lucky enough to find them.

START HERE:

globalbucketlist.com/ chocolatehills

Unusual Natural Wonders for the Bucket List

Chamarel, Mauritius: When molten rock cooled down and turned into clay, various chemicals created this small dune field with seven distinct colours. Whether you actually see the "Seven Coloured Earths" depends largely on sunny weather.

The Richat Structure, near Ouadane, Mauritania: Venture into the vast Sahara Desert and you'll find this strange natural feature, 40 kilometres in diameter. Minerals and gases give it a distinctly alien appearance. Initially attributed to an asteroid, scientists now believe it is the result of erosion.

Pancake Rocks, New Zealand: Alternating layers of sandstone and limestone, along with 30 million years of earthquakes and erosion, have resulted in this popular road stop in Punakaiki. Compressed water blasts through blowholes surrounding the multi-layered rocks.

Socotra, Yemen: Isolated in the Indian Ocean, the island of Socotra has unique flora that make it one of the weirdest places on the planet. Over 30 per cent of its plants are endemic, including the umbrella-shaped and wonderfully named dragon blood tree. Ancient cultures believed its sought-after red sap was the blood of dragons.

Sossusvlei, Namibia: Sossusvlei, a landscape of bright red and yellow dunes and semi-petrified trees, sits inside Namib-Naukluft National Park. Arrive late in the afternoon to watch the sun cast shadows on the dunes, some of which rise as high as 100 metres.

Spotted Lake, British Columbia, Canada: New Brunswick's Hopewell Rocks, Quebec's Mingan Archipelago, Saskatchewan's Crooked Bush—Canada has no shortage of natural weirdness. Nor is it short on lakes; it has over 3 million of them. The strangest one is outside Osoyoos, British Columbia. Hundreds of circular spots stretch across the aptly named Spotted

Lake, containing highly concentrated minerals that "paint" the pools with different colours.

The Wave, Coyote Buttes, USA: Near the Arizona-Utah border is a remarkable sandstone formation known as the Wave. Access is extremely limited: you can win 1 of only 20 daily permits either through an online lottery or by just showing up early in the morning. From here it's a 12-mile hike without trail or map.

Yehliu Geopark, Taiwan: Erosion, wind and water have caused unusual hoodoos to blossom on the north coast of Taiwan. Walk among phallic formations with names like the Queen's Head, Beehive and Sea Candles.

319

Find Peace with a Temple Stay

I'm sure there are more than a few readers who'd love to lose themselves in the world, perhaps with the ironic goal of finding themselves. Any break in routine—whether it's meant to bring relaxation, spike the amount of adrenalin running through one's veins or trigger spiritual enlightenment—provides a welcome mental holiday. This is one of the reasons South Korea's largest Buddhist order established Temple Stay Korea—a chance to leave behind the cell phones, social media and traffic, and plug into a different way of life.

The Lotus Lantern meditation centre offers Zen Buddhist teaching in an impressive temple surrounded by forest and farms. Introducing visiting foreigners to Buddhism, it offers basic but well-maintained accommodation, complete with picturesque garden pagodas. The overall atmosphere is one of tranquillity; the mere act of raising your voice would seem to violate some unspoken rule. I am given a training uniform of grey pants, T-shirt and waistcoat, to be worn at all times. I forsake all the trappings of materialism, the delights of earthly pleasure, in the quest for illumination. Inside the main temple, overlooked by a golden statue of Buddha, a Russian monk named Aleksander introduces me to the basic concepts of Buddhism, explaining that enlightenment is the ultimate goal of meditation. He calmly explains that if I feel physically uncomfortable during any of the practices, I should just relax at my own pace, and if I have any questions, I should just ask.

Visitors can choose the weekend program, an intense week of meditation or to stay for a longer period of rest. Each day's schedule

involves chanting, meditation, garden work, slow walks, calligraphy classes and several other options for those who need to keep themselves busy. All meals are vegetarian, eaten in strict silence, though a monk's cell phone did ring during dinner, leading to muffled giggles among the visitors. Monks eat to sustain themselves on their path to enlightenment, not for pleasure. I'm told that I must finish everything on my plate, avoid waste and consume consciously.

After washing up in silence, I head to the hall for my first lesson in meditation. I fold my legs into the lotus position until the strain becomes too much—after about eight seconds. Aleksander tells the group to count to 10 repeatedly, and to be aware of any errant thoughts that flow in our minds. If we think about anything other than the number, we must reset to zero. I don't make it past 3. Large mosquitoes cloud above my head, raining bites on my bare arms. I ask if mosquitoes constitute a sentient life form, a sly-handed way of inquiring whether I'm allowed to squash the buggers in a Buddhist temple. "Monks do not kill mosquitoes," says Aleksander, waving a couple

away from his face. This could well be the single biggest obstruction to me ever becoming one.

Like learning to play piano, meditating takes time and practice. After a few minutes, I give up altogether and spend the next half-hour enjoying the silence, the space to breathe. The resonating sound of a *moktak*—a traditional wooden instrument—signals that the session has ended, and we have some free time before lights out at 9:30 p.m. Thin mattresses and blankets are provided, and mosquito netting mercifully keeps out the bugs while letting in a cool forest breeze.

I wake at 3:30 a.m. to the sound of the *moktak*, signalling it is time for chanting in the temple. Monks and weekend spiritual warriors have gathered in the glow of candlelight. I try to follow with the helpful English guide provided but end up focusing on the slightly closed eyes of the golden Buddha up front, the smiles on the deity statues that surround it and the bright colours painted on the dragons above. Prostrating oneself is a form of meditation and a sign of devotion. Korean Zen Buddhism has 108 prostrations, each performed to a different chant. Bending down onto the knees, head to the mat, hands turned upward, stand and repeat—it is a strenuous, dizzying physical challenge to keep up. I notice that sweat begins to stain the mat where my forehead touches, but together with the rhythmic sound of the *moktak* and the chanting, the overall effect is almost hypnotic.

Garden work, cleaning or simply strolling into the surrounding forest is also viewed as a form of meditation. You can even put on a personal Do Not Disturb sign, in the form of a wearable "Quiet Time" tag that asks everyone to respect your vow of silence. With each meditation session it becomes a little easier to focus on my breathing, to see the numbers click over in my mind. The outside world floats away, save for the clear calls of birds, the buzz of insects. Concluding my overnight stay, I exchange my training uniform for my jeans and sweater, bow my head in thanks to the monks and volunteers. My temple stay had little to do with religion and everything to do with finding a way to create the time and space for reflection. No matter what spiritual path you follow, or even if you don't follow one at all, a Korean temple stay is an experience worthy for your bucket list.

START HERE:
globalbucketlist.com/templestay

Pluck Tea in Ceylon

When ancient Arab traders discovered a fertile, teardrop island in the Indian Ocean, they called it Serendib. We still use the word *serendipity* to describe the phenomenon of finding something valuable that was not expected. It's a word stuck in my mind as I drive into Sri Lanka's Central Highlands, passing dense rainforest, milky waterfalls and playful monkeys. Even as the temperature drops with the rising altitude, the smiles and waves of locals radiate with cultural warmth. Soon enough, unkempt mountains transform into a rich carpet of manicured plants, green waves rolling smoothly with the foothills. We have arrived in the heart of Sri Lanka's most famous export: tea.

Our destination is Ceylon Tea Trails, originally residences built for the tea barons who ruled over the estates, now a luxury bungalow resort. Owned and operated by Dilmah, one of the world's largest tea brands, Ceylon Tea Trails is a love letter to anyone with a passion for tea, tranquillity and Sri Lanka itself. Resembling large country estates, the four bungalows are several kilometres apart, serviced by butlers and private chefs, and encircled by gardens that offer superb views of mountains and lakes. Entering the colonial Tientsin Bungalow, constructed in 1888, it feels as if you're stepping into another era thanks to its polished wooden floors, high ceilings and plush four-poster beds. Uniformed staff wait for me with an evening cocktail in a lounge that smells of old, expensive leather. Faded paintings of tea barons hang on the wall. The fireplace is blazing, the cool night a relief from the humidity on the coast. It feels like I've intruded on a royal escape.

I drink coffee when there's work to do and tea when I want to relax. Since the first tea leaf accidentally fell into a Chinese emperor's boiling water, millions around the world have enjoyed their tea too. Oddly enough, the British first planted coffee in Ceylon (present-day Sri Lanka), but it failed to take hold. Tea quality, on the other hand, is dependent on soil, climate and altitude. These all blended perfectly in the Central Highlands, and Ceylon tea quickly became a valuable global commodity. Certainly, I've never enjoyed a fresher cup of tea than the one waiting for me with breakfast on the patio. The flavour is clearer, richer, more satisfying than any cup of tea I've tasted before. Adding to the ambiance is the early-morning sun brightening up evergreen tea terraces painted like Monet brushstrokes onto the surrounding mountains.

"What are those yellow and blue specks moving around up there?" I ask the butler. I've never had a butler before, and I think he rather suits me.

"Those are the tea pluckers, sir."

Thus begins my education in tea.

Ceylon Tea Trails offers hiking, mountain biking, tennis, croquet and a spa—plus the opportunity to visit a working tea estate and learn about the finest tea in the world. The estate's guide is Andrew Taylor, a quick-witted tea master and direct descendant of Sri Lanka's first tea planter. We start in the fields, where I learn how tea is gathered, the plucker seeking the desired two

leaves and a bud. Left alone, these waist-high plants will grow over 6 metres. The estate's army of tea pluckers consists of short, skinny women wrapped in colourful saris, each with a wood basket balanced on her head. With lightning fingers, they pluck up to 15 kilograms of tea leaves a day. They're paid according to weight. I ask one plucker if I can give it a try, which solicits cackles. Even though the basket is empty, its weight strains my neck. I clumsily pluck away for a half-hour before deciding that this is work best left to wispy women with necks of steel.

Since its inception, Dilmah has prided itself on the ethical treatment of its employees. Through its foundation, it supports some 1,500 community projects, including child care, geriatric services, arts programs, counselling, and even prisoner rehabilitation. The company also provides free housing, education and medical services for its tea estate workers. On the slopes, the mood is light as the women chatter away, moving between rows of bushes, gathering the leaves that will find their way to 92 countries.

At the nearby factory, I learn about the processes of withering, rolling, fermentation and drying.

Appreciating a Fine Cuppa

Many factors determine the quality of tea, including the region, the rainfall, the season of plucking and the soil composition. Brewing techniques depend on the type of tea itself. The tasting and enjoyment of tea is a ritual one can follow at home. First, take a small sip to clear your palate of tastes, and absorb the full experience. The second sip is to appreciate the taste across the vegetal (grass, spinach, leafy), fruity and spice spectrum. Next comes texture and mouthfeel, the sensation of liquid sloshing around your tongue and inside your mouth. Some teas are heavier, smoother or woodier than others. Small cups allow many infusions of the same leaf. A good tea leaves a pleasant aftertaste that can positively (or negatively) impact additional tastings later in the day. Once that's over with, simply enjoy the refreshment. Like our bucket list, tea is generally best appreciated in good company, without distraction and with plenty of time.

Andrew explains how leaves are classified and graded, and, finally, how to make the perfect cup of tea: water just to a boil, one spoonful of tea per person, one for the pot. Never add sugar, which negates the considerable health benefits, and only a dash of milk if any. We taste different grades, letting the liquid roll around the tongue and expelling mouthfuls into a spittoon, much like wine tasting. There's still a lot to learn, but my appreciation for tea has deepened, and no afternoon break will taste the same again.

Back at Tientsin Bungalow, named after the Chinese village from whence the tea seedlings came, a fine mist rolls across the hills. I consume my afternoon tea without sugar, enjoying its aroma, robust flavour and bright colour. A guitar strums in my head, perhaps inspired by a former Tientsin guest, Paul Simon. In a country scarred by war, the peace and serenity is tangible. Finding something valuable not originally sought after? Serendipity indeed.

START HERE:
globalbucketlist.com/ceylon

TAIWAN

Order the Number Two

In my ongoing quest to prove that sometimes you can actually believe what you read on the Internet, let's head to Taiwan and get to the bottom of the legend about a toilet-themed restaurant. Yes, toilet. Not bathroom, washroom or even WC. Modern Toilet, in Taipei's trendy Shilin District, sees no reason to excuse itself to powder its nose. The small restaurant is brightly decorated with designer toilet seats for customers to sit on—lids closed, of course. Glass covers a large sink, serving as an adequate table to debate the merits of eating on the potty. Cartoon characters on the wall and menu take the form of friendly curls of excrement, happily offering specials, competitions and club memberships for regular regulars. I am not taking the piss, I assure you. Menus are in Mandarin only, so we'll sit down on the throne, get to our business and order the number two.

Modern Toilet is a successful chain flush with new franchises around Taiwan. Today there are a dozen Modern Toilets, providing an unusual eatery for local hipsters and confusing the hell out of everyone else. This is not the place to walk in and ask if you can use the loo. Everything here is bright and cheery, from the fluorescent orange-green decor to the decorative shower curtains to the pretty staff. Napkins take the form of toilet rolls on the wall.

Number two arrives in a miniature porcelain toilet bowl and turns out to be an adequate, somewhat spicy chicken curry. Carrots and corn float on top, bringing back truly awful college memories (of those times when alcohol necessitated a visit to the toilet for a different reason). My questionably flavoured, appropriately coloured citrus juice is served in a miniature plastic bedpan. Other drinks might arrive in urinal-shaped cups. Such attention to detail is impressive. Ironically, I need the loo before tucking in and am somewhat relieved to find the men's room free of edibles.

The owner, Cheng, tells me the restaurant was inspired by his love

of comics and the coiled shape of ice cream. Indeed, Modern Toilet is renowned for serving massive "ice shavings"—a porcelain urinal loaded with ice cream, crushed ice, marshmallows, jelly, candies and other sweet goodness beyond identification. The ice cream is chocolate, shaped like a turd, as befits the overall theme. There's no room for the prudish here. Various forms of poo-shaped merchandise are displayed in the window, from plastic sweet containers to key chains and plastic toys for the kids. Prices appeal to the core clientele of trendy students, faithfully supplied by Taipei's many universities, with most dishes less than US$10. Besides hot curries, the restaurant offers noodles and stews, and I'm happy to report that just because the food is served to look like crap, it doesn't have to taste like it.

Modern Toilet has thought of just about everything to make your short stay comfortable, from various seating arrangements (a toilet bar, anyone?) to magazines available to read while you do your business (eating and otherwise). The Taiwanese are fond of theme restaurants. There's a jail-themed restaurant in the south, where "inmates" are handed prison overalls before being shown to their table. There's a dinosaur restaurant too, somewhere, but if it involves being trampled by a T. Rex, I think I'll give it a miss.

I ask Cheng why he decided to get into the business of scatological dining. "Just for fun," he replies. Ask me why on earth eating from a toilet bowl in a Taiwanese toilet-themed restaurant belongs on the Great Global Bucket List and the same answer applies.

START HERE:
globalbucketlist.com/toilet

Volunteer with Rescued Elephants

After oil and automobiles, tourism is the world's largest industry. Travellers make an enormous impact with their choice of transport, accommodation, activities and interests. It's been heartening to see the rise of the ethical traveller and eco-conscious tour companies. "Leave only footprints" is now a serious objective. Organizations like Projects Abroad and GoVoluntouring match travellers with community, environmental, wildlife, education and youth programs in dozens of countries. Meaningful travel (and unforgettable bucket list memories) are made when you give something back. Which brings me to a very small woman with a big heart in northern Thailand.

Most visitors to Chiang Mai inevitably find their way to an elephant park. Once a mainstay of the Thai logging industry, elephants today are found primarily in tourist camps, where they dance, take rides and make paintings with their trunks. Not all the elephant parks are as ethical as their brochures might suggest, and there have been ongoing reports of mistreatment. Lek Chailert once worked in the elephant tourism business, helping trekking companies locate unemployed elephants. After discovering what awful conditions these elephants had to endure, this firecracker of a woman dedicated her life to improving living standards and rescuing elephants in need. Her efforts led to the establishment of her Elephant Nature Park—a rehabilitation sanctuary for abused animals from both the logging and tourism industries. There are no rides or circus tricks, but it is an ideal place to get face to face with Asian elephants on their own terms.

Hearing the stories behind the 40-odd elephants living in the sanctuary can punch your heart. Some were rescued from the streets of the cities, where they were used by people to beg for money. (Urban elephants quickly become sick from eating garbage and sleeping in parking lots. A few even become addicted to amphetamines fed to them by unscrupulous owners as a means of extending their work hours.) Other elephants in the park were donated by owners who could no longer afford to keep them. Abandoned, injured or just retired from other elephant camps—without a refuge, they all faced a tragic future.

Today, international volunteers help with the day-to-day activities of this elephant haven, whether it's building fences, feeding, washing or helping the sick. The nature park is open to those of all ages and physical capabilities, and volunteers can stay overnight for weeks at a time (accommodation and meals are on-site) or just visit on a one-day excursion to learn about the plight of the Asian elephant. Donations from around the world are accepted, and the project has expanded to include hundreds of rescue dogs, happily sharing space with the elephants in the 100-hectare sanctuary.

Although there are fewer than 4,000 Asian elephants remaining in the country, the elephant remains the proud national symbol. I meet Max, renowned as one of

the tallest elephants in Thailand. His story reads like a screenplay: sent off to the logging camps, abandoned, ended up on the streets as a beggar. Max was the victim of a terrible accident: this giant was dragged underneath the wheels of an 18-wheel truck. Lek found him and nursed him back to health. He has several female companions (elephants have complex emotional relationships) and now walks tall, with eyes that bespeak pain and struggle, but ultimately redemption.

Hand-feeding elephants is a surprisingly tender experience. Using their trunks, they gently take bunches of bananas and oranges from my hand and shovel them into their mouths, peel and all. Lek shows me how to hand-feed bread, putting it into the enormous mouth of a male that could swing its head and crush her like a beer can. Feeding the elephants doesn't come cheap. One elephant can consume up to 300 kilograms of food and 200 litres of water per day. The nature park has an online donation program through which people can adopt an elephant; fees from volunteers and day visitors also help sustain the program.

I take an opportunity to bathe two elephants down by the river. Staring one in the eye, I know instinctively that a creature of intelligence is staring right back at me. Elephants have the largest brain of any land mammal, and its hippocampus—the part of the brain responsible for emotion and spatial awareness—is more developed than any other animal. They are known to grieve for their dead, laugh, show compassion, play, learn and recognize themselves in the mirror. In the wild, elephants typically live in close-knit matriarchal societies, which makes isolation and abandonment even more devastating for them. I scrub the elephant behind his ears, rubbing the sandpaper-coarse skin and pin-sharp black hairs on his hide, feeling the pink, wet goo on his nostrils. He rewards me with a spray from his super-soaker trunk, an act of mischievous play if ever there was one.

It's easy to see why volunteers love it here, why they develop bonds with the animals in their care, as well as with staff and other volunteers. Each elephant has a *mahout*, a local guardian who cares for it. As the sun set across the beautiful Mae Taeng Valley, I watch a lone *mahout* walk his elephant back to the camp. They trudge in the water at the same pace, two vastly different creatures understanding and respecting each other, an image forever copied to my brain's memory card.

It's disheartening to read about the increase of elephant poaching in Africa, where an estimated 20,000 elephants were slaughtered in 2013 alone. Thirty per cent of the 40,000 Asian elephants in existence live in captivity, yet the illegal ivory trade continues to grow. Fortunately, there are people like Lek, who really do make a big difference in the lives of both the animals in her sanctuary and the volunteers who keep it going.

Build a well in Ghana. Work with marine turtles in Costa Rica. Care for orphans in Mongolia. Plant seeds on an organic farm in Argentina. Teach a class in India. Adopt an endangered animal in Bolivia. Commit just one day of your holiday to supporting a community organization; it will likely be the most memorable day of your entire trip. Every Great Global Bucket List should make a positive impact on the world. Voluntourism, however you choose to participate, is an experience that stays with you long after the tan fades.

START HERE:

globalbucketlist.com/elephants

Voluntourism with Animals

Bolivia's Comunidad Inti Wara Yassi relies solely on volunteers to rehabilitate big cats, monkeys, birds and other animals rescued from the illegal exotic-pet trade. Sharing a room in simple accommodations, you'll be assigned an animal or tasks for a minimum stay of two weeks.

China's Louguantai Wild Animal Breeding and Protection Center invites international volunteers for a minimum two-week stay to look after rescued or captive-bred bears, as well as other animals. The centre is located a couple of hours' drive outside Xi'an.

Costa Rica's Marine Turtle Conservation Project needs volunteers to give endangered sea turtles a fighting chance. Patrol the sandy beaches under the moonlight to fend off poachers and predators, protect the nests and enjoy the tropical rainforest.

South Africa's Cango Wildlife Ranch offers two- to four-week volunteer programs to assist with the conservation of big cats, lemurs, storks, pygmy hippos and other animals. Expect plenty of animal interaction, ongoing maintenance and cage cleaning.

Yukon's Muktuk Adventures is a dog lover's dream. Living onsite in rustic countryside cabins, volunteers from around the world assist with the care and exercise of over 100 spirited sled dogs.

Release a Sky Lantern

THAILAND

Bucket listers arriving in Bangkok find themselves at a crossroad. Do you head south to the famed paradise islands or point your compass north toward the country's culture? With the luxury of having done both on several occasions, I place my trifecta bets on the sticky-fried air of the northern jungles. Not that the beaches of southern Thailand are terrible, but should you find yourself in Phuket, you might indeed find yourself phuket (if you get my meaning). I found the town to be an overcrowded mess of a beach town, with aggressive touts picking off boorish European clientele chasing prostitutes of dubious gender. Granted, Phuket (pronounced "Poo-ket") is the gateway to more tranquil islands in the south, mere straits away from Krabi, high-end Phi Phi, Koh Samui and Koh Phangan, which hosts the legendary and overrated Full Moon Party. Sure, you'll find glitzy resorts and backpacker paradises in the south, but for the most part, it's "same-same but different."

Visitors to Thailand become intimately familiar with this slogan because just about every market stall and restaurant offer the same products and menu. Even the fantastic Buddhist temples slowly blend into each other. The same is true in Chiang Mai, the largest city in the north, though the city is far more appealing than Phuket. Traffic is less frenetic, touts less desperate. You'll inevitably find your way to an elephant park (see page 333), casual Thai cooking classes, some of the more impressive temples and authentic kick-boxing contests. Some of you will head further north to Pai, a backpacker favourite with those who enjoy outstanding food, cheap booze and late-night dancing under the stars. Myself included.

You'll meet enough expats in northern Thailand to wonder why you too don't just pack it all up and move here. Rent is dirt cheap, an hour-long massage costs less than five bucks, politics are relatively stable (unlike in Bangkok), the food is extraordinary and Singha-sunburnt package-tourists are stowed away in the south.

Like silky coconut milk in a red curry, the bucket list experience that brings it home is a festival called Loi Krathong. It takes place throughout Thailand under a full November moon and is particularly special in Chiang Mai. Out come the masses to make wishes and honour the water gods with decorated baskets made of wood, banana leaves and flowers. The city's night market

Get Cooking

It's fun to learn things abroad, like capoeira in Brazil, surfing in Australia, diving in the Caribbean and yoga in India. The culinary arts sizzle in Thailand, which has (a) the best cuisine in the world and (b) fantastic cooking schools to accommodate all types of tourists. Chiang Mai's Chilli Club Thai Cooking Academy, a terrific no-frills option, is located in a popular budget guesthouse. It allows you to choose your own dishes from a vast selection, then commences with a visit to the local market to purchase the ingredients. Crush some lime or Thai basil between your fingers, dare to bite a raw chili, learn about fruits and spices you never knew existed. Each wannabe chef gets his or her own cooking station and is shown how to cook five dishes. You'll learn that every Thai meal should be balanced with salty, spicy, sour and sweet tastes, and that presentation is crucial. Eating alone is considered bad luck, and dishes should be shared between everyone at the table. Fortunately, you'll find hungry new friends at their own cooking stations, ready to oblige.

becomes particularly festive, hosting a beauty pageant that traditionally accompanies the festival. It's exotic and warm and good-spirited, but the true magic is overhead. Floating above, like glowing marshmallows in a lava lamp, are thousands of sky lanterns. Constructed of rice paper with wood or wire frames, these lanterns have a lit candle in the centre that creates hot air, raising the lanterns up much like hot-air balloons. Lanterns are for sale everywhere. The custom is to write a wish on the rice-paper walls before releasing the lantern to the night. How thousands of flaming lantern bombs don't eventually descend on Chiang Mai or burn down the surrounding farms is one of the miracles of the festival. (Accidents and injuries proved to be the case in Bangkok, which now bans sky lanterns during the festival under penalty of death.) Chiang Mai, meanwhile, glows under the spell of these floating stars, a scene so radiantly exotic, you can expect your travel buzz to light up the streets.

Here's my true story: I had spotted a stunning girl, a fellow traveller, thick in the crowds, our eyes meeting for but a second. Single at the time, I kept looking over my shoulder to see if I could spot her

again, but with hundreds of thousands of people about, I resigned myself to it being a case of ships passing in the night. Along with some friends, I purchased a sky lantern and we scribbled our wishes on its side. Three of us each took a side and suspended the lantern at eye level for a moment, our faces lit by the soft orange glow of the candle. We closed our eyes, made our wish and watched our lantern slowly rise with the grace of a bubble. Our next offering was in the form of live fish in a plastic bag, procured for a few baht, which we would release down at the river. Squeezed among the masses, we let the crowd carry us to the river's edge to free our fish. Standing next to me, as if by magic, was the girl I had seen earlier.

"Funny thing," I told her. "Just a few minutes ago I wrote a wish on the side of a sky lantern that I would see you again." With an opening line like that, is it any wonder we spent the remaining two weeks of her holiday exploring Southeast Asia like a pair of lovesick swans?

There are crossroads in travel, just as surely as there are crossroads in life. Each decision we make is accompanied by pros and cons,

many of them beyond our control. All we can do is trust that wherever we are, it is exactly where we're supposed to be. Wherever you end up in Thailand, I hope you too will find your sky lantern, make your wish and watch it materialize beneath a bucket list evening sky.

START HERE:
globalbucketlist.com/chiangmai

Enjoy a Sunrise with the Gods

Asandstorm sweeps in from northern Syria, blanketing the old ruins of eastern Turkey's Harran in a fine, powdery dust. Although the temperature is scorching at this time of year, the sand dims the sun. An orange glow covers the ruins of an Islamic university, a great mosque, a glorious palace. These buildings were once renowned throughout Mesopotamia, but time pays them no respect. I see these ruins in sepia tones, and the atmosphere is thick. It might just be the dust, but you can taste the history in southeastern Turkey.

I am in the land between the legendary Euphrates and Tigris Rivers, where modern civilization was born. Together with Iraq and parts of Syria and Iran, this is the Mesopotamia where great biblical empires were born, ruled and conquered. From the plain, I see a flat, dry terrain baking in the summer heat.

It started with the Hittites, who were the first to establish an agricultural economy governed by a political kingdom. In an age of iron and an age of conquest, the Assyrians moved in, followed by the Persians, the Macedonians of Alexander the Great, the Seleucids, the Romans,

the Byzantines—the list goes on. Mesopotamia, like modern-day Turkey, was the gate between East and West and as such has always been a prized trading route.

As the tour van barrels further into the sun-dried streets of Adiyaman, I wonder how anyone survived without air conditioning. It is 42°C, with no respite from the heat in the shade. Following a lavish lunch of traditional grilled kebabs, breads, dips and salads, I explore the city by foot. It is currently booming with the economic benefits of the nearby Southeastern Anatolia Project. Men sit on low wooden stools in

the open courtyards, sipping small glasses of sweetened tea. Their thick moustaches, flat berets and traditional grey loose pants have changed little in centuries. Kurdish men sell nuts and fruits from their carts, and everywhere I walk, locals ask "Hello, where you from?" with a sincere curiosity you'll find

throughout Turkey. Public television sets and white satellite dishes attached to apartment blocks bring me back to the present. The call to prayer echoes under the shadow of a 14th-century minaret. Eastern Turkey has always been more conservative than western Turkey. Parts of Istanbul resemble a European city, but here one's foot is firmly planted in Asia. I hear the call-to-prayer lullaby and settle in for an early night. Tomorrow morning, I will leave the city at 2 a.m. to join the gods for sunrise.

Discovered by a German geologist in 1881, the statues that face the sunrise and sunset atop Mount Nemrut are an under-the-radar historical wonder. At 2,206 metres, they recall an age when kings aspired to join the pantheon of gods who ruled their lives. After a two-hour early-morning drive from Adiyaman, I arrive at the parking lot of Nemrut eager to stretch my legs on the short 500-metre hike up to the eastern terrace. The early-morning wind is invigorating, the dark night sky slowly brightening with the violet of dawn. To Turks, witnessing the sunrise atop Mount Nemrut is marketed as an emotional experience in itself. After all,

Bucket List Sunrises

Light from darkness, colour from void. Sunrises bring hope, potential, beauty and the cool whispers of wonder—fine spectacles to enjoy anywhere. Below is a list of sunrises that sparkle on the Great Global Bucket List:

- Ahu Tongariki, Easter Island, Chile
- Angkor, Cambodia
- Bagan, Burma (Myanmar)
- Haleakala National Park, Hawaii, USA
- Ipanema Beach, Rio de Janeiro, Brazil
- Machu Picchu, Peru
- Masada, Israel
- Masai Mara, Kenya
- Santorini, Greece

this is a nation quite familiar with historical ruins. As for the rest of us, caught between the sunrise and a throne of 2,000-year-old giant stone gods, it is pure bucket list.

I stroll up the stone path beneath the pre-dawn stars, slipping silently under the cover of light. Above me is a 55-metre-high pyramid of crushed limestone, painstakingly assembled to honour and entomb King Antiochus I, who ruled in the century before Christ. To join the gods of his faith—Zeus, Apollo, Fortuna, Hercules—Antiochus had giant statues built on either side of the pyramid,

adding a statue of himself to join their throne. Not only would he be an equal of his gods, but the sun would forever rise and set beneath their feet. Scarred and cracked by age, the king and his gods still remain, their heads decapitated but carefully positioned to face the sunrise below. Greek inscriptions behind the throne explain the site for an eternity of visitors, urging them to remain true to their gods. But all eyes are on the mountains. Dozens of Turkish tourists stroke their cameras, ready for the sun. Some are wrapped in blankets, having made the pilgrimage hours ago, when the desert air was crisp. With each passing second, the sky transforms. Mauve, lavender, the soft veil of amethyst. Finally, a perfect golden egg yolk appears, cracked against the jagged rim of the mountains in the distance. I hear the excited *oohs* and *aahs* typically reserved for fireworks, the clicks of cameras recording the moment for posterity. The first golden ray strikes the statue of Zeus, and the king of Greek gods sparkles in the light, as he has for millennia. Without doubt, it is one of the most magical sunrises I have yet seen. Fifteen minutes later, the Turks have all departed. They came for the sunrise; I'm staying for the history.

Standing 8 to 10 metres high, the limestone statues exude their own type of magic. There is Apollo, god of light and reason. Fortuna, goddess of luck, fortune and fertility. Mighty Hercules, born to Zeus and a human mother, is broken beneath his thick beard. Joining the gods are an eagle, their traditional messenger, and Aslan, the proud lion, recognizable from *The Lion, the Witch and the Wardrobe.*

A temple once stood here, and whatever rituals took place within it certainly left an emotional resonance. After a packed breakfast, eaten while gazing upon the distant mountains of northern Syria, I walk around the scattered limestone to the western terrace, where Antiochus replicated the pantheon of his gods. In eight hours, they'll watch the sun set beneath their feet. I hike up a nearby hill and take it all in. Empires, wars, earthquakes and tourists—they will come and go, but the heads of Olympians will always follow the sun.

From Adiyaman, we drive to the city of Diyarbakir, its old town surrounded by a 5.5-kilometre basalt wall dating back to the Byzantines. This is the longest ancient wall after the Great Wall of China. Diyarbakir was a prize battled over by Romans and Persians, before falling into Byzantine, Arab, Turkish, Mongol and then Persian hands. The Ottoman Empire took control in the early 1500s. From atop the old wall, crumbling in parts, restored in others, some of that history can be seen, along with the narrow streets and wider boulevards of the city. In the distance, the Tigris River flows and a fertile patch of crops forms a crescent of green against the rocky, sandy desert.

Sanliurfa, also known as the historical city of Urfa, is the City of Prophets. It is here that Abraham, the founding father of monotheism, was born. Biblical scholars debate whether the town of Ur, mentioned in Genesis, is, in fact, Urfa or somewhere else in Iraq. Regardless, Muslim tradition holds that Abraham was born in a local cave, and here he survived being burned at the stake by King Nimrod for tearing down pagan idols. A miracle is said to have occurred, with Allah turning the wood into fish and the fire into water. This spot, Baliki Gol (Pool of Abraham), or the Lake of Sacred Fish, is a holy destination for Turks.

Drinking sweet tea on a restaurant patio, I gaze at the layers of Urfa's history, recognizing empires the way geologists might recognize eras in sedimentary rock. On the hill, the remains of a 1st-century castle, with two pillars dating back even further. A 6th-century church tower to the right, a 13th-century mosque on the left and another 17th-century mosque closer to the front, courtesy of the Ottomans.

And I can see the cave where the prophet was alleged to have been born over 4,000 years ago. In the middle, a giant Turkish flag rolls with the wind. Turkey, the latest empire to dominate this region.

Sepia dust from the encroaching desert relented briefly during the 40-kilometre drive to Harran, a town mentioned in the bible and known as one of the oldest settlements in recorded history. This is where Abraham, under the directions of God, decided to move to the land of Canaan. This is where Rebecca drew water from the well for Jacob, where Roman armies were squashed in battle, where a pagan people known as the Sabians existed until the 11th century. Ancient bricks are scattered along the landscape, enduring one more desert storm. I pick up a chunk of rock and am surprised to see a blue colour on the other side. Rinsed with water, it is clearly ceramic—the shard of an ancient pot? Archaeological teams continue their investigations behind fenced-off areas, but one can still literally tread upon relics of the past.

Unlike in Istanbul, with its heavy tourist traffic, eastern Turkey has few tour buses, touts and men trying to sell you carpets. Yet it serves up everything that makes the country such a remarkable destination—the hospitality, food, landscape, culture and, most of all, the history.

START HERE:
globalbucketlist.com/nemrut

Paraglide in Southern Turkey

Eighteen hundred metres below me, the Mediterranean sparkles like sequins on a disco queen dancing beneath a mirror-ball sun. I stand atop a cliff, surveying the view, feeling my nerves pickle with sweat. A brief countdown, an awkward run, the ground vanishes beneath my feet and, suddenly, I am flying. Not like Superman, mind you, but comfortably seated in a paragliding harness. My tandem pilot, Alper, begins to hunt thermals, warm pockets of air that boost the parachute up with such force it leaves my stomach reeling. As we level out and gently drift seaward with the breeze, the liberating sensation I feel is matched only by the scenery. Located on Turkey's south coast, Ölüdeniz is known as one of the world's best paragliding destinations for good reason.

I first heard about Ölüdeniz in Rio de Janeiro, where I tried hang-gliding for the first time. Instructors and clients were bantering over which form of gliding is better. Much like skiers and snowboarders, those who choose to *hang* and those who choose to *para* share a friendly rivalry as they argue which delivers a better sensation, the purer form of the glide. Ölüdeniz's reputation had spread as far as Brazil because of its perfect weather conditions through much of the year, its impressive height and the unbeatable views. Below the peak lies a popular resort town with dozens of hotels and a packed, pebbly beach alongside the turquoise Mediterranean.

It takes us over an hour to drive up the steep, rocky slopes in an all-terrain truck. "We do this five times a day, seven days a week, six months a year," explains Alper, looking suitably bored, as do the other instructors seated in the back of the truck. He works for Hector Tandem Paragliding, which shepherds thousands of tourists up and down the mountain each summer, as many as 50 a day. Guests like me will sit in the front harness while the pilot takes care

of the technicalities. This means no training or experience necessary; in fact, you don't even have to hold on. Alper tells me that his youngest client was a three-year-old girl who fell asleep in her harness halfway down the mountain.

We finally reach the peak, which is buzzing with solo paragliders and staff of tandem companies in the thralls of high season. I suit up in thick overalls, feeling the familiar nerves kick in, though watching the graceful takeoff of other gliders helps keep the jitters at bay. Unlike with hang-gliding or bungee jumping, it won't feel like I'm jumping off a cliff. Alper simply waits a few minutes for the right wind and together we run forward. The ground gives way to air. It's a

procedure as simple as wading into water. Paragliders are designed to keep you flying as long as possible, not slow your decent. Thermals provide the lift, allowing the pilot to stay in the air for hours with an incredible measure of control. Alper guides us toward another glider so that our parachute tips touch. My free hands means that I can snap some great photos.

There are a few things I really don't want to hear from any guide, pilot or instructor. At the top of the list is "Brace for impact," but not far behind is "Do you want to see what this baby can do?" That's exactly what Alper says, and before I can answer, he nose-dives the paraglider into a death spiral. In the seconds it takes Alper to halt the descent, I have turned as green as a toasted pistachio. Thrill-seekers will be in their element, but I prefer to leave somersaulting head over chute to the professionals.

After half an hour, we slowly descend toward the landing zone on the beach. The paraglider touches down so softly I don't realize we've landed until I'm standing on solid ground.

Paragliding has boomed in recent years, largely because of the ease of set-up, the undeniable thrill and the sport's excellent safety record. Since Turkey, I've glided over an emerald-coloured lake in Slovenia's magnificent Julian Alps, high above New Zealand's Queenstown and against the orange cliffs that buttress the Pacific in San Diego's Torrey Pines. Spiral dives notwithstanding, experiencing the genteel art of floating under a parachute should be enjoyed at least once in your lifetime. Southern Turkey's beauty merely provides the bonus thermal to keep us flying high on the Great Global Bucket List.

START HERE:
globalbucketlist.com/paraglide

Troglophytes—Not Just a Cool Word

Medieval troglodytes (aka cave dwellers) carved homes, churches and even cities into the soft tufa of central Turkey's Cappadocia. For bucket listers, there's much here to appreciate, from spending the night in a quiet cave hotel to riding a romantic hot-air balloon over fairy chimneys and other unique rock formations. Two thousand years ago, the Hittites lived here in an underground city, carved deep into the earth. During the Dark Ages, persecuted Christians returned to these same Kaymakli caves for sanctuary. Eight levels deep, with one room for each family, these caves, linked by low narrow tunnels, hid some 5,000 people beneath the ground. In 2015, a housing development in the regional capital of Nevsehir stumbled upon an underground city that archaeologists estimate housed tens of thousands of people.

Go to Hell

While it might be cute to visit Hell (Michigan) or Hell (Norway), give this bucket list a little credit. If visiting places with weird names is something to do before you die, I'd have to include chapters about Intercourse (Pennsylvania), Saint-Louis-du-Ha! Ha! (Quebec), Anus (France), Humpty Doo (Australia), Gogogogo (Madagascar) and, yes, even Austria's very own Fucking. Seriously, there is a village named with that unfortunate adjective. I once went to school with a prickly fellow by the similarly unfortunate name of Dougal Dick. He was often telling us to go to hell, and I don't believe he was talking about Turkmenistan.

You see, in this particular case, Hell has a doorway, and it is located near a village called Derweze in central Turkmenistan. The Door to Hell, also known as the Derweze gas crater, has belched out flames, sulphur and menace since 1971. Funny story, really: Soviet engineers discovered one of the world's largest gas reserves and promptly got drilling. Then the ground collapsed, creating a large crater spewing poisonous gas. The solution: light the gas leak and let it burn out, which the engineers estimated would occur within a couple of weeks. Here we are, many decades later, and the resulting hellfire is still flaming, boiling mud and intensifying the crater so that it is now 70 metres in diameter. The sight of an ominous burning hole in the Karakum Desert continues to terrify the hell out of everyone who sees it. In 2010, the Turkmenistan government announced plans to stop the burning of untold volumes of valuable natural gas. Like many things in Turkmenistan, that didn't go so well. Then tourists started

showing up, drawn by tales of an otherworldly inferno burning in the ground, including my über-traveller friend Rus Margolin, who has visited over 200 countries.

"Hell is literally in the middle of nowhere. You might see an occasional wild camel crossing the desert road, but that's it. It's best to time it so you get there for sunset and the night fires." Another friend, acclaimed explorer George Kourounis, is the only man to ever step foot on the bottom of the crater.

"It is as hot as Satan's breath and stinks to hell too," George tells me. "You feel like a gladiator in a coliseum of fire."

Turkmenistan's president, Gurbanguly Berdymukhamedov, his name a curse for spelling bees everywhere, has changed his strategy to create a protected nature reserve, preserving the fiery Door to Hell so that bucket listers can show up and impress their Facebook friends with photos. Note that the Prince of Darkness himself would need the correct paperwork, since Turkmenistan is the only country in the world that requires a visa from *everyone*. And while it's not easy getting to Turkmenistan, much less driving 270 kilometres from the appropriately named state capital of Ashgabat, there are a couple of local tour operators who can get you to the gates of hell.

For those of you chasing weird place names who would prefer the relative accessibility of Llanfairpwllgwyngyllgogerychwyrndrobwllllantysiliogogogoch, Wales; Dildo, Newfoundland; or Boring, Tennessee—well, there's nothing wrong with ticking those places off the list either.

START HERE:
globalbucketlist.com/derweze

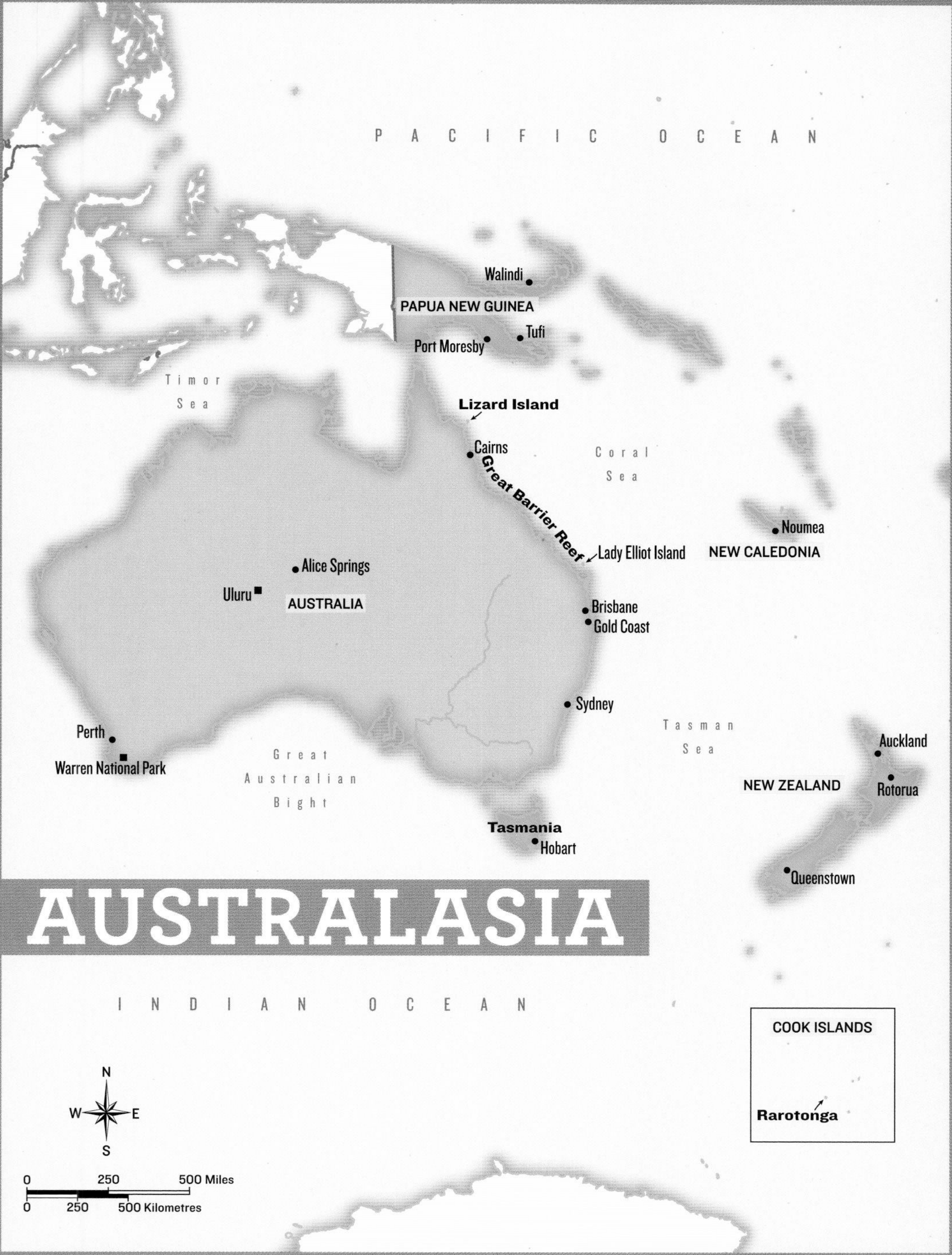

PACIFIC OCEAN

Walindi

PAPUA NEW GUINEA

Tufi

Port Moresby

Timor
Sea

Lizard Island

Cairns

Coral
Sea

Great Barrier Reef

Noumea

Lady Elliot Island

NEW CALEDONIA

Alice Springs

Uluru

AUSTRALIA

Brisbane

Gold Coast

Perth

Sydney

Warren National Park

Great

Australian

Bight

Tasman
Sea

Auckland

Rotorua

NEW ZEALAND

Tasmania

Hobart

Queenstown

AUSTRALASIA

INDIAN OCEAN

COOK ISLANDS

Rarotonga

N
W   E
S

0   250   500 Miles

0   250   500 Kilometres

Meet a Tasmanian Devil

Tasmania. Home of the devil, sanctuary for the wombat. Before the last ice age, it was connected to the mainland by a land bridge but now sits apart in the southeast corner of Australia, an island state in an island nation. "Tassie" is a road less travelled for most visitors to Australia, but then, bucket listers don't represent most visitors. We want peace, we want quiet, we want beauty; we want nature and adventure and unique animals—human and otherwise—we'll never forget.

Tasmania was discovered as early as 1642 by a Dutch navigator named Abel Tasman. Not much happened in Van Diemen's Land, as it was known, until the British decided to settle convicts on it in 1803. Australians can be sensitive about their origins, though it should be said that many founding convicts were victims of corruption or involved in the pettiest of crimes. Van Diemen's Land, on the other handcuffed hand, was reserved for hardcore and repeat offenders. The entire island was a brutal experiment in prisoner reform and punishment. Convicts were initially assigned to work and support the free settlers, but this was deemed not harsh enough. Hard-labour camps were introduced and prisoners put to work as slaves, with only gruel and God for sustenance. Port Arthur, the most infamous prison on the island, was founded as a "machine to grind men honest."

Located about an hour and a half from the capital of Hobart, Port Arthur today is Tasmania's premier tourist attraction, a convict theme park complete with wax models and bad period actors. By the mid-1800s, the island convict machine had ground to a halt. The British stopped sending prisoners, and harsh Van Diemen's Land became beautiful Tasmania, and lo, all was good. With a population of about half a million, Tasmania is an outdoor lover's paradise, offering abundant hikes, beaches, biking, fishing and climbing. It is also blessed with an indigenous creature straight out of everyone's favourite Saturday-morning cartoon.

The Tasmanian devil is synonymous with the island, as ubiquitous as Mickey Mouse in Disneyland. Unlike rodents, they are nocturnal and shy, not to mention ugly, smelly and bad-tempered. Good thing they don't have sharp jaws that clamp down four times harder than a pit bull's. Oh wait, they do. Tasmanians love their ferocious, hairy devil, especially since the species is going through its own special form of hell. A rare form of contagious cancer has wiped out an estimated 70 per cent of the population since 1996, with no cure in sight.

The devils' plight is not aided by their knack for ending up as a popular item on the roadkill menu. While the roadkill is impressive in Western Australia, the sheer amount of dead kangaroos, wallabies, wombats, possums, devils and other indigenous wildlife on Tasmanian roads suggests carnage.

"It's unfortunate that the first animals most tourists see in Tasmania are dead ones," says Matt, my enthusiastic guide for a three-day tour. Fortunately, we visit a nature park where we can check out a few live ones. There are many things to be grateful for in the world, and the fact that kangaroos are herbivores is among them. Forester kangaroos are enormous, built like heavyweight boxers with sharp talons that can tear a man to shreds like a used lottery ticket. I hand-feed one particularly friendly beast, and when he grabs hold of my arm with his claws, *cuddly* is the last description that comes to mind. Later that day I order a tasty kangaroo burger for lunch, just to reassure myself of my place on the food chain.

Freycinet National Park, home of Wineglass Bay and striking red granite mountains, is the island's natural highlight. Wineglass Bay got its name from the shape of the inlet—and from the fact that whalers used to slaughter whales here, turning the colour of the water to Cabernet. But fortunately those days are long gone, replaced by a protected national park and

mirror-clear turquoise water buttressing an empty white-sand beach.

"This is why people come to Tasmania," explains Matt. "You may have natural beauty like this on the mainland, but here we have it all to ourselves."

We visit misty Cataract Gorge, outside Launceston, and the

Is That a Tasmanian Tiger?

The thylacine was the largest carnivorous marsupial of modern times. It lived in Australia, Tasmania and New Guinea until farmers eradicated the species to extinction. Described as a large shorthaired dog with a hyena's gait and tiger-like stripes on its back, this predator was mostly shy and avoided human contact. The last known Tasmanian tiger, as it was more commonly known, died at the Hobart Zoo in 1936. Yet there have been hundreds of unconfirmed sightings reported since. Huge rewards have been offered over the years for the physical evidence of its existence. Despite several claims and blurry photographs, the thylacine is considered extinct. If there are any tigers running about in the remote bush of northwest Tasmania, they've learned to stay well clear of any humans looking for them. Keep your eyes peeled anyway, just in case.

Painted Cliffs on the former prison colony of Maria Island. We then walk across a land bridge to a small island to spot local penguins. The tide comes in on the way back, and I find myself swimming in rough currents to the safety of the beach. As with the tiger snake that slithered across my path earlier in the day, the result could have been dangerous but was far more exhilarating. Tasmania is an easy choice for those seeking an alternative to the holiday meccas of Australia's east coast. Should you need another excuse to add Tassie to your bucket list, you can confess, truthfully, that the devil made you do it.

START HERE:
globalbucketlist.com/tasmania

Explore the Great Barrier Reef

Although you may not actually be able to see the Great Wall of China from space (see page 263), you can certainly see the Great Barrier Reef. At 2,300 kilometres, it is almost *ten* times longer than the next longest barrier reef, found in Belize. Running up the east coast of Australia and covering an area of approximately 348,000 square kilometres, it shields the mainland with a wall of 2,900 reefs and 900 islands, home to more than 1,500 species of fish, 400 species of hard coral, 4,000 species of mollusc and 240 species of birds. That's a lot of creatures, and a lot of numbers, which is why I've flown down under to investigate the best way to chalk up one of earth's natural wonders on the bucket list.

We'll start in Port Douglas, a winding drive up the coast from the gateway of Cairns. Affluent Port Douglas also serves as a hub for the Daintree National Park, a UNESCO World Heritage Site and the world's oldest tropical rainforest. But I've arrived to board Quicksilver's wave-piercing high-speed catamaran to the outer reef. Operating 365 days a year, the full-day excursion is one of the most popular activities in all of Australia. The catamaran deposits guests on a permanent pontoon, from where they can snorkel, dive, putter about in semi-submersible vessels, enter an underwater observation station, feast on a buffet and even take to the skies in a short helicopter ride.

From above, I begin to grasp the size and staggering beauty of the reef. Crystal turquoise water barely conceals mounds of living coral as far as the eye can see. Back on the pontoon, I sign up for the Ocean Walker, a chance for non-swimmers to experience the reef Captain Nemo–style. With air piped in, a heavy fishbowl-like glass helmet is placed over my head. I walk down to an underwater platform, enjoying a wet-body, dry-face sensation as a diver feeds a monstrous Maori wrasse in front of me. All in, the outer pontoon is a grand day out for the whole family, though it can be quite busy, especially when a cruise ship is in town. Far more peaceful is the sea-kayak excursion I take

from the beach of my jungle escape, the lovely Thala Beach Lodge.

The water is calm this early in the morning, and an overcast sky has coloured the turquoise seas silver. Sea turtles pop out of the water just metres from my paddle to see who's visiting their turf. It's been a pleasant introduction to the reef; now it's time to take it to the next level.

Lizard Island is a true slice of paradise. A 45-minute charter flight from Cairns takes me to this barrier reef island that consists of a protected national park, a five-star all-inclusive luxury resort and an important marine research station. It is also one of the best places to scuba dive on both the inner and outer reefs. Seemingly everyone who works here is young, tanned and fetching, from the staff at the resort to the international scientists studying how climate change is impacting the ecosystem.

"They should rename the resort 'Perseverance,'" I suggest during an outstanding dinner of duck confit and lobster lasagne. Not too long ago, a cyclone had torn across the island, wrenching vegetation out at its roots and causing millions of dollars of damage. After extensive renovations at the resort and just one month away from its reopening, *another* cyclone came along and did just as much damage. After many more months of repair, the resort is now built to withstand a category 5 cyclone. I suppose practice makes

A Crayola Box of Coral

Living coral reefs form when there is warm water and lots of sunlight. Hard corals have a limestone skeleton and are named after how they look. Of the 350-plus known hard coral species on the Great Barrier Reef, look out for staghorn, plate, mushroom, brain and boulder corals. Soft corals lack a skeleton but are typically more colourful than hard corals. Snorkellers and divers may notice that the reef does not appear as bright as it typically looks on TV or in magazine pictures. This is because of light absorption in water, red and yellow being filtered out within the first few metres of the surface. Professional underwater photographers use artificial lights to capture those famous, rainbow-coloured hues.

perfect, and in this case, the beautifully designed 40-suite resort is among the finest I've stayed at anywhere. But as much as I enjoy snorkelling over giant clams off the talcum beach in front of my villa, I'm more excited to dive one of the reef's best-known sites, the Cod Hole. No sooner am I in the water than hundreds of barracuda surround me. Minutes later, I'm gliding between technicolored canyons of coral, chasing docile whitetip reef sharks. Luminous fish are everywhere. The diversity of the ecosystem is staggering.

Before I bid farewell to the lizards after which Captain Cook was inspired to name the island, international scientists at the nearby research station give guests a tour to explain their field experiments, all designed to conserve the reef and measure the impact of human behaviour. Ocean acidification, pollution and increasing temperatures leave no doubt that the Great Barrier Reef is under threat. Passionate about even the most minute of plankton, the strapping researchers and marine biologists are working hard to save the oceans, and they just might do it too.

Seair's 12-seater C208 is flying low enough that I can see herds of dugongs grazing on underwater seagrass below. I had departed the surf mecca of Gold Coast early that morning for the two-hour, low-altitude flight to Lady Elliot Island. A small coral island located at the southern tip of the Great Barrier Reef, it's famous for its breeding turtles and manta rays. The eco-resort on the island is renowned for its clear waters, snorkelling and diving. Owned and operated by the Australian government, it is a more rustic and family-friendly affair than what I found on Lizard Island. Think less champagne and more beer. The beach cabins are just steps away from the coral. Greeting visitors is the chirpy white-capped noddy, along with barking bridled terns and cheeky buff-banded rails pecking for scraps on the dining patios. Within an hour, I'm snorkelling in the lagoon among Picasso triggerfish, yellow trumpetfish, steephead parrotfish and mimic leatherjacket—a fish that looks as strange as it sounds. A few hours later, I'm 18 metres below the surface, swimming through tunnels of coral, trying to keep my breath steady in the presence of graceful manta rays,

curious hawksbill turtles and ghostly blacktip reef sharks. Some guests are experiencing the same on a "discovery dive," which most resorts offer to guests interested in diving but not committed to the certification . . . yet.

"That was . . . I didn't know it could be like that!" exclaims a guy from Sweden, seduced by the magic of the Great Barrier Reef. Now you know too. Experiencing this marine marvel—above water or below, in luxury or on a budget—is a sizeable drop in our bucket list ocean.

START HERE:
globalbucketlist.com/barrierreef

Climb out of Your Tree

Thin metal rods poke out of the Dave Evans Bicentennial Tree, spiralling up toward a wooden platform, seventy-five metres in the Western Australia sky. These karri trees are among the tallest hardwoods in the world, and this particular tree, sitting inside Warren National Park, is the tallest in the forest. Climb 130 erratically staggered thin black rods, thrusting yourself between ever-widening gaps while your knees become as wobbly as a Central African government. Just when you're pickled with fear, you'll see a sign that reads, "That was the easy bit, mate!" The climb to the lookout takes about an hour and is far scarier than any tree you ever tackled in your childhood. There isn't even an official around to call an ambulance should you drop out the sky. Although if there was, he'd probably just say, "It's just a tree, mate! In Australia, we have spiders bigger than this."

START HERE:
globalbucketlist.com/bigtree

Explore an Ancient Burial Cave

It's not the darkness. It's not the tight squeezes. It's not the sharp rock, the dampness or the fact that I'm so far off-grid. No, it's the fact that each nudge forward reveals more and more bones, scattered and broken and unmistakably human. Some skulls are missing jawbones, others have huge cracks where a weapon made impact. Whoever these people were, their deaths were certainly violent, and their bones do not rest in peace.

The burial cave of Rimarua is found on the island of Atiu in the Cook Islands—a postcard-perfect island paradise in the South Pacific typically associated with honeymoons, hammocks and dreamy turquoise water. The Cooks, as they are affectionately known, consist of 15 islands in an area of ocean covering a staggering 1.8 million square kilometres. Traffic on the main island of Rarotonga follows two circular roads: an inner ring and an outer ring. To go one way, take the Clockwise Bus, to go another, take the Anti-clockwise Bus. Better yet,

hire a scooter, which you can ride without a helmet, to feel the warm sea breeze in your hair. I appreciate the value of helmets. My own helmet cracked in the scooter accident that started my global journey. But I appreciate that sometimes we need personal freedom, space, beauty, adventure and everything else that is the antithesis of a choking urban centre. If the city's getting you down, take two weeks in the Cooks and you won't need to call anyone in the morning.

There is not a single glitzy resort chain in the country. With

barracuda wasn't very impressive, but Mike from Black Pearl Charters did what islanders seemed to do naturally: smile wide, laugh deep and make visitors feel jolly good about life.

Most tourists stick to Rarotonga or the stunning Aitutaki Lagoon, where luxury hotels set up dinner tables on the beach under the stars. Atiu (pronounced "A-choo"), an island with just 400 inhabitants, is accessible by prop plane. A sign at the local airstrip reads—and I am not making this up—"Will passengers please hand their AK-47s, bazookas, grenades, explosives and nukes to the pilot on boarding the aircraft. Airport Management thanks you for your cooperation."

Captain Cook was the first European to explore Atiu in 1777. He was welcomed by the indigenous locals in much the same way I was welcomed by its current tribal chiefs—with the sound of a ukulele and a coconut cup of home brew, shared in one of the island's eight bush pubs. Atiu islanders are an exceptionally friendly bunch, eager to show visitors the natural beauty and wonders of their home. A handlebar-moustached character named Birdman George points

boutique being the rage in the world of hotels, here is a boutique island. Tiny craft shops sell colourful Polynesian fare; the festive weekend market smells of flowers and homemade barbecue. Fun fact: by law, the tallest building on the Cook Islands cannot be taller than a coconut tree.

On the water, I cast a line during my first deep-sea fishing adventure, hooking the biggest barracuda you've ever seen. When it comes to big-game fishing, I am told that exaggeration is a key skill, and fishermen tell no lies. Actually, my out flying endemic swiftlets, and instructs me how to climb a coconut tree. Another guy shows me how to peel a coconut with my teeth. I attend a festive local birthday celebration, eat sweet papaya for breakfast and stargaze in the warm, breezy night. It doesn't take long to fall in love with the authenticity of the place.

Very little is known about the Rimarua burial cave, as no formal archaeological studies have been undertaken. Marshall Humphreys, an Englishman who went "troppo," has been leading tours to the burial cave for years. Returning to the island with his Atiu-born wife, Marshall has rare permission from the landowners to take tourists into the cave, parts of which he continues to explore with his kids. Marshall parks his pickup along a dirt road and explains that life may not have always been as peaceful on Atiu. Legend holds that warriors from another island had the misfortune to underestimate an attack on a local tribe. After a massacre, their bodies were dumped into a hole in the ground. Centuries later, we carefully lower ourselves into this very hole, using slippery tree roots as footholds. Marshall admits it is

not an adventure for everyone, especially the overweight, squeamish or claustrophobic. Within seconds, I'm muddied and ducking under low rock. Avoiding sharp coral limestone overhangs, I make my way further into the dark, my headlamp lighting up piles of skulls and bones.

"There's more over here," says Marshall from up ahead. "And here . . . and here."

Since nobody has studied the cave or its history, nobody knows how old the bones actually are.

Unchain My Heart

Paradise islands that depend on tourism are easy to recognize. You typically see resorts operated by familiar names (Fairmont, Hilton, Hyatt, Four Seasons) and restaurants, coffee shops and fast-food joints similar to your local strip mall. There are no chains or mega-brands in the Cook Islands. Move over, Margaritaville, Starbucks and Sheraton. Governed by tribal chiefs with a strong emphasis on retaining its culture, all land must be family-owned and cannot be sold to foreign entities. Unique hotels, restaurants and stores are a welcome treat for visitors looking for something different, especially from a culture that takes its hospitality seriously. Unchain your heart. Set it free.

"Mind you don't step on any skulls," instructs Marshall cheerily, as if it were the most natural thing in the world to say.

I slide on my belly down one particular shaft and find yet more bones, over the years swept into a pile by heavy rain. I am face to face with a skull sporting a large hole in the cranium, the fatal impact of a Stone Age weapon. Could either of us have ever imagined we would meet across time, space and culture? I squeeze around, slither up the shaft and make my way back to the cave entrance. Mosquitoes are waiting in ambush, so we jump in the pickup and beeline for the chief's orange hooch in a bush pub. The crazy adventure, the sincere hospitality, the sheer beauty of the place—it warms my heart every time I revisit that day in my memory.

Some books, movies and songs stay with you long after they're over. Put the Cook Islands on your bucket list and you'll understand why some destinations stick with you too.

START HERE:
globalbucketlist.com/cookislands

Feed Fish by Hand

NEW CALEDONIA

Gourmet mustard, fine wines, patisseries, prominent noses . . . ah, France. Now add coconut trees and white, sandy beaches. Welcome to a cigar-shaped island in the South Pacific, a little slice of French paradise floating 16,000 kilometres from Europe. With a currency linked to the euro and local government controlled in Paris, New Caledonia might be only a two-hour flight from Sydney, Australia, but it's a world away.

The island is not swamped with foreign visitors. There are folks from France, figuring that a long flight is well worth it for a tropical island where you can still procure stinky cheese. There are a few Japanese honeymooners, taking advantage of direct flights from Tokyo. Otherwise, given its high cost, its remoteness, its inaccessibility and its, well, Frenchness, most South Pacific travellers prefer Fiji. Locals, immersed in their "We have the cake and we're eating it every day" paradise, prefer it that way. Here's a fun fact: Simon Fraser originally wanted to call the new British Crown colony he discovered on Canada's west coast "New Caledonia," since the coastal mountains reminded him of the Scottish Highlands. Alas, Queen Victoria nipped that idea in the bud, as Captain James Cook had already claimed his New Caledonia in the South Pacific, inspired too by its resemblance to his Scottish homeland.

I am here to visit my friend Philippe, a third-generation New Caledonian I had met travelling in Bolivia. Less than half an hour from the airport en route to a hunting lodge, he insists I refresh with a swim in a warm, clear mountain stream. Yes, I said hunting lodge. Before you start packing bags of blood to splatter me with on my next book tour, know that deer are a plentiful pest in New Caledonia—in fact, there are far more deer than people here. Local environmentalists *encourage* hunting to keep the deer population under control, for they are as abundant as chemicals in a hot tub (and just as deadly to plant life).

After our swim, we pick up cheese and fresh baguettes and continue our drive north to the lodge. That evening, the kitchen needs more meat. We're sitting on the patio, so our host picks up his rifle, shines a flashlight, pulls the trigger and, voilà, venison is ready to be collected by kitchen staff. I get the impression there are so many deer on the island, you can basically shoot in any direction and you're bound to hit one. We sit around a large bonfire under a beauty pageant of galaxies, grilling the meat over a wood fire.

Damn, these people have it good. There aren't even any mosquitoes. I pass up the offer to hunt, since I don't travel with a storage fridge for meat, nor do I have any experience, skill or desire to skin Bambi. Instead, I sit on the porch blasting empty beer cans, in the time-honoured trailer-park hick tradition. I prefer to shoot with my camera and kill with my photographs. Still, trophy hunters aside (especially those who practise dentistry), it's somewhat hypocritical to enjoy hamburgers while begrudging a chef who pulls the trigger.

When a New Caledonian asks you to guess what it is you're eating, shut up and keep chewing. My veal is delicious, and then I'm told I'm eating giant sea turtle. All I can think about is chewing on Yoda. Strong in the taste it is. The chef, a friend of Philippe's named Michel, has a storage freezer stocked with all manner of wild creatures, the strangest of which are fruit bats. Philippe is determined to flaunt the island's culinary offerings, both French and indigenous. We eat a traditional *bougna*—a stew of starches (sweet potato, taro,

Holland in Venezuela

In Bolivia, I meet a Frenchman born on an island in the South Pacific. I also meet a Dutch couple, Herman and Wilna, both born and raised on an island off the coast of Venezuela. New Caledonia, Bonaire and other islands are the last remaining colonial enclaves, operating as political and economic districts of other nations thousands of kilometres away. Most use foreign currencies, and have easy access to products from the motherland. If you're looking for more examples of "tropical" France, try Martinique, Guadeloupe, Réunion in the Indian Ocean, or French Guiana. You can also spend your euros on the islands of Saint Pierre and Miquelon, located just 25 kilometres off the coast of Newfoundland. The Netherlands controls the Dutch Antilles (including Bonaire, Saba and Curaçao), as well as Aruba—all in the Caribbean. Britain rules tropical Bermuda, Anguilla, Montserrat, the Cayman Islands and the British Virgin Islands. Hawaii is a state, but the United States also controls Puerto Rico, Guam, American Samoa and the US Virgin Islands.

manioc) and meat cooked with coconut milk in an earth oven for two hours. New Caledonians "cook" raw fish in the acid of strong lemon juice, much like Peruvians "cook" fish to make ceviche. The result—a parrotfish salad with coconut milk and garlic—is absolutely sumptuous. But this isn't parrotfish bought at the local fishmonger. On a hot, windy day, we jump in a boat and motor out a couple of kilometres to the reef that protects the island from heavy waves and hungry sharks. Snorkelling above, I watch Philippe and his friend Jan spear colourful parrotfish and one enormous lobster that put up an impressive fight. Back on shore, I gut my first fish, cut a finger posing with the lobster (as heavy as a break-up conversation at the altar) and soak in the sun with the number one local beer, creatively named Number One. That night, I hear a gunshot in the distance. One less deer walks the plains.

During my stay, I will feast on foie gras, various local deep-fried delicacies, chocolate croissants, fruits, tropical fish, octopus and a cheese that leaves my breath as noxious as the underwear of a coal miner. The island is an unexpected foodie delight, even if you're not too fond of fruit-bat stew.

Noumea, the capital, boasts all the modern trimmings: French supermarkets, global-brand stores, parks, billboards, beaches and nightclubs. It is odd to find gourmet French products a third of the price of those found back home in Canada, which is a lot closer to France than New Caledonia. Noumea's spaghetti streets lead to a downtown refreshingly free of tourist propaganda, a clear indicator that islanders are content to let Fiji take the German package tours, so they can just get on with living in paradise.

An early two-hour fast ferry drops us off on the adjacent Île des Pins (Isle of Pines), where Philippe insists I hand-feed luminous fish in a natural aquarium. Through a freak of nature, the deep ocean crashes against a shallow reef on this island, creating a sparkling, shallow clear pool bubbling with life. With a slice of bread, mask

and snorkel, I stand in the water as thousands of tropical fish swim in and around me, biting bread held between my fingertips. The beaches of Île des Pins are as fine and as white as flour, the water as bright as the innards of a blue lava lamp. We hike along a sea channel, and I feel that special buzz one feels when discovering a glowing jewel hidden deep down planet Earth's cleavage.

New Caledonia is the perfect melange of exoticness, natural wonders, gastronomic delights and South Pacific bragging rights. As Philippe drops me off at the airport, a bright rainbow arches over the lush green mountains into the sparkling blue sea. A fitting au revoir for an island that substitutes for France itself on our Great Global Bucket List.

START HERE:
globalbucketlist.com/ newcaledonia

Tickle Your Adrenalin Glands

It's perfectly normal to jump off buildings, planes, canyons and bridges in New Zealand. No other country compels their visitors—of all ages—to tackle extreme sports, egged on by slick marketing and unusual activities packaged together so convincingly that Grandma suddenly finds herself with a parachute on her back. Likewise, I'm going to package the highlights into one chapter, although I can already feel the soft breeze from your head shaking as you think, *I'd never do that!* Oh, but you will.

Canyon Swing: While the bungee folks are trained to promptly get you off the bridge before any second thoughts, the folks at Shotover Canyon Swing have turned their leap of faith into a performance. Jumpmasters ensure that your confidence is utterly shattered, your nerves shot and you're quadruple-guessing yourself before they facilitate your 60-metre free fall into a 200-metre arc at 150 km/hr. Jumpers can choose from a variety of styles, like being upside down, somersaulting, wearing a bucket or pin dropping off the edge. I chose a method called the Upside Down Gimp, rated five out of five on the soiled-underwear scale. Hanging with a teddy bear between my legs, the jumpmasters start the countdown. Five, four, three . . . the bastards dropped me before the countdown ended!

Swoop: Many activities are located on the North Island's Rotorua, a town seemingly designed to trim the weeds of boredom. Introducing the Swoop, a flying terror machine that hoists me up 40 metres by crane in a hang-gliding cocoon. All I have to do is pull a little red piece of plastic to pop the cable and send the cocoon hurtling in an arc at 130 km/hr with the G-force of a fighter jet. It's quite peaceful up there at the

top, with views of the surrounding green countryside, some cows in a nearby field. Pulling the ripcord is in my control, a thought that has me chewing on my aorta. Well, you can't hang off a crane forever. Life stops for the split second between my pull and the drop. Then it slams me in the face, leaving my breath, body and soul behind.

Zorb: Nearby in Rotorua, the Zorb is yet another enterprising Kiwi invention, consisting of a large plastic ball with a hollow core. Suitably protected from the elements, the ball is rolled down a 250-metre-long grass hill with one or more lucky Zorbonauts inside. The dry Zorb has me strapped into the innards of the ball. After rolling head over tail, I turn as green as the grass outside. They tell me nobody has puked in the Zorb. Yet. The wet Zorb, in which I am unhinged and allowed to slosh around, is akin to getting rinsed in a large washing machine. You know, for good, clean fun.

Jetboating: In the 1950s, a Kiwi farmer needed a quick way to survey his land from a shallow river. He invented jetboating, a technology that has since evolved to 1,000

horsepower machines faster than Formula 1 cars. What's more, they can cruise on just inches of water and turn on a penny. Today there are jetboat tours around the country, but my favourites are Rotorua's Agrojet (which hits 100 km/hr in 4.5 seconds on a 1-kilometre course), Queenstown's Shotover Jet (which takes a dozen passengers through a narrow canyon) and Dart River Jet Safaris (which visits *Lord of the Rings* and *Chronicles of Narnia* film locations). All enjoy ripping a 360-degree Hamilton Turn, a manoeuvre that soaks most passengers in the boat. The tours are open to all ages and bodies, but inevitably, everyone ends up shrieking like a teenage banshee.

It's one thing trusting yourself to jump off a bridge, another watching jetboat pilots shave rock faces in a speeding piece of heavy equipment you happen to be attached to.

Sledging: On the Wairoa River, you can raft over the world's highest commercial vertical drop. Essentially, this means your inflatable raft will be airborne before submerging on

impact below. Hang on, because there's a very good chance of capsizing. To ensure you really get soaked, consider an activity the Kiwis call sledging. Using flippers, a heavy kickboard and a crash helmet, you forgo the raft altogether and meet the rapids at eye level. Of course, this means you have to use your body to navigate rocks, undertows and whirlpools, but that's all part of the fun. Never let go of your board, and unless you feel like drinking half a river, keep your mouth shut.

Bungee Jumping: Much like nobody could have anticipated Chris Pratt becoming a movie star, who would have thought that tourists would pay good money to leap off

a bridge attached to a heavy elastic band. A Kiwi named A.J. Hackett invented the commercial bungee jump in 1988. Kawarau Gorge Suspension Bridge outside Queenstown is not the highest bungee in the world (see Macau Tower, page 294), or even the highest in New Zealand (that's the Nevis). It is, however, the home of the world's first commercial bungee operation, which carries its own bragging rights. Line up to plummet 43 metres, and ask to dunk your head in the river below.

Caving: Although it started with a quick zipline into a cave, blackwater rafting is the most genteel of our Kiwi bucket list activities. I'm deep in a limestone

cave, floating on a rubber tube, headlamps off. A Milky Way of glow-worms covers the rocks above my head. Our guide silently drags our group forward, our legs linked like a chain of human doughnuts. It feels like we're navigating deep space. Located about an hour from Rotorua, the Waitomo region has over 300 caves—a spelunker's wet, damp and dark dream. This deep in the earth, the water is clean and freezing, but the wetsuit keeps me toasty (along with the hot coffee and biscuits carried by the ever-friendly Kiwi guides). Caving is always fun, but it is the starlike glow-worms (more accurately, maggots with phosphorescing poop)

that steal my heart. As they light up the dark tunnels with thousands of twinkling, green LED-like lights, catch a glimpse of life in space, deep in the earth.

Skydiving: If I were to take all the above thrills and mould them tightly between my palms, the ball of nerves would look like a skydiver. Nothing comes close to that moment when you gather your wits during the free fall and experience the sensation of terminal velocity. Skydiving in New Zealand is exceptional because of the stunning scenery and the pro-fessionalism of the sport's operators. NZONE Skydive, the best of the lot, runs operations in both Rotorua and Queenstown and counts grand-parents among its biggest fans. The rolling green fields of the North Island, and the fjords and mountains of the South Island, really show off at 3,500 metres. Sixty seconds later, the chute opens, and it's a gentle float down to earth. Not only have you conquered your fear, but you'll feel like you've conquered New Zealand too.

START HERE:
globalbucketlist.com/kiwi

Learn to Dive in Papua New Guinea

Chronic ear problems put the kibosh on my underwater dreams long ago. Travelling to Malaysia, the Philippines and the Maldives, I could only listen to recreational divers talk about their experiences exploring the world's best reefs. My accursed, rotten and largely cosmetic right ear doesn't hear much and is prone to infection. If only the damn thing worked like it is supposed to. Enter TV's Survivorman, Les Stroud.

In an episode on his show, Les gets ready to dive in Borneo. He too has chronic ear problems. The solution, he reveals, is a tiny piece of Kraton, a type of polymer plastic, fashioned into a product called Doc's Proplugs. These vented plugs have a tiny hole that allows equalization while keeping out water to avoid ear infections and ruptured eardrums—useful for sufferers and healthy divers alike. Since the plugs allowed Les to dive, they might be my ticket to underwater adventure too. I quickly procure an inexpensive pair and seek out an exceptional destination where I can test them out.

Papua New Guinea (PNG) is the world's most ethnically diverse country, with over 700 tribes speaking an incredible 800 languages. It is a country vastly rich in resources yet remains poor and undeveloped. Although PNG is blessed with pristine natural beauty, tourism accounts for just 30,000 visitors a year. Disneyland gets that many visitors in a single day. One million highlanders, previously unknown to civilization, were discovered as late as the 1930s. PNG *still* has undiscovered tribes, animals, minerals and insects deep in the bosom of its jungles. No wonder scientists, anthropologists and mine speculators are drawn like moths to a wildfire. Tourism's diminished status is evident upon my arrival at the airport in the capital city. Instead of tourist brochures, there are free mining maps. Instead of resort billboards, there are advertisements for mining equipment.

The Airways Hotel, located just minutes from the airport, has armed guards at the entrance. With a terrible reputation for crime, Port Moresby is a potholed sprawl of a capital, stretching over hills with few landmarks. I've never stayed in a hotel guarded by men with shotguns. Great showmanship, but do they have to clutch their weapons so readily? Truthfully, the only killers I worry about are mosquitoes, since the whole country is cursed with malaria. Having connected through Brisbane, I expected Australians to think of PNG as a tropical getaway, their own Hawaii down under. Instead, PNG is viewed as backward, hostile and politically turbulent. Most Australians visit only to tick off from their list the gruelling yet world-renowned 96-kilometre Kokoda Trail, retracing a turning point in the Pacific Campaign of World War II. The area was a hot

spot for heavy fighting between
the Allies and Japanese, and World
War II plane wrecks still litter PNG
and its surrounding waters, as if the
1940s were only a few years ago.

Joining me is a group of experienced female divers who happily
take me under their wetsuited
wings. Among them are the Scuba
Diver Girls, a San Diego–based
diving club that boasts hundreds
of thousands of online followers.
Together, we hop on a small plane
to the Tufi Dive Resort, overlooking
a gorgeous fjord. It's the only place
in the area with electricity, and it
owns the only two cars to drive
the few dirt roads. Roaming the
modest grounds is a large hornbill

named Coco, a wallaby and a pair
of cuscus, possum-like creatures I
recognize vaguely from my night-
mares. With a neurotic twitch, Coco
is prone to nipping my toes under
the dinner table.

The girls immediately head out
with their flippers, and I hit the
books. Most dive resorts offer PADI
or NAUI qualification courses, and
Tufi is an exceptional classroom.
Back home I'd have to learn my
skills in a swimming pool. Here I
practise in the resort's house reef,
sharing my school desk with giant
lionfish, parrotfish and luminous
coral. There is typically an incredible 30 metres of visibility; the water
temperature hovers between 26°C

and 29°C all year round. In the world of diving, that's about as good as it gets. I learn about equalization and pressure groups, buoyancy and hand signals. I learn that divers don't consider any marine animals to be dangerous so long as you keep a respectful distance. Encountering sharks and whales is a lucky bonus, not a terrifying ordeal. Modern dive computers calculate how much air you have, how deep you are and how long you have to recover between multiple dives. That, along with being accompanied by professional, experienced divemasters, all but removes the dangers of

decompression illness. Reminded to keep checking my gauges, I realize there really is little to worry about. I pass my written exam and practical skills with flying colours, the girls throw me a party, and, finally, after all these years, I am ready to submerge myself in another world.

Unlike your latest operating system, the earplugs work exactly as advertised. As I effortlessly defy gravity, floating alongside more colour and life than I've ever imagined, on this, my first certified dive, tears well up beneath my mask. As I dish out underwater high-fives with the girls, my grin is so wide,

water almost gushes into my regulator (I am well trained on how to clear it). Oprah would call it an "aha moment." Those of you who dive know what I'm talking about. I only hope the rest of you will have the opportunity to find out.

Based at Australian-owned Walindi Plantation Resort, we explore the reefs of Kimbe Bay, off the coast of New Britain. Over half the world's coral species can be found in this one bay, as well as 900 species of fish. Surrounded by active volcanoes, I dive my first deep-water swim-through, a reef tunnel teeming with life 34 metres beneath the surface. I encounter my first big animals: grey reef sharks gliding like shadows. We explore a submerged Japanese World War II Zero fighter and take turns sitting in the cockpit. Despite coral latching onto its wings, the fighter is in remarkable condition. I hover over giant barrel sponges, red whip gorgonians, moray eels and nudibranchs, and beneath schools of barracuda and countless neon tropical fish. Clownfish comically guard their anemones. I have found Nemo at last.

I learn to dive with a distinct feminine grace. The Scuba Diver Girls believe male divers often miss the

Bucket List Diving Spots

Margo Sanchez, co-founder of the Scuba Diver Girls, shares her 10 favourite dive spots to put on your bucket list:

- Bahamas: Tiger Beach
- Bonaire, Leeward Antilles: the east coast
- Cook Islands: Aitutaki Island
- Fiji: Beqa Lagoon Resort Shark Dive Experience
- Mexico: cenotes in the Maya Riviera
- Mexico: Isla Mujeres
- Micronesia: Yap
- Papua New Guinea: Walindi Bay
- Southern California: La Jolla
- Virgin Islands: St. Thomas

point, aggressively chasing goals while the sheer delight of being underwater eludes them. Women, they tell me, are more patient divers, more in tune with the world of water. Dozens of dives later, I believe they are right, and continue to "dive like a girl," as a male divemaster recently told me. I took that as a compliment, and continue to do so.

On our return to Port Moresby, I pick up souvenir masks from a craft warehouse. There are no tourists, and the fantastic hand-carved tribal masks, bowls and statues are inexpensive. Sometimes things are too touristy, and sometimes things are not touristy enough. There's so much potential here. Papua New Guinea has the resources to be the richest country in the South Pacific. Corruption, crime, mismanagement and the outflow of wealth into foreign operations are challenges for the country to overcome. It reminds me of Africa—the crowds, the atmosphere, the tribes. It reminds me of Central America—the jungles, the volcanoes, the beaches. But in the end, of all the countries in the world, Papua New Guinea is distinctly, and utterly, itself.

Scuba diving, from the South Pacific or Caribbean to the cold waters off Canada, is a bucket list adventure that doesn't discriminate based on weight, age, physical ability or even your aquatic experience. Within one week, I had transformed from someone who had barely swum underwater to a scuba diver exploring shipwrecks and sharks, and even doing night dives. Modern equipment has greatly improved personal safety, and strict worldwide standards for dive shops and schools ensure the quality of equipment, instructors and guides. As for me, just when I thought I'd seen the world, it turned out I'd hardly seen any of it at all.

START HERE:

globalbucketlist.com/png

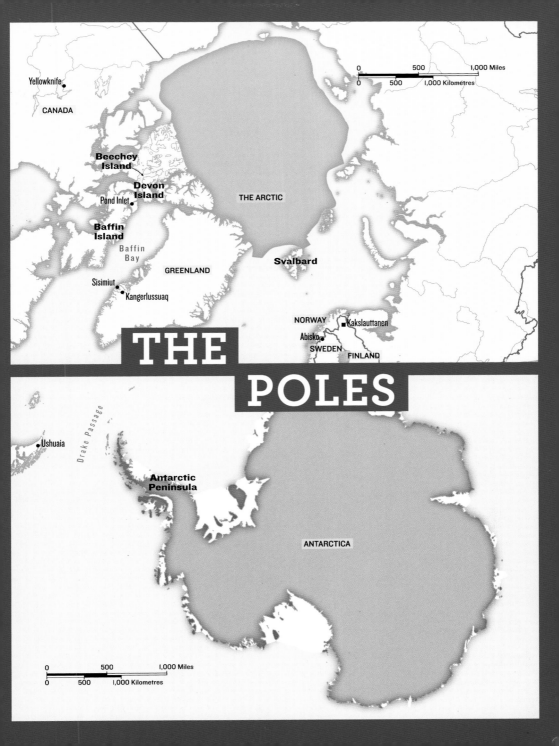

THE
POLES

Camp on the Seventh Continent

ANTARCTICA

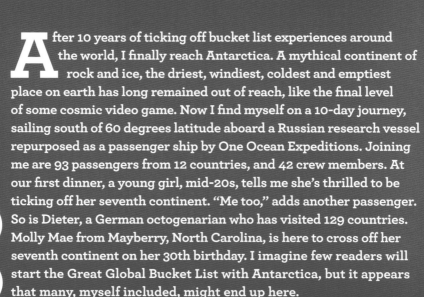

After 10 years of ticking off bucket list experiences around the world, I finally reach Antarctica. A mythical continent of rock and ice, the driest, windiest, coldest and emptiest place on earth has long remained out of reach, like the final level of some cosmic video game. Now I find myself on a 10-day journey, sailing south of 60 degrees latitude aboard a Russian research vessel repurposed as a passenger ship by One Ocean Expeditions. Joining me are 93 passengers from 12 countries, and 42 crew members. At our first dinner, a young girl, mid-20s, tells me she's thrilled to be ticking off her seventh continent. "Me too," adds another passenger. So is Dieter, a German octogenarian who has visited 129 countries. Molly Mae from Mayberry, North Carolina, is here to cross off her seventh continent on her 30th birthday. I imagine few readers will start the Great Global Bucket List with Antarctica, but it appears that many, myself included, might end up here.

Over the years researching this book, I have met thousands of people. When I tell them what I do, the reaction typically runs the gamut of "You have my dream job" to "You're a lucky bastard." The reality of travel writing is a story best left to another volume (and forms the basis of my television show, *Word Travels*). In the presence of such seasoned company on board the *Akademik Sergey Vavilov*, the reaction is no different. My travel partners ask a question that speaks volumes about the nature of Antarctica. To paraphrase: "As a writer, how on earth can you describe something like this?"

It doesn't take very long for Antarctica to throw down a challenge. Photographs might paint a picture worth a thousand words, but in merely 1,000 words, how do I describe a place so magnificently unlike anywhere else on the bucket list? Snow-capped mountains? Pu-leeze, we've seen plenty of them, from the Rockies to the Andes. Huge glaciers? We toasted them from a much larger, swishier cruise ship in Alaska. Seals and whales? No shortage of them in Canada's Haida Gwaii, not to mention Iceland. If Antarctica embodies all the above, isn't that enough to give one an idea of what to expect? Perhaps,

but that would be akin to describing Burning Man as an arts festival, a Lamborghini as a car, and China's Mount Hua as a day hike. The scale of Antarctica—with its frostbitten history and remoteness—is simply overwhelming. Awaking from a feverish dream of seasickness after crossing the notorious Drake Passage, we slowly drift down the Gerlache Strait. Blackened rocky peaks, crystal-blue sea ice, and the sheer beauty of our isolation leave hardened travellers speechless.

As a writer, I'm at a loss for the similes and metaphors to explain why every human being on earth should experience what the seventh continent is all about. Greater men have tried before. Polar legends like Robert Falcon Scott, doomed to failure and death, beaten to the South Pole by Norwegian Roald Amundsen. Explorers like Sir Ernest Shackleton, a mighty leader of men who survived one of the great adventures of modern times. Sir Douglas Mawson, Jean-Baptiste Charcot, James Clark Ross, Frank Wild—men of remarkable tenacity and human endurance. Others have wintered on the ice, driven mad by the darkness, the chill, the nothingness. Many kept diaries,

The Drake Shake

To reach the Antarctic Peninsula, all boats must cross the notorious Drake Passage. This 1,000-kilometre-long waterway is the bridge to the polar region, a bridge with gale-force winds, massive swells and the world's strongest currents. It's known by sailors to be the roughest stretch of water in the world, so take whatever seasickness remedy you have and huddle down until the boat stops pitching and rolling. The legendary Drake Shake is an ocean purgatory you might experience before reaching polar paradise. Fortunately, you might also experience Drake Lake, when the waters are calm and pleasant. Much like your personal susceptibility to seasickness, you won't really know how bad it is until you get there. However bad your Drake Passage, what awaits you on the other side is definitely worth it.

and Antarctic literature makes for fascinating reading, from the rudimentary logbooks to journals of philosophical despair. Men who starved, froze, drowned and yet embraced their fate with courage.

"For God's sake, look after our people," wrote Robert Falcon Scott, concluding his final journal entry. It was the end of a heroic age, when men faced the extreme forces of nature with remarkable hardiness. We have come a long way from those early journeys to discover the icy continent. I'm drinking a cold beer in a hot tub surrounded by the sweeping vista of the Lemaire Channel—and buxom ladies in bikinis. A four-course meal awaits in the dining hall, along with a dram

of fine Oban single malt. If he saw me, Shackleton would be spinning in his grave on South Georgia. Or maybe not? Perhaps the region's relative accessibility would have pleased him greatly.

Visitors to Antarctica—and there are some 40,000 a year—become its greatest ambassadors. We ultimately spread the inspiration we feel and champion the importance of this wilderness remaining a rare sanctuary from the ugliness of geopolitics. Governed by the Madrid Protocol, a treaty that gives one hope for the future of this planet, Antarctica is protected

from exploitation and ownership. A cynic might argue that's because oil has yet to be discovered or that the land is so barren, it has no value to anyone. Still, the International Association of Antarctica Tour Operators has strict guidelines for passenger ships, landings and encounters with wildlife: leave only footprints; preserve the ecosystem above all else.

Under the midnight sun, my eyes finally adjust to the searing splendour of the ice, and my mind begins to process the space. Twice the size of Australia, Antarctica is the world's fifth-biggest continent. Polar exploration might have changed, but our expedition still provides a taste of the misery of

yesteryear. Passengers can elect to camp one night on the ice itself, which is too good an opportunity to pass up. It is snowing lightly as we board the Zodiac boats from the gangway, a snow we hoped would stop, and never did.

Provided with a sleeping bag, Therm-a-Rest and bivouac, we are dropped off on a small island, where we will flatten the snow with our boots and lay our one-person coffin-like coverings on the ice. Surrounding us are mountains, glaciers and penguins, but this takes an immediate back seat to staying warm and dry, a feat hardly anyone manages to accomplish. A long, dark-less night of deep discomfort draws protests from some of the tourists, who eventually succumb to resignation and acceptance when told there is no going back to the ship until morning.

Squeezed into my sleeping bag, I think about Shackleton's men surviving on the ice in far worse conditions and with far inferior gear. Endurance, the very name of their doomed ship, is the quality most needed for survival in the Antarctic. At 4 a.m., the sky is still bright, the snow is still falling. Previously concealed by the pretty sights and the ship's comforts, the true face of Antarctica has revealed herself. Remote, hostile, bitterly cold— nature's fortress of solitude.

Lined up like sullen refugees, we await the first Zodiac, wondering if

we'll ever feel warm again. Shackleton would be horrified at the lack of some of the passengers' spirit, their hope so easily vanquished. I found the whole experience challenging, unforgettable and entirely authentic. Returning to the comforts of the *Vavilov*, our less-than-happy campers are congratulated for seeing the experience through. Within a couple of days, we find ourselves laughing about our memorable adventure on the ice.

On the way back from a shore excursion, two large humpback whales circle our Zodiacs, close enough for me to feel their blowhole spray land on my face. Throughout our journey, we have seen orca, minke whales, jumbo-winged

albatross, basking elephant seals, serpentine leopard seals lazing on the ice and thousands of penguins. I expected to see more whales in these protected waters, but the rotting remains of old whaling stations are a reminder of the massacres that took place in the past. It is estimated that in Antarctica alone, more than 2 million whales were butchered in the 20th century, more than all the whales that exist worldwide today. One Ocean's *Vavilov*, and its sister ship, the *Akademik Ioffe*, do visit South Georgia, where the waters boil with life, but that is a different, longer itinerary.

After a week, I've settled into the routine of life on board an expedition cruise. The enthusiastic intercom announcements recall a high-school camp: "Good morning, team! It's a beautiful day to meet the chinstrap penguins on Half Moon Island. We love chinstraps, because they've got *attitude*!" The lineups to enter the dining room. Happy hour, with Hilary tending the bar, meticulously DJing appropriate tunes from her iPod. I've grown particularly fond of the scorching Finnish sauna, then refreshing in icy seawater in the adjacent plunge pool. There have been a couple of birthdays, some anniversaries, raucous Chinese karaoke and discreet romances blossoming out of sight. The Russian crew live below, serving guests above, like an aquatic Downton

Abbey. Meals are tasty and always welcome. There's often storytelling at the bar in the evenings, the most fascinating tales always told by the ship's doctor, Dr. Joan. One of the world's foremost penguin researchers provides an answer to a question that has been bothering me for some time. No, penguins don't taste like chicken. Their meat is closer to liver. Just in case you were wondering too.

It is the penguins that capture most imaginations, anthropomorphized as they are in movies as overweight bureaucratic administrators with pot-bellies and hunched gaits. Awkward on land, graceful in water. You can stare at the Adélie, chinstrap and gentoo penguins for hours. Scientists on board confirm that penguin numbers are high and healthy. By the end of the trip, we no longer marvel at the penguins, unless we have not encountered them before, like the errant Macaroni (distinguishable by its yellow bushy eyebrows) lost within a sea of chinstraps. Just a week ago I knew little about penguins. Now I can tell my gentoos from my Adélies—squawking on land, hobbling about like Friar Tuck after raiding the liquor cabinet.

For 10 days, we receive no news from the outside world. While it's possible to send and receive email on board, there is no Web, no social media. Any major news? What's happening in the Middle East? Which three celebrities died? None of it matters down south. It probably never will.

From the onboard library, I pluck an anthology of Antarctic writing—what struggle and strife those early explorers went through! Frostbite, exhaustion, starvation . . . how they would have envied us today, with our Gore-Tex, sunblock and onboard salad bars. I have to remind myself to pause, look around. "If this bay were accessible and located in North America, people would come from all over the world just to see it," remarks Jeff, our photographer-in-residence. Dwarfed by glaciers and smoothly sculptured icebergs, we're on the Zodiac slicing a path through the sea ice. It's just another bay, on just another day.

Antarctica has delivered, without doubt, the most staggering views I've found on the Great Global Bucket List. Immersing oneself in the history of the continent's discovery only deepens one's sense of wonder and appreciation. As always, the people joining you—passengers and crew—will shape your experience just as surely as the strong wind shapes icebergs. Whether you visit Antarctica for the wildlife, the photography, the company or the sheer exoticness, prepare to be positively overwhelmed. This is not your typical adventure, and One Ocean's *Vavilov* is not your typical cruise. Every bucket lister is better off for it.

START HERE:
globalbucketlist.com/antarctica

See the Northern Lights

Surveys have asked thousands of people what's at the top of their bucket list. Familiar natural and ancient wonders float to the top: the pyramids in Egypt, the Grand Canyon, Niagara Falls. Typically taking pole position, however, are nature's celestial fireworks known as the aurora borealis. It appears our imaginations are enamoured by the idea of solar storms smashing into earth's magnetic fields. *Imaginations, ideas*—I use these words only because I have failed in numerous attempts to actually see the fabled northern lights. For those who live in high northern latitudes, witnessing shimmering colours dancing in the night sky is a certainty. For bucket listers hoping to see the lights, it is something of a crapshoot.

The northern lights are best seen in the early-morning hours during the coldest, darkest months.

I spent two freezing nights at an aurora-watching lodge outside Whitehorse, in Yukon. No dice. I spent five November days in bitterly cold Yellowknife, a city that sits directly below the aurora oval and is therefore one of the best places worldwide for aurora viewing. No dice. When I camped in a yurt in northern Saskatchewan, the night sky was gloriously clear. Tonight's the night! Except it wasn't. Sailing in remote Alaska late September? Nope. Iceland? Try again. Visiting the high Arctic got me excited, except it was summer and no lights shine in the midnight sun. You can see why I've come to believe that the northern lights are nothing more than a mass hallucination. Actually, they're more like the Dave Matthews Band.

Grammy-award-winning Dave Matthews is originally from Johannesburg, and during the height of his popularity, he would often pop home to visit family. At the time, I was a huge fan of the Dave Matthews Band. Its music made my ants march, and my 1990s crash, crush, spoon, two-step and say goodbye.

"I can't believe I met Dave Matthews!" a friend would tell me. Then another. Then another. Dave was turning up everywhere—at gigs and restaurants and pubs and events around the city. Try as I might, I never saw him. Visit after visit, it felt like God simply did not want me to meet Dave Matthews in person.

After 10 fantastic opportunities, it feels like God does not want me to see the northern lights either. Not so for my Facebook friends. They post incredible photos of green, and occasionally red and blue, waves crashing in the night sky. Sometimes these pictures are taken a day or two after I visited! Point being: you simply can't rely on ever seeing the northern lights. Granted, you can stack the odds in your favour by visiting aurora hot spots and consulting solar-flare charts. However, as hundreds of disappointed Japanese tourists in Yellowknife will testify, the aurora dances to its own tune. Heading north with the expectation of seeing the aurora is like going on safari hoping to see a crocodile and lion battle over a baby wildebeest. You don't schedule a visit with the lights. The lights . . . just happen.

Fact is, unless you can hop on a plane to Scandinavia or northern Canada or remote Russia on a moment's notice, the northern lights are simply not as accessible as other experiences in this book (and some of these experiences, I'm fully aware, are not very accessible at all). Aurora viewing camps are designed to make the experience

as comfortable as possible, but they cannot guarantee the lights will show up any more than a barman can promise you'll personally meet Dave Matthews.

Of course, bucket lists needn't be grounded in reality. We can dream of visiting the moon, going on an electric-car road trip with Elon Musk (another South African!) or unlocking the vault at Fort Knox. This Great Global Bucket List, on the other hand, is as tangible as the book or device on which you're reading it. Perhaps one day I *will* see ethereal ribbons of light twirl in the heavens, dancing in a celestial ballet. Perhaps one day I *will* meet Dave Matthews. That's the beauty of our bucket list. It is patient, evergreen and inherently rational. Just knowing an experience is out there waiting for us is all the inspiration we need.

START HERE:
globalbucketlist.com/aurora

Best Places to See the Northern Lights

Deciding where to go to see the aurora depends on many factors. Some places are further north, some are inexpensive, some have fewer clouds, some have minimal light pollution. Some might be more accessible or scenic than others. While there's no guarantee the lights will come out to play, stack the odds in:

Abisko, Sweden: This national park in Swedish Lapland is internationally renowned for its aurora viewing. Hop on a chairlift to the viewing station, exhibition station and four-course gourmet meal. There are daily flights from Stockholm.

Kakslauttanen, Finland (pictured below): There's a myth that procreating under the northern lights is good luck for any resulting babies. In which case, couples will appreciate the stunning glass igloos at this Arctic resort. Lie back, watch the sky, do what you gotta do.

Svalbard, Norway: Way up north of the Arctic Circle, the Svalbard Islands do not see daylight between mid-November and end of January. The aurora illuminates the polar night above a stunning landscape popular with European tourists.

Yellowknife, Northwest Territories: Yellowknife sits directly under the auroral oval, with flat terrain and few clouds. There's a strong chance of seeing the lights between January and April. Book a heated chair with one of the wilderness lodges located just outside the city.

Cross the Northwest Passage

For over 500 years, the Arctic has tempted (and in many cases, tortured) adventurers. With the Northwest Passage promising a faster trade route between Europe and Asia, one across the roof of the world, early explorers set out to find a reliable line through the labyrinth of desolate islands, barren peninsulas and hull-crushing sea ice. Despite the Arctic's reputation as a frozen wasteland, it is home to enthralling creatures (A tusked whale! Polar bears!), staggering vistas and the people who have survived here for millennia—the Inuit.

Over the years, I've had the good fortune to explore the vast territories that make up the Canadian Arctic, finding no shortage of bucket list–worthy experiences. Camping in northern Yukon, I've dodged grizzly bears to hike up granite tors, looking down on sweeping valleys carved by teal-hued glacial rivers. Thousands of beluga whales have swum at my feet near Arctic Watch on Somerset Island, the world's most northerly eco-lodge. I've sampled unusual Inuit culinary delights, like raw baby beluga, dried beaver and boiled tundra swan. (Melt-in-the-mouth Arctic char sashimi is understandably more agreeable for southern palates.) I've strolled on tundra beneath the midnight sun, swum in ice-cold waterfalls and gazed on the ruins of Thule and Dorset settlements stretching back thousands of years. Despite the starkness of permafrost, summers north of 66 degrees flourish with life. Fluffy white balls of Arctic cotton—along with colourful poppies, willows, wildflowers and luminescent lichen—sprout as if imagined by Dr. Seuss.

The Canadian territory of Nunavut is larger than Western Europe, yet just 36,000 people call it home. The Arctic's enormous space results in rare but rewarding wildlife encounters. Powerful shaggy

muskox recall the now-extinct woolly mammoth. Hundreds of thousands of caribou complete the longest land migration anywhere on the planet. Much like that of the Arctic fox, Arctic hare, ermine and rock ptarmigan, the fur of barren ground caribou turns white for the long winter, offering greater protection against predators.

Even in summer, weather up here is famously unpredictable, making travel expensive and somewhat difficult. Your safest and most comfortable bet is cruising Norway's Svalbard Islands or along the jagged coastlines of Greenland and Baffin Island. From my previous journey to Antarctica, I knew One Ocean

Expeditions' ice-strengthened *Akademik Sergey Vavilov* would be the perfect expedition ship for the Arctic and, with favourable ice conditions, a crossing of the mythical Northwest Passage itself.

One Ocean Expeditions' east-to-west itinerary follows in the footsteps of the Franklin Expedition, the Arctic's greatest maritime tragedy and most endearing mystery. One hundred and twenty-eight men, aboard two of the most technologically advanced ships at the time, went searching for the passage in 1845 and promptly disappeared. Their fate inspired dozens of failed rescue missions (the lives and boats lost looking for Franklin's *Erebus* and *Terror* number more than the original casualties), as well as songs, books, movies and conspiracy theories. As the scattered bones of Franklin's men began appearing on islands further south, morbid rumours of cannibalism captured the public's fascination. Poor weather, lead poisoning, spoiled canned food, weak leadership and the refusal of the Royal Navy to adapt or adopt Inuit survival techniques are just some of the theories for the expedition's failure.

Norwegian Roald Amundsen finally completed a passage through in 1905, and the RCMP's *St. Roch* found a west-east deep-water corridor as recently as 1942.

Seventy-three years later, as I find my berth on the *Vavilov* in Kangerlussuaq, Greenland, fewer than 300 ships have successfully made the crossing. The 12-day voyage ahead might not take us all the way from Baffin Bay to the Beaufort Sea, but we will snake through the most difficult channels, skirting icebergs, visiting historical sites and searching for wildlife. If they could see our fresh salads, cappuccino maker and stocked Scotch bar, Franklin's men would be rolling over in their permafrost graves. Well, those lucky enough to have been buried anyway.

Culturally, the Inuit communities of Greenland and Canada

HMS *Erebus* Is Found

In September 2014, the flagship of the Franklin Expedition was discovered in Victoria Strait off the west coast of King William Island. Since vanishing in 1845, *Erebus* and its sister ship, *Terror,* have been the subject of major naval searches, resulting in many more lives and ships lost. The breakthrough finally came with the help of Inuit testimony, modern technology and a committed partnership between Canadian public- and private-sector parties. Remarkably intact, the 33-metre-long wreck sits upright beneath just 11 metres of water, a sunken treasure for historians and underwater archaeologists.

are similar, but life is distinctly different. In Greenland, just 55,000 people live on the world's largest and least-populated island, clinging to a ragged coastline. A sprawling ice sheet covers over 80 per cent of the country. Sisimiut, Greenland's second-largest town, is distinctly Scandinavian, its apartment blocks, stores and houses painted in vibrant colours to combat long winters of endless darkness. Across the Davis Strait on Baffin Island, the Canadian town of Pond Inlet feels like an isolated northern outpost. Broken snowmobiles, discarded

lumber, furniture and equipment are strewn throughout town.

We officially enter the passage by sailing into Lancaster Sound, passing towering, sparkling blue icebergs, the captain carefully navigating the ship through pancake ice, bergy bits and dense growlers. The ever-capable (and perfectly named) Captain Beluga consults satellite ice charts to determine which channels might stop us in our tracks. Franklin had no such luxury. His ships were trapped for two dark winters, eventually crushed like peanut shells by shifting ice. Hauling heavy sledges south, his men succumbed one by one to the elements and, eventually, to one another's appetites. Although Inuit testimony of starving men boiling human bones was repulsed by 19th-century British sensibilities, forensic scientists have confirmed that recovered human remains show clear signs of cannibalism. On desolate Beechey Island, I stand at the bone-chilling graves of three of Franklin's men, immortalized with eerie grave markers. Onward to Prince Leopold Island, where I'm rejuvenated by hundreds of thousands of seabirds living in vibrant colonies on

striking limestone cliffs. In Coningham Bay, our Zodiacs chance upon two adult polar bears feasting on several baby belugas, trapped by a shallow sandbank during low tide. Dozens of belugas swim further in the bay. Life and death are never too far away from each other in the Arctic.

Scientists believe melting Arctic sea ice, permafrost and ice shelves will impact the world's climate dramatically. From the *Vavilov*, we can clearly see glaciers receding. A reliable, ice-free passage through the Arctic is becoming increasingly more realistic. Given the potential impact for shipping and oil and gas discoveries, several northern nations are sharpening

their lawyers to make a claim. For the first time in years, the *Vavilov* is able to make a safe, ice-free evening crossing through the narrow Bellot Strait, leaving the Atlantic for the Pacific while skirting the edge of North America and the start of the Canadian Arctic Archipelago. Tonight, the strait is as clear and calm as a vodka martini. Basking in the orange glow of evening sunshine, my fellow passengers toast the climax of our northwest passage. It is also the final trip on my Great Global Bucket List, the conclusion of a decade-long journey to experience the very best of the world, pole to pole.

Exploration and discovery have come a long way since Frobisher,

Hudson, Franklin and Amundsen found the edge of human endurance (and occasionally fell off it). Today's travellers are not seeking to discover and name new lands, to bask in the glory and immortality that follows. Even if I did tenderize myself earlier in the trip by falling down the deck stairs on my way from the hot tub to the sauna (the horror, the horror), bucket listers needn't take any more risks than necessary. We live in a remarkable age where the wonders of the planet are accessible in a manner our ancestors could only dream of. The ghosts of salty sea dog explorers have paved the way for us to follow.

Every passage, wherever and however we choose to do it, is meaningful. As we cross the Bellot Strait, behind me is the past— 10 years of adventures, conversations with thousands of interesting people and the realization of my wildest dreams. Ahead is the unknowable future, with all the joy and heartbreak that come with it. Why sail forward at all? We cannot allow uncertainty to stop us cold, nor fear to glue us to the couch. Sure, Franklin's passage ended in disaster, but mine concluded with chilled pink champagne and a maritime toast to the final, incredible tick on my bucket list. Final, that is, for now.

START HERE:
globalbucketlist.com/
northwestpassage

Epilogue

More than one traveller I've met has voiced their distaste for the term *bucket list*. They criticize the absurdity of creating wish lists driven by our mortality, believing it can only lead to unrealistic goals and crushing disappointment. Anti-bucket-list articles are popping up with increasing frequency. One online magazine called bucket lists "America's most idiotic new pastime." The backlash in response to the exploding popularity of bucket lists is not entirely without basis, and yet it's not entirely apt either.

Television shows and articles (and books) that convince you life is not complete without doing X or visiting Y tend to be less about inspiration and more about braggadocio. Clickbait headlines such as "Top 10 Meals to Eat before You Die!" and "Top 10 Beaches to Visit before You Die!" exploit our curiosity and penchant for lists and countdowns. More accurately, these stories should be headlined "Top 10 Meals the Writer Loved" or "Top 10 Beaches the Writer Wants to Visit!" But you probably wouldn't click on that link. Other than regarding the originality of the destinations, the activities and the storytelling itself, this particular book makes no judgments. And while I might have been jolly proud of myself for surviving that crazy plank path in China, I certainly don't think anything less of anybody who would rather give it a miss. Missing it would be, after all, the sane thing to do.

How we travel and what we get out of our journeys are intrinsically personal. Three individuals might visit the same destination and have three different experiences. I've had heated discussions about what constitutes visiting a country. One seasoned traveller believes you have to spend a week in the country; another, an hour. It is ludicrous. Life is not a race, and the only person refereeing your international exploits is you. As for bucket lists, they can be silly or seasonal, focused on far-flung adventures or chores around the house. Nobody, and least of all me, can claim to know what you should be doing with your life. Much as guidebooks merely make suggestions with the filter of quality control, so *The Great Global Bucket List* picks out unique experiences I feel are worth knowing about. In both cases, the quality of the advice depends greatly on the quality of the advisor. If you've read this far, I'm hoping you've come to know, enjoy and trust me as a guide. It's a responsibility I do not take lightly.

Many years ago, I was wandering about a Hungarian music festival, as one does, and stumbled into a tent that offered some warmth from the cool evening breeze. I struck up a conversation with a woman, falling into a familiar chat about what I do and how many countries I've visited.

"Well, you've certainly seen and done a lot," she said. "Tell me, what have you learned?"

That question floored me. Typically, I'm asked for travel advice or about the countries I haven't visited yet. What *have* I learned?

A great deal, as it turns out. I've learned that wherever I go, people prefer to help me rather than hurt me. I've learned to hear and listen to my instincts, and how much power is contained in a sincere smile. I've learned that the

people I meet will always shape the experience I have. Perhaps, most importantly, I've learned that wherever I am is where I'm supposed to be. Along with other insights, how I came to realize all this will one day fill another book, but the adventures contained within this one will—I hope—impart a realistic (and optimistic) view of the world we live in.

I'm constantly discovering new bucket list experiences, in new countries, regions and cities. It is readers like you who often point me in the right direction, alerting me to the fact that *going there* or *doing that* should be on my radar. Since I don't plan to quit exploring anytime soon, I expect that *The Great Global Bucket List* will continue to grow and evolve, both in print and online. It will continue to generate discussion and debate, dreams and derring-do. Use *The Great Global Bucket List* as a guidebook if it suits you—just keep in mind that each experience will be your own. Gift it to your recently retired parents, your soon-to-graduate kids or anyone you hope to inspire. In a media-saturated world where fear, chaos, corruption, epidemics, wars and tragic accidents dominate the news cycle, bucket lists can evolve to become wellsprings of optimism, gathering our innermost hopes and dreams. Silly as bucket lists may appear to some, I believe every one of them builds a better future, an opportunity to learn about the world—and ourselves—through authentic and meaningful experience. Item by item, tick by tick.

"Inspire the world with my global adventures." Thank you for letting me cross that one off my list.

robin@robinesrock.com

Acknowledgements

This book has been many years, and many more miles, in the making. A full list of thanks would have to include everyone from my grade-six teacher, who told me I'd one day be writing books, to the distracted driver who crashed into me, setting off the unlikely chain of events that would lead to my career in travel writing. It must include every pilot who landed the plane safely, every driver who didn't collide with a truck, canyon floor or wild animal, and every lodging that put a roof over my head. I would of course have to thank my outrageously supportive family, including parents who let me chase down my dreams, trustworthy friends who stuck around when I did and siblings who put the *brother* in *brotherhood*. And because many of the stories in this book were the result of filming a 40-part television series, it would be a slim volume indeed without the broadcast executives and production team that made that happen. Likewise, I'm grateful to the newspaper, magazine and online editors who commissioned stories and provided the purpose (and purses) to keep me chasing bucket list stories.

Behind the scenes, I've built a team of talented individuals and trusted advisors who have allowed me to create a new generation of guidebook (inspiration on the page, information online) and spread the message across a diversity of platforms. It would be a great injustice if their names don't appear in this book, along with the photographers who generously donated their images to illustrate some of the chapters. I'd give a heroic shout-out to the wonderful folks at HarperCollins Canada who created the great-looking book (or ebook) you're holding in your hands and helped get the word out so you knew it existed in the first place. I'll tip my hat to the sponsors and brands that have supported me over the years, and to the readers of my previous books who encouraged me to write new ones. I'll use this opportunity to say thank you to my family across time and space, the ancestors and grandparents who took bold risks to ensure better lives for their offspring and encouraged me to take chances before it is too late. Finally, the list would conclude by acknowledging the two most important girls in my life: a daughter who has taught me

ACKNOWLEDGEMENTS

more than the world ever could, and the wife of my dreams. So yes, I'd expect
there would be lots of names on this list, and here they are:

Argentina: Martin Klee **Bolivia:** Alistair Matthews, Transturin **Brazil:**
Roberto and Gabi Castro, Ernest Magalhães, FSB, Embratur **Chile:** Turismo
Chile, Ski Arpa, Santiago Adventures, Arson Clothing, George Cogan,
Russell Kling **Colombia:** Proexport Colombia Trade Commission, Maria
Fernanda Guzman **Ecuador:** Haugan Cruises, Katie Beckwith, Palmar
Voyages, Chris Lee **Peru:** Peru Treks & Adventure, Aqua Expeditions,
Suzanne Flores, LAN Airlines, Carla Perroni **Belize:** Ian, Larry and staff at
Caves Branch Jungle Lodge **Canada:** Frontier North Adventures, Travel
Manitoba, Tricia Schers, Travel Alberta, Bluewater Adventures, Randy
Burke, Destination BC, Susan Clarke **Cuba:** Connor Gory, Ian MacKenzie,
FITCuba, Ken Hegan, Dave Dormer **Mexico:** Tucan Tours, Mexico Tourism
Board **Nicaragua:** Val Murray, Tucan Tours, Bigfoot Hostel **United States
of America:** William Byrnes, Jarrod Levitan, Sean Aiken, Bruce Voyce,
Poipu Beach Resort Association, Seasport Divers, Arthur Yannoukos,
Princess Cruises, Guy Glaeser, Karen Candy **Ethiopia:** Muluken Tamirat,
Joseph Kabir **Kenya:** &Beyond, Bateleur Camp staff, Kenya Tourism Board
Madagascar: Rus Margolin **Rwanda, DRC and Uganda:** Rothbart, Russell
Kling, Ruslin Margolin **South Africa:** Yvonne van Tal, Greater Addo
Marketing, Sun International, Nambiti Hills **Tunisia:** Mohsen Maatoug,
Tunisian Tourist Office **Zanzibar:** Bradley Kalmek, Debre Barrett, Air
Zambia, *SL* magazine, the guy who never did serve us the cake of the day
Zimbabwe: Bradley Kalmek, Debre Barrett **Croatia:** Philippe Renauld
Czech Republic: Peter and his road trip **England:** Thomas Fussing **Finland:**
Visit Helsinki, Rovaniemi Tourism **Germany:** Visit Berlin, Trabi Safari
Hungary: Barlangaszhat **Iceland:** Adventure Center, Dave Calder **Italy:**
Emilia Romagna Region Tourist Board, Modenatur **Latvia:** Latvia Institute
Lithuania: Regina Kopelevich, Ann Rabinowitz, Michael Pertain **Norway:**
Troels Branth Pederson **Poland:** My grandmother, Fanny Esrock **Portugal:**
Azores Tourism **Romania:** the hashers of Bucharest **Russia:** Sundowners
Travel, my Vodkatrain travel buddies, Intrepid Travel **Slovenia:** Slovenia
Tourist Board, Tilen Gabrovšek **Spain:** Russell Kling **Ukraine:** Solo East
Travel **Burma:** Russell Kling **Cambodia:** The girl who kindly rescued me

from an angry mob, Minesh Tanna, Laura Sanin **China:** China National Tourism Office, Greg Lewis, Sundowner Travel **India:** A cast of millions **Indonesia:** Russell Kling **Israel:** Ministry of Tourism, Dan Hotels, Gideon Har Hermon, Ken Hegan **Jordan:** Jordan Tourism Board **Laos:** Minesh Tanna, Jessica, Tara, Lindsay, Paul, Alissa and Harry **Macau:** Macau Tower **Malaysia:** Tourism Malaysia, Rama and Mr. Khabir **Maldives:** Gili Lankanfushi Resort, Kurt Berman **Mongolia:** Sundowner Travel, Nomin **The Philippines:** Philippines Department of Tourism, Rene de los Santos, Malapascua Dive Resort **South Korea:** Lotus Lantern International Meditation Center, Korea Tourism **Sri Lanka:** Dilmah Tea, Sri Lanka Tourism, Thomas Fussing **Taiwan:** Government Information Office **Thailand:** Minesh Tanna, Jessica Waal, Tara and Lindsay Irwin, Alissa, Ellen and the Elephant Nature Park **Turkey:** Anatolia Travels, Cercis Murat Conagi, Gizem Kökten **Turkmenistan:** Rus Margolin, George Kourounis **Australia:** Tourism Australia, Devil's Playground Tours, the Radus and Ende clans of Sydney, Jessica Waal, Alison Beer, Erin Georgieff, Jennifer Nguyen, David Brodie **Cook Islands:** Cook Islands Tourism, Air New Zealand, Ally Stoltz, Ken Hegan, Ross Borden, Lesley Sauls, Joanne Haugen **New Caledonia:** Philippe Renaud **New Zealand:** Tourism New Zealand, Destination Queenstown, Tourism Rotorua, Ruth Atherley, Paul Holman, Air New Zealand **Papua New Guinea:** Margo, Stephanie, Bronwyn, Christina and Scuba Diver Girls everywhere, PNG Tourism Promotion Authority, Laura Matar **Antarctica:** One Ocean Expeditions, Jeff Topham, Elyse Mailhot, Boris, Eva and the Antarctic crew and passengers of the *Akademik Sergei Vavilov* **Arctic:** One Ocean Expeditions, Jeff Topham, Elyse Mailhot, Aaron, Nate and the Arctic crew and passengers of the *Akademik Sergei Vavilov*

While I am grateful for the support of many destination-marketing organizations, they did not review or approve the content of this book.

Many of these stories were researched while filming the television series *Word Travels*. Including them would not have been possible without Heather Hawthorne-Doyle, Julia Dimon, Leah Kimura, Caroline Manuel, Sean Cable, Chris Mennell, Neil MacLean, Ian MacKenzie, Deb Wainwright, Mike Bodnarchuk, Mary Frymire, Peter Steel, Zach Williams, Paul Vance,

ACKNOWLEDGEMENTS

Brian Hamilton, Michael Chechik, Gabriela Schonbach, Lori Aldcroft, Omni Films and Patrice Baillargeon. Filming a TV show in 36 countries—now, that's an adventure!

Some of these stories have appeared in different form in a variety of publications. Special thanks to Zebunnisa Mirza, Melissa Morra, Andrea Kolber, Jim Byers, Sarah McWhirter, Catherine Dawson-March, Matt Robinson, Liza Finlay, Randy Curwen, Manjari Saxena, Stephen McCarty, Winnie Chung, Jon van den Heever, Jim Eagles, Diana Plater, Andrea Lowe, Ross Borden, Gemma Bowes, Jason English, Jessanne Collins and the travel editor who graciously kicked this all off, Linda Bates. A young travel agent named Valoree Bloomfield helped me take the plunge as a 30-year-old backpacker, and Kimberly Morton and Minty Thompson helped me keep the momentum as an upstart writer and public speaker.

Special thanks to the following photographers, travellers and friends for generous use of their images: Ruslan Margolin; Jeff Topham; Russell Kling; Paul Vance; Neil Maclean; Julia Dimon; Christina Koukkos; Bronwyn Dickey; Chris Lee; Minesh Tanna; Philippe Renauld; Ryan Bray; Ian MacKenzie; my wife, Ana Carolina Esrock; and all those strangers who happened to be around when I really needed someone to take a shot with me in it (even if it didn't always work out).

My visionary editor, Patrick Crean, first recognized the potential for a bucket list many years ago. Neither of us could have expected it to take me so far, both at home and abroad. Thanks to Alan Jones, Susan MacGregor, Laura Dosky and everyone at HarperCollins Canada for getting the inspiration out (and making it look so good). Judy Phillips did a fantastic job sharpening my words, imagery and facts too. Thanks to Kelly Jones and Deborah Viets for their careful proofreading, and to Noelle Zitzer for project management. I'm grateful for additional fact-checking by Natalie Meditsky and Stephanie Nunez. Thanks to my literary agent, Hilary McMahon, and all at Westwood Creative Artists; my speaking agent, Cathy Hirst, and all at the Lavin Agency; my friend and sounding board Jon Rothbart; Sherill Sirrs, rtCamp and the exceptional efforts of David Rock in helping me build the extensive video library and companion website. Thanks to Jeff Topham for adding his trademark "tickle" to the photographs in this volume.

Special thanks to Ford Motor Company of Canada, who have allowed me to Go Further, and to KEEN Footwear, who have been there from the very beginning. Tip of the travel hat to Heather Taylor, Lauren More and Matt Drennan-Scace. My gratitude to Tourism Australia.

I type these words in a quiet ship library, windows facing the bow of the Russian-flagged vessel, the *Akademik Sergey Vavilov*. Outside is Devon Island, an Arctic desert with the kind of striking landscape difficult to describe. For the past 10 years, this has been my challenge when returning home. It's one thing to write a story, but how do I convey to my friends and family what I've experienced? I learned pretty quickly that I'd have to create two worlds: the one out there, and the one at home. Balancing this scale has been critical to my success as a human being, a traveller, a friend, son, brother, husband, cousin, nephew and father. My eternal gratitude to the Kalmeks of Vancouver, Fanny and the late Abie Esrock, Alex Esrock, the Raduses, the Levitans, Barons and Resniks. So much of this book is for the friends and colleagues who stuck around, and for the ones who didn't. You know who you all are.

My daughter, Raquel, dramatically changed my bucket list. Wild experiences have been replaced simply with: be a great dad. But this book is dedicated to my wife, Ana Carolina. We met halfway through this journey, and I know it wasn't easy staying behind, holding the fort, raising Raquel while Daddy runs off to the Great Barrier Reef. Eventually, every traveller finds a warm, loving home. My own means more than the world to me.

Photo Credits